Myth and Identity in the Epic of Imperial Spain

Myth and Identity in the Epic of Imperial Spain

Elizabeth B. Davis

University of Missouri Press
Columbia and London

Cataloging-in-Publication data available
from the Library of Congress.
ISBN 0-8262-1277-8

♾™This paper meets the requirements of the
American National Standard for Permanence of Paper
for Printed Library Materials, Z39.48, 1984.

Design and composition: Vickie Kersey DuBois
Printer and binder: Thomson-Shore, Inc.
Typefaces: Stuyvesant, Syntax, Palatino

A fragment of the introduction appeared in the *Bulletin of Hispanic Studies* 71 (1994): 339-57, under the title "The Politics of Effacement: Diego de Hojeda's Humble Poetics." A shortened version of chapter 3 appeared in *Calíope* 2 (1996): 36–57.

Publication of this book has been supported by a contribution from the Program for Cultural Cooperation between Spain's Ministry of Education and Culture and United States' Universities.

To my parents, Milton Davis, Jr., and Lillian S. Davis,
and to the memory of Steven N. Bogard

Contents

Acknowledgments

This project came to fruition due to a generous seed grant from the Ohio State University, a grant from the Program for Cultural Cooperation between Spain's Ministry of Culture and United States' Universities, and a travel grant from the Tinker/Latin American Studies Program at the Ohio State University. These grants allowed me to do archival research in Spain and to compare the accessible editions of the five epic poems I treat to the generally more reliable first editions. As I pored over the many editions of the poems at the Biblioteca Nacional in Madrid, the letters of Don John of Austria at the Archivo General de Simancas, and letters from the Archbishop of Lima at the Archivo General de Indias, this project began to take its final form. I wish to express my gratitude to Pilar Lázaro de la Escosura of the Archivo General de Indias and to Isabel Aguirre of the Archivo General de Simancas for their meticulous assistance. For the joy and good fortunes of that Spanish sojourn, heartfelt thanks also go to Antonio Coloma, Pedro Álvarez de Miranda, Pura Silgo, Santiago Gallego-Aguagil, Amparo Cano, and Miguel and María Dolores Beltrán.

It is impossible to name all the people who have contributed in various ways to this project. Frank Pierce encouraged me from the very beginning. My book on the epics of imperial Spain would have been impossible to write had his work on epic poems not preceded it, and I mourn his passing. I will always be indebted to Norman Austin and to the participants in the NEH Arizona Homer Institute. The luminous verses of Homer have made it difficult for me to reconcile myself to literary epic, but the learning experience of the institute has made my work on Spanish-language Renaissance epic more meaningful. I am truly fortunate to teach in a university where there is a strong and vibrant Center for Medieval and Renaissance Studies. Its director, Nicholas G. Howe, read the manuscript in its entirety and made many useful suggestions. I treasure his wisdom and his friendship. The chapters that touch on the Spanish American colonial experience benefited from the invaluable perspective and enthusiastic support of Maureen Ahern. Donald R. Larson generously read the manuscript and provided feedback. David T. Gies offered information on the connections between Spanish Romanticism and European literary history, and constant encouragement. I can never repay Frances R. Aparicio for the intellectual prodding, the love, and the support she has given me since the early "single mom" days in Tucson. Her intelligent reading strengthened my chapter on

Juan Rufo. James R. Nicolopulos has been my faithful interlocutor on things epic for the last few years. I am grateful to him for sharing his knowledge and good humor with me. The outside readers for the University of Missouri Press suggested ways to strengthen the manuscript, and Clair Willcox, Jane Lago, and Sara Davis, also of the University of Missouri Press, helped me turn it into a book. Eliana S. Rivero and Reynaldo L. Jiménez read and critiqued work that ended up in this book, and I thank them for the moral support and affection they gave me during the years in which the manuscript was written. I am very grateful to family and friends who provided childcare on many occasions so that I could write. My greatest debt, however, is to my daughter, Eliana Veronica Davis, for her patience, understanding, and love. This book is also hers, in a way.

Editions Consulted

Except where otherwise indicated, I have relied on the following editions of the five epics. For ease of reading, I have modernized spelling and punctuation in all quoted passages from the poems and other sources, except in Corcoran's edition of *La Christiada* and Entrambasaguas's edition of *Jerusalén Conquistada*. All translations from Spanish are my own.

Alonso de Ercilla. *La Araucana*. Edited by Isaías Lerner. Madrid: Cátedra, 1993.

Diego de Hojeda. *La Christiada*. Edited by Sister Mary Helen Patricia Corcoran. Washington, D.C.: Catholic University Press, 1935.

Juan Rufo. *La Austriada*. Edited by Cayetano Rosell. Biblioteca de Autores Españoles 29. Madrid: Rivadeneyra, 1854.

Vega Carpio, Lope Félix de. *Jerusalén Conquistada*. 3 vols. Edition and critical study by Joaquín de Entrambasaguas. Madrid: Consejo Superior de Investigaciones Científicas, 1951.

Virués, Cristóbal de. *Historia del Monserrate*. Edited by Cayetano Rosell. Biblioteca de Autores Españoles 17. Madrid: Rivadeneyra, 1851.

Myth and Identity in the Epic of Imperial Spain

Introduction

When Garcilaso de la Vega, called the "Prince of Castilian poetry," dedicated his "First Eclogue" to the viceroy of Naples, he seemed to have qualms about offering pastoral verse, rather than a more prestigious poem such as an epic, to Don Pedro de Toledo of the house of Alba. In the dedication, the poet declares his intent to write not about great deeds or demonstrations of martial prowess, but rather about the vicissitudes of shepherds and shunned lovers. The poet's request that the viceroy exchange the hero's laurel for ivy is tantamount to a rejection of epic, with its high style and lofty language, in favor of a less grand, but more novel, kind of poetry. However, he seems to feel obligated to justify his pastoral project by promising to write about Don Pedro's exploits in the future:

> then will you see my pen trained
> in the infinite, countless sum
> of your virtues and famous works . . .

> (luego verás ejercitar mi pluma
> por la infinita, innumerable suma
> de tus virtudes y famosas obras . . .)[1]

The poet's posture constitutes more than affected modesty.[2] Garcilaso's disavowals and justifying strategies leave little doubt about the outlook of the times in the matter of the hierarchy of literary types. For the poets of Golden Age Spain, epic was the premier genre.

Garcilaso de la Vega's apparent self-consciousness about writing "rustic" poetry is evidence of a lost literary and cultural matrix from which the epic was eventually separated, thereby causing a very real distortion in our perception of the whole. Other sixteenth- and seventeenth-century genres are better read and more properly appreciated against a backdrop of epic that they themselves invoke. Yet, despite its importance as a precursor of the modern novel and a major narrative site of early nationalism and Golden Age cultural identities, the epic of imperial Spain

---

1. "Égloga Primera," stanza 2.
2. For the affected "modesty formula," see Ernst Robert Curtius, *European Literature and the Latin Middle Ages*, 83–85.

suffers from neglect. This is not the case in broader academic circles. David Quint's *Epic and Empire* (1993) and Michael Murrin's *History and Warfare in Renaissance Epic* (1994) are proof of the genre's current appeal and of important new readings of Renaissance epic, in general. These scholars' treatment of Spanish-language epics, however, is limited by the constraints of their own discipline, and Hispanists have not done much to remedy the situation because, by and large, their attention remains fixed on genres that enjoy a canonical status, such as lyric poetry.[3] This state of affairs could be considered acceptable during the decades when formalist and structuralist literary theories constrained readers to focus on the inner workings of briefer texts. But from the perspective of recent literary theories that are more intertwined with history (such as the New Historicism), it no longer seems sufficient that the tortured, introspective sonnets embraced by poets at the court of Charles V should have the last word on the subject of Golden Age literary culture, or on that of poetry and empire, despite the recent work that a few scholars have done to historicize Spanish Petrarchism.[4] Even when reexamined as the product of a specific political and cultural milieu, the Italianate lyric of Garcilaso and his followers cannot presume to narrate the story of Spain's new imperial polity in search of legitimizing myths. That narrative function corresponds more properly to the epic, a genre central to Golden Age cultural practice but not read much today. The removal of epic from the usual curriculum of Golden Age studies is, in reality, a recent occurrence. The rationale for omission of a once-privileged genre is complex. William Melczer has suggested that a number of the Spanish epics were so topical that enthusiasm for them was necessarily short-lived.[5] Because the canon is a later construct that is superimposed onto the sixteenth and seventeenth centuries, it is reasonable to think that the most allusive of these texts remained isolated from it by virtue of the fact that the immediate pretext

3. I call attention, however, to two important Ph.D. dissertations, that of James Robert Nicolopulos ("Prophecy, Empire and Imitation in the *Araucana* in the Light of the *Lusíadas*"), forthcoming as a book at Pennsylvania State University Press, and that of Felisa Guillén ("Épica, historia y providencialismo en la España del siglo 17: El caso de la *Jerusalén conquistada*"). Elizabeth R. Wright's dissertation "The Poet as Pilgrim: Lope de Vega and the Court of Philip III, 1598–1609" (forthcoming from Bucknell Press as Pilgrimage to Patronage . . .) also contains chapters on epics.
4. See Ignacio Navarrete, *Orphans of Petrarch: Poetry and Theory in the Spanish Renaissance*; Alicia de Colombí-Monguió, *Petrarquismo peruano: Diego Dávalos y Figueroa y la poesía de la Miscelánea Austral*; and Roland Greene, "'This Phrasis is Continuous': Love and Empire in 1590."
5. See William Melczer, "Nationalisme et Expansion Impérialiste dans la Littérature Espagnole," in *Stage International de Tours, 1966*, 349–63. I owe this reference to Gilberto Triviños.

for their composition was forgotten. However, not all of the learned epics from this period are so restricted in their appeal. There are a respectable number of texts that celebrate the conquest of America or the glories of Lepanto, for example, or that have a sacred theme perceived as eternal. Such poems embody an ideology of ethnic and state identity that feels surprisingly recent, and a religious belief system that obtains to some degree still.

John Beverley has suggested that the epic already began to feel outmoded in the context of Baroque aesthetics:

> Something like the conceit in "Angélica y Medoro" preserved the range and sublimity of epic as a form of class discourse, in a situation where the actual narration in interminable *octavas reales* of a military expedition or foundation was beginning to be felt not only as anachronistic, out of fashion, but also as potentially confusing or destabilizing, given the new realities of power politics faced by the Spanish monarchy and colonial viceroyalties in the seventeenth century.[6]

This is a thoughtful and provocative view of seventeenth-century literary practice. However, Frank Pierce's work on Golden Age epic strongly suggests that due to its prestige, the epic continued to enjoy editorial privilege well into the seventeenth century, whereas it was relatively difficult to publish lyric during the same period. Consider, for example, Lope de Vega's dogged determination to write the national epic that he thought Spain still lacked, and the immediate success of his attempt: *Jerusalén Conquistada* (*Jerusalem conquered*) was printed four times in the space of ten years (twice in 1609, once in 1611, and once in 1619). But it is unnecessary to resort to anecdote. There is a very considerable body of epic appearing in Spain and the colonies at this time: Pierce lists some 150 epics published in the seventeenth century alone, a figure that does not include reprintings or translations. Golden Age translations of classical epic (Homer, Virgil, Lucan) and of Renaissance "literary" epic (Sannazaro, Boiardo, Ariosto, Camões, Tasso, Tansillo) numbered approximately thirty.[7]

This bountiful Golden Age genre consists of narrative poems of significant length, though there are cases of shorter heroic poems sometimes classified as "minor epic." If the foundational texts of the genre (the *Iliad* and the *Odyssey*, *Beowulf*, the *Chanson de Roland*, the *Poema de mío Cid*) can be

---

6. John R. Beverley, "Gracián and the Baroque Overvaluation of Literature," since published in Spanish in *Relecturas del Barroco de Indias*, ed. Mabel Moraña (Hanover: Ediciones del Norte, 1994).

7. Frank Pierce, *La poesía épica del Siglo de Oro*, 340–69.

called "primary epics," as Arthur Terry has done, the Renaissance epics belong to the category of "secondary" or "literary epic," which has its deepest roots in Virgil's *Aeneid* and the *Pharsalia* of Lucan. Chevalier and others refer to this type as *"épica culta."* With rare exceptions, the poems are written in *octavas reales* (eight hendecasyllables ending with a rhymed couplet, ABABABCC) and divided into books, or cantos (as few as twelve, as many as thirty-seven). According to Aristotelian precepts, which enjoyed great prestige among sixteenth-century Spanish literati, the epic poem was supposed to recount the feats of a single hero (although in practice this was not always the case). Furthermore, the epic action was to be unified, though it might contain several parts, and the story was supposed to be verisimilar.[8]

During the early modern period, especially in Italy, there was an important debate about the nature and precepts of epic. Ariosto's *Orlando Furioso* offered the possibility of radically revitalizing the classical epic paradigm, while Tasso insisted on the superiority of historical (or historicoreligious) epic. A parodic tendency in the *romanzi* gave rise to additional tensions in the epic genre. To a certain extent, developments in Spanish epic of this period reflect these tensions. Menéndez y Pelayo, for example, points out two dominant schools within Spanish epic poetry of the Golden Age: the historical epic and the novelesque, or "fantastic," epic. According to Menéndez y Pelayo, historical, or *verista,* epic emerges in the second half of the sixteenth century and includes works such as Jerónimo Sempere's *La Carolea* (1560), Luis Zapata's *Carlo Famoso* (1565), the first part of Ercilla's *La Araucana* (1569), and Juan Rufo's *La Austriada* (1584). These poems are seemingly imbued with the conviction that Spanish military commanders were living during intrinsically epic times, so all that was necessary was to narrate historical events. Ercilla, a veteran of the campaigns in Arauco, characterized his poem as "a narration taken from the truth without corruption, and cut according to its measure" (relación sin corromper sacada / de la verdad, cortada a su medida, *Araucana* 1.3.5–6). The poet of *La Araucana,* as we know, finally tired of a historical narrative, and in the end, he incorporated several amorous episodes that point in the direction of a novelesque tendency closer to the spirit of Ariosto. It is significant, however, that Menéndez y Pelayo does not trace the beginnings of fantastic epic to poems much earlier than Bernardo de Balbuena's *El Bernardo, o victoria de Roncesvalles* (1624). John Van Horne disputes this position, claiming to find fantastic elements in Hispanic epic that predates the "historical" poems. In particular, Van Horne cites Ercilla and Lasso de la Vega (*Mexicana*) as evi-

---

8. My definition of epic expands the one given by Pierce; see his *Poesía épica,* 12–13. On primary and secondary epic, see Arthur Terry, *Seventeenth-Century Spanish Poetry: The Power of Artifice,* 180–81.

dence that the fantastic school of epic was gaining ground in the latter part of the sixteenth century.[9]

A careful reading of many epic poems of this period suggests that Menéndez y Pelayo was correct in his finding that Ariosto could not be imitated without serious qualms until the early seventeenth century, Alonso de Ercilla's celebrated protestations about the difficulty of sticking to arid historical truth notwithstanding. The poems of the mid-sixteenth century do indeed attempt to exclude elements that might distract from the narration of great deeds, but even the most historical poems (*La Austriada*, for example) allow for the intrusion of some novelesque episodes or ingredients. That Ercilla allows us to view his dissatisfaction with the dryness of historical epic indicates his extraordinary talent and his desire for a free rein, but in the end, he always resumes a historical narrative. The only poem analyzed in this book that does not manifest conflict about having been strongly marked by Ariosto's influence is Lope de Vega's *Jerusalem conquered* (1609), an epic that worries about historicity for other reasons. Judging by their work, it is simply not clear that Spanish poets of the second half of the sixteenth century felt especially torn or confused, either about the genre or about their own poetic projects. Lerner notes that the strain between historical and fantastic (Ariostesque) epic does not seem to have been intense in Spain, at least initially, while Pierce observes that in Spanish literary experience, epic theories do not come together in a consistent way until Tasso's time.

> In Spain, the general rule was indifference toward all manner of epic rules about theme and structure, while practicing adherence to the *octava*, the division of the poem in cantos, and the use of epic ingredients such as the *exordium*, the simile or the scene of the dawn, not to mention others which are more complex, such as hell, prophecies, epic harangues, military reviews, etc.[10]

Thus, the epics themselves recommend an elastic definition of their genre. No matter how impure some of these Spanish poems may seem to us, they evince a conceptualization of epic that is fluid yet precise.

From the above, it is clear that the seventeenth century shows no inclination to disown this large and varied corpus of texts. There is undoubtedly

---

9. See Bernard Weinberg, *A History of Literary Criticism in the Italian Renaissance*, 2:954–1073; Marcelino Menéndez y Pelayo, *Historia de las ideas estéticas en España*, 2:237 n. 2; and John Van Horne, *"El Bernardo" of Bernardo de Balbuena*, 150–52.

10. Pierce, *Poesía épica*, 264. On the belated preoccupation with epic theory in Spain, see Pierce, *Poesía épica*, 232. On the negligible early impact of the Italian debates in Spain, see Isaías Lerner, introduction to *La Araucana*, by Ercilla, 9.

truth, however, in the notion that writers began to find the form of epic increasingly constrictive, and it seems plausible that minor poetic types such as the ballad (*romance*), always the eponymous form of popular heroic verse, began to replace the learned epic. But so did prose fiction.[11] The swelling enthusiasm for the idea of "writing epic in prose" (*Don Quijote*, 1.47) brought a kind of formal liberation to Golden Age writers, but it should be remembered that for these same literati, epic remained the most prestigious poetic type. Pierce asserts that writers such as Cervantes and Lope de Vega were so influenced by the literary agenda of humanism that for them, the epic would have been the noblest genre. Basing his argument on the "superabundance of epics or pseudo-epics" published during this period, he concludes,

> However much *El Quijote, La Vida del Buscón* or *La Vida es sueño* may seem to us to be amongst the supreme literary achievements of the time, we cannot see . . . the entire sixteenth and seventeenth centuries, in their true historical perspective, if we do not remember that such works as the above did not in any way represent for their contemporaries the best that could be done in literature.[12]

Our canon, of course, does not retain this bias. Most of us avoid reading the epics of the Golden Age because of their length and because we lack a context in which to understand them. This inattention has generally isolated the texts, though a curious set of circumstances partially salvaged *La Araucana*. Ercilla's poem was deemed the accep:able epic, the best of its kind, and this privileged status resulted in its being frequently cited and reprinted. In addition, while the unwieldy size of the epics militated against their inclusion in class reading lists, professors of Spanish American literature, in particular, have traditionally reserved some space for Ercilla's text, of which there exist many anthologized versions. This fact alone probably contributed to the survival of *La Araucana*, since a work's pedagogical expedience has a direct relationship to its inscription in the canon.[13] All these forms of cultural

11. While not finding the "roots" of the novel in epic, Mikhail Bakhtin argues that the modern genre displaced the ancient form, whose "completedness" and "immutability" felt unreal to the modern mind. See his "Epic and Novel," in *The Dialogic Imagination*, 3–40; and Georg Lukács's "The Epic and the Novel," in *The Theory of the Novel*, 56–69.

12. Frank Pierce, "'La creación del mundo' and the Spanish 'Religious Epic' of the Golden Age," 31.

13. For an overview of the history of anthologized versions of *La Araucana*, see Hector Romero, "*La Araucana* a través de los antologistas." Hugh Kenner, in "The Making of a Modernist Canon," and Barbara Herrnstein Smith, in "Contingencies of Value," address some of the complexities of canon formation. The latter two essays, as well as that of John Guillory, all cited in this chapter, are included in *Canons*, ed. Robert von Hallberg.

reproduction certainly protected Ercilla's text from the disregard that befell the other learned epics, fallen to a neglect from which Pierce's *La poesía épica del Siglo de Oro* could not entirely rescue them. But if Pierce did not succeed in rekindling interest in the literary epic, he did underscore the fact that, by dint of their exclusion of this genre, the twentieth-century Golden Age curriculum and canon are less than representative of Spanish literary culture of the period. And he reminded us that earlier readers were more generous in their consideration of Renaissance and Baroque epic.

In the Spanish-speaking world, the eighteenth and nineteenth centuries still read the epics of the Age of Gold, and read them well. Pierce's book documents this, as does the study accompanying Entrambasaguas's critical edition of *Jerusalem conquered*. On the Spanish American side, as González Echevarría has written, the nineteenth century recuperated the epics of the imperial age and subjected them to a "monumentalizing" reading that turned them into foundational texts of the various national literatures.[14] But though the 1800s still accorded a place of honor to the literary epic of the six-teenth and seventeenth centuries, the attitude of the times was no longer unequivocal. Beyond the confines of Spain, the reception of Spanish epic had not been unqualifiedly favorable since Voltaire's *Essay on Epic Poetry* (English version, 1727). Following the lead of Cervantes, who had the poems of Ercilla, Rufo, and Virués saved from the bonfire in *Quijote* 1.6, Voltaire included *La Araucana* in his essay, comparing it favorably to the *Iliad*, while at the same time making disparaging remarks about Ercilla's text. This mixed judgment nonetheless rescued *La Araucana* from oblivion. As for the poems of Rufo and Virués, Voltaire wrote that Cervantes's "overweening inclination towards his countrymen" had clouded his judgment of those works.[15] The same opinions, had they been expressed by a lesser pen than Voltaire's, might have had little effect. The Frenchman's knowledge of Spanish was just passable; indeed, there is no evidence to suggest that he did more than leaf through *La Austriada* and *El Monserrate*. George Ticknor did not believe he had read even *La Araucana*; "if Voltaire had read the poem he pretended to criticize," wrote Ticknor in 1849, "he might have done some-thing in earnest for its fame." [16]

---

14. For representative eighteenth- and nineteenth-century readings, see Pierce, *Poesía épica*, and the critical study by Joaquín de Entrambasaguas (vol. 3 of his criti-cal edition of Lope de Vega's *Jerusalem conquered*). On the importance of epic for the origins of a literary tradition, see Roberto González Echevarría, "A Brief History of Spanish American Literature," in *Cambridge History of Latin American Literature*, 1:7–32.

15. Voltaire, "An Essay upon the Civil Wars of France and Also upon the Epick Poetry of the European Nations from Homer Down to Milton," 123–29.

16. George Ticknor, *History of Spanish Literature*, 2:464 n. 9.

It now behooves us to examine the ramifications of Voltaire's words in the context of canon formation and the articulation of canonical positions in literary history. While it is not clear what immediate effect Voltaire's judgments had inside Spain, there can be little doubt that they carried enormous authority elsewhere in Europe, and that they were influential in swerving the European epic canon away from Spanish epic. In the nineteenth century, the translated literary histories of Frederick Bouterwek and J. C. L. Simonde de Sismondi were read and discussed by Spanish intellectuals of the romantic period. Romanticism, of course, had an agenda of its own from which to read the Golden Age, one that did not favor the literary epic: as early as 1808, August Wilhelm von Schlegel had called for a reevaluation of the period centered above all in the theater of Calderón, while Agustín Durán's 1828 *Discurso* privileged the popular element found in the theater and in the ensemble of ballads from the oral tradition (*el romancero*). Neither Bouterwek nor Sismondi challenged the validity of Voltaire's assessment of *La Araucana* or of the other Spanish epics; however, both historians granted at least a certain generosity of space to Spanish epic. The German writer (whose history was translated to Spanish in 1829) claimed that the "spurious heroic style" of narrative poems such as Boscán's "Hero y Leandro" (Hero and Leander) constituted an obstacle to the development of true epic in Spain, as did the grave "national spirit of chivalry," which would not allow Spanish writers to imitate the "romantic epopee of the Italians." Bouterwek also criticized the Spaniards' inappropriate choice of epic materials from recent historical events. In a section titled "Fresh Failures in Epic Poetry," he gave one page to the Spanish incapacity for epic, three to *La Araucana*, wherein he invoked Voltaire's favorable evaluation of the speech of the cacique Colocolo, and one to a list of ten other epic titles.[17] Conspicuously missing from his list are *El Monserrate*, *La Christiada*, and *El Bernardo*, the last two of which Pierce considers literarily superior to *La Araucana*. Sismondi (1813) did little more than echo the opinions of Bouterwek.[18] Though he dedicated some twelve pages to *La Araucana*, whose celebrity he attributed to Voltaire, he spent much of his time pointing to what he saw as the flaws of the work. He never mentioned any other Spanish epic of the period.

Ticknor, on the other hand, gave a total of twelve pages to "historical narrative poems," starting with *El poema de Mío Cid*. Six of these went to *La Araucana*.[19] He, too, found Spanish epic wanting, but he examined

    17. Frederick Bouterwek, *History of Spanish and Portuguese Literature*, 1:263–64, 1:407–3.
    18. Bouterwek's translator, Thomasina Ross, affirms that Sismondi "implicitly adopts the judgments passed by Bouterwek." See her preface to Bouterwek's *History*, 1:7.
    19. Ticknor, *History*, 2:459–64.

more texts than the earlier historians did and had laudatory things to say about Ercilla and Virués. He included Hojeda and Barahona de Soto, and if what he had to say was not always positive, his criticism was more thorough and evenhanded than that of Bouterwek and Sismondi. But all in all, once the nineteenth century had spoken, there remained very little that could incite a student of poetry to devote time and energy to the learned epic. The received opinion continues to be that, save perhaps Ercilla, Spanish-language epic of the imperial age is not fit to be read or taught because it lacks literary merit.

Perhaps even more than the romances of chivalry, which made no claim to high literary status, the epic thus brings us straight up against the thorny problem of evaluation. The fact that it was allowed to drift from the canon in the first place already suggests that Golden Age epic is less than excellent: the canonical text is assumed to be inherently superior,[20] and this assumption of essential superiority remains deeply rooted in our discipline, despite recent work on canon formation that suggests literary scholars need to be more circumspect about their criteria for evaluating excellence. Barbara Herrnstein Smith argues that evaluations of artistic merit usually conceal judgments of contingent value: the evaluator estimates how well a given object has performed certain particular functions for a particular set of subjects under a particular set of conditions. Because the relationship between the object and a new set of subjects is always different, any attempt to assign unchanging merit to a literary text becomes problematic: as Herrnstein Smith puts it, "It is thus never '*the same* Homer.'" [21] And, of course, there is always the possibility that a text can be valued for its performance of different functions, as new conditions warrant. Surely Maxime Chevalier meant nothing less than this when he called for a reevaluation of the learned epic:

> From an aesthetic point of view, the production of epic in the eighteenth and nineteenth centuries, excluding the verses of Alonso de Ercilla, Luis Barahona de Soto, Bernardo de Balbuena, Lope de Vega, and one or two others, warrants the oblivion in which we allow it to sleep. But if we make a distinction between . . . critical evaluation and cultural history, we will see that two basic errors derive from this deferment and neglect: the idea that learned epic did not have great importance in the cultural life of Golden Age Spain, and the notion that it was marginal to that same cultural life.[22]

20. John Guillory, "The Ideology of Canon-Formation: T. S. Eliot and Cleanth Brooks," 338.
21. Herrnstein Smith, "Contingencies," 31.
22. Maxime Chevalier, *Lectura y lectores en la España del Siglo 16 y 17*, 104–5.

Challenging us to distinguish between evaluation and cultural history, Chevalier's 1976 essay did not elicit much response from specialists in the field. By and large, Golden Age specialists continue to study the literary types that were privileged by the nineteenth century: lyric, the *comedia*, and the novel. And, as Keith Whinnom and others have suggested, the Golden Age canon continues to reflect not the cultural experience of sixteenth- or seventeenth-century Spain, but that of our own time.[23] The destiny of Golden Age epic, therefore, might prove especially fascinating for historians of canon formation, because it shows that organizing the past according to an image with which we, ourselves, are comfortable purges from the canon not only the writings of marginalized groups, such as early modern women writers, but even a highly canonical genre like the epic.

One premise of this book is that Hispanists can no longer afford to ignore the epic if, as they claim, they desire to understand early modern Spanish culture through its various discourses. In recent years, as noted above, there has been a move to examine Renaissance Petrarchism within the context of global empire and to make of it a sort of imperial poetics. Indeed, Petrarchism flourished throughout Europe, spreading from Spain to her colonies in the sixteenth century. Thus, Petrarchism might appear to be the obvious object of study for those Hispanists preoccupied with the relationship between art and power in the Spanish Renaissance. More to the point, perhaps, Petrarchist verse still occupies a privileged position in the national canon of virtually all Western powers, a fact that, by itself, predisposes us to perceive a strong connection between Petrarchism and European expansionism. The relationship between imperial power and the epic, however, is much stronger because it is intrinsic to the genre and more directly expressed.

In very reduced form, the thesis of this book is that the epic, due to its ancient prestige and its ability to expound an idealized form of the political program of the state, was invaluable to the ruling circles of the imperial monarchy, who used it to forge a sense of unity and to script cultural identities during the period of expansion and conquest. Centuries of cultural as well as chronological difference separate us from the moment of conquest, making it is easy to forget that the government of the Catholic kings did not have a set plan for empire. Instead, they more or less invented one as they went along. By the reign of Charles V, the imperial administration and its bureaucracy were much stronger and more organized, but the notion of Spain as an imperial power was still somewhat new and awkward. This

---

23. See Keith Whinnom, "The Problem of the Best-seller in Spanish Golden-Age Literature"; and Elizabeth Rhodes, "Spain's Misfired Canon: The Case of Luis de Granada's *Libro de la oración y meditación*," 62.

book focuses on the decision of five authors, each of whom represented the interests of imperial Spain to one degree or another, to use the epic genre as a vehicle for the construction of an imagined ethnic and political identity for Spain, metonymically represented by the ascendant Castilian monarchy and its elites. I will argue that their poems figured forth an unmistakable Spanish "sense of self" long before the crystallization of nineteenth-century nationalisms, and that they took full advantage of well-fixed epic conventions to ground this newly forged "Spanish" identity in imperial myths that served to legitimize it.

Another premise of this book is that this collective subjectivity or imagined self is not readily susceptible of direct representation, but rather that the epics derive Spanish heroic identity negatively, in a way analogous to that in which Orientalist texts create a sense of identity for the Westerner by positing "an imaginative geography and history [that] help the mind to intensify its own sense of itself by dramatizing the distance and difference between what is close to it and what is far away." [24] In other words, these poems define the Spaniards not by what they are, but according to what they are not. One ramification of this is that, because it is dominant in the system, the male Western self is not as much in evidence in these poems (or not in the same manner) as is the "othered" enemy. It does not have to be, because it is unmarked. A second ramification is that the Spanish-language epics of this period inscribe otherness according to representational patterns that are hauntingly repetitive. It is not news, of course, that a similar writing of alterity appears in other genres of the times. Due to the epic's warlike ethos and inherent dualism, however, these charged representations of Spain's "others" are starker and more transparent in the epic than in other genres (though within this dominant pattern, inconsistencies occur). In part, this is true because epics invariably entail travel and contact with peoples whom the poems themselves constitute as objects of conquest, usually expressed in the terms of religious conversion and submission to the authority of the Spanish crown. In these texts, thus, cultural fictions relating to an "other" that is deliberately associated with a broad process of symbolization of evil become attached to group identity and the state. This construction of the enemy as "barbarian" and the self as "nonbarbarian" is not an ethereal action that can exist apart from the subjectivity of historically situated writers, for it is that subjectivity which makes a certain kind of plot thinkable and a certain kind of racialized attitude acceptable.

The epic genre itself places some restrictions, or at least some parameters, on the ways in which subjectivity is made manifest. Since the epic has

24. Edward W. Said, *Orientalism*, 55.

always participated in the public arena in a way that other poetic genres could not, it is not surprising that the poems in question should be programmatic and ideological. More intriguing is the occasional unexpected twist in the epic narrative. The fact that contradictions or subversions of epic codes can arise at all in a genre that by definition tends to privilege creating an illusion of moral absolutes and unitary subjects is quite remarkable. Yet perhaps it should not surprise us to find loci of intense conflict and a certain dualism in the epic. For even though these poems, generally, are foundational narratives that do not tolerate internal ideological divisions well, they cannot entirely suppress those divisions, either. Furthermore, epic poems are narratives of war that demand military parity between the warring parties. This means, among other things, that the enemy is never completely contemptible and that, on occasion, he or she earns the reader's best sympathy. Just as in many other kinds of myth that ultimately glorify foundations, what first fuels the epic plot is the violence of civil war, betrayal, rape, and murder. Brother against brother, man against woman, Christian against infidel: conflict seems to be inextricably bound up with foundational stories and with epic, generally.

In focusing on the linkage of culture to identity and imperial monarchy, this book may appear to de-emphasize humanism, a dominant cultural movement in Renaissance Spain. In truth, humanism was indispensable for the development of literary epic. Not only was its class base roughly the same as that of the epic—educated men and literate aristocrats with an austere taste in reading material—but in some ways, its project was also the same: appropriation of the writers of Greek and Roman antiquity according to its needs. Although the influence of Tasso and Ariosto on Spanish epic writers was very significant, it was from Lucan and particularly Virgil that they learned how to imagine and to image the empire. The Golden Age knew Homer largely through Virgil. From both bards the authors of Spanish epic took their sense of the importance of military expeditions against peoples perceived as different, of shipwrecks and foundations. From Virgil, writers like Alonso de Ercilla, Cristóbal de Virués, and Lope de Vega learned the boundless dimension of epic time and the literary devices for connecting a contemporary state to an immemorial past. Even for a writer like Diego de Hojeda, whose relationship to earthly power is admittedly ambivalent, Virgil remained the primary model through Marco Girolamo Vida's Christianized imitation of the *Aeneid*. Hojeda's *La Christiada*, like so many of its nonreligious counterparts, boasts a sustained critique of greed and other excesses of imperial expansion which is not only an epic topos, but a humanist one, as well. That critique, however, was never intended to call into question the rightness of the imperial enterprise itself.

Ultimately, Spanish epic of the sixteenth and seventeenth centuries promoted an idea of imperial monarchy that is a Castilian and Catholic version of the empire constructed in the epic of antiquity. In the Spanish texts, the conquest and domestication of the "other" and the resulting fabrication of a fictional group identity for both correspond to similar processes of subject-fashioning that already appear in the poets of Greece and Rome.

Spanish epic of the late sixteenth century does not, as a rule, use the word *empire*, yet its acceptance of Habsburg expansionism is everywhere apparent. From this one might infer that the idea of a universal polity with the Castilian monarch at its center was well established inside Spain by midcentury, but according to Elliott, the Castilian populace proved resistant to this notion at first.[25] The transient imperial monarchy needed myths to make it appear universal, enduring, and stable. As Frances Yates has shown, the ideal underpinning for Habsburg empire would lie in the old imperial idea, now revitalized in the new world ruler (*Dominus mundi*), Charles V. Through its identification with the Holy Roman Empire, Habsburg monarchy was linked to venerable myths of imperial predestination and fulfillment, such as the renovation and translation of the empire, the return of the golden age, the reign of peace and justice, and the recuperation of prelapsarian harmony.[26] In this context, the epic offered advantageous self-justifying strategies to the pro-Castilian upper echelon of the Iberian Peninsula that attempted to narrate its history and its agenda in the face of abiding pressure from both the peninsular semiperiphery and the periphery. Not only could the epic effectively incorporate and mobilize the myths of imperial culture, it could also draw on the prophecies and genealogies that were conventions of Greek and Roman epic to link the Castilian monarchy to a remote past, and, thus, manufacture the illusion of permanence. All epic shares this feature: part of its fiction is a backward gaze in search of validating legends. Epic shares this strategy with the nation-state and with some incipient form of national consciousness at least as far back as the Renaissance.

Although it would be anachronistic to invoke the nineteenth-century national idea here, there was a nationalism before the nation-state. Furthermore, the Spanish nation-state could be said to be precocious in some respects. In *Nations before Nationalism*, John A. Armstrong argues that

25. John H. Elliott, *Imperial Spain, 1469–1716*, 150.
26. See Frances A. Yates, *Astraea: The Imperial Theme in the Sixteenth Century*, Part 1, "Charles V and the Idea of the Empire"; and Marie Tanner's *The Last Descendant of Aeneas: The Habsburgs and the Mythic Image of the Emperor*. For the relationship between myth and state in the novel, see Timothy Brennan, "The National Longing for Form," in *Nation and Narration*, ed. Homi K. Bhabha.

in the early modern period, evangelizing religion, messianic myths that encode cultural superiority, and codification of what will be the national languages all contribute to the emergence of a national subjectivity. For specific reasons, several of these aspects show up comparatively early in Spain. The role of religion in connecting Spain's language to her military might is well documented. For Elliott, the preservation and extension of the faith constituted the mission that justified Habsburg hegemony in Europe and beyond.[27] Something of the same zeal accompanied the efficiency with which Charles V's reign elevated the Castilian language to a hegemonic position within the peninsula. Perhaps due in part to the foreign-born king's eagerness to establish his legitimacy on the Castilian throne and throughout his realm, the case of Spain shows comparatively early diffusion of the language of the court. In this period, Castilian Spanish was already becoming the "national print-language," to use Benedict Anderson's term. While the abandonment of nondominant vernaculars is usually identified as a later phenomenon coinciding with the period of nation-state consolidation, the language of Castile had already spread to the viceroyalties of the semiperiphery in the sixteenth century. Elliott claims that "Castile's cultural predominance derived from the innate vitality of its literature and language at the end of the fifteenth century." [28] Surely there were other considerations, such as Charles's determination to render the courts of the semiperiphery friendly to his throne. This early tendency toward Castilianization of the imperial monarchy would prove difficult to sustain and reaffirm as opposition grew within the semiperiphery and beyond in the later Habsburg years. But the reign of Charles V shows sufficient evidence of centralization to suggest that preconditions already existed for subjects from different points of the empire to suppose themselves part of a larger whole, which they believed to be consubstantial with imperial monarchy. It was the epic poets' job to render this larger whole—which was, in reality, a vulnerable construct—as predetermined and immutable.

Recent accounts of the origins of nationalism and theories of nation building place in the foreground the role played by literature of the imagination and by culture, generally, in fixing group identity. In

27. John H. Elliott, *Spain and its World, 1500–1700: Selected Essays*, 165. The contemporary political theorist Tommaso Campanella similarly emphasized the role played by religion in linking sword and language, the two "instruments of Empire." See Anthony Pagden, *Spanish Imperialism and the Political Imagination: Studies in European and Spanish-American Social and Political Theory, 1513–1830*, 59.

28. Benedict Anderson, *Imagined Communities: Reflections on the Origin and Spread of Nationalism*, 67; Elliott, *Imperial Spain*, 118.

Imagined Communities, Benedict Anderson emphasizes the genre of the text in building the nation; yet, because he wants to arrive at nineteenth-century nationalism, Anderson does not treat the epic, which he considers prenational, except to insist that epic time, simultaneous and distant, differs markedly from the "homogenous, empty time" of the novel.[29] What is significant about Anderson's argument is the connection it forges between text and state, and the role he attributes to the imagination in the process of actively creating a community.

Both Anderson and the theories of postcolonial discourse that draw on his work and sometimes criticize it focus unremittingly on the modern, usually on the novel. In this they are reminiscent of Bakhtin, whose essay on "Epic and Novel" mapped out a very lucid reading of the epic in order to arrive at a methodology for the study of the novel, which he finds open-ended by comparison, a genre in which "time and the world become historical," a literary type characterized by "an eternal re-thinking and re-evaluating." [30] All of these theories share a common bias in favor of modernity and a kind of archaeological argument: the epic gave us the novel, but the epic is extinct and imperfect, a sort of australopithecine national narrative. These backward-looking theories, which depend to one degree or another on the epic for their whole understanding of how national identities are forged, consistently slight and even misunderstand the earlier genre. (It is clear, for example, that these theorists have never read Virgil in his Roman context.) Yet obviously the epic does not exist only to herald the novel with its nation-building strategies. The epic is valid in and of itself, and it functions in analogous fashion much earlier. Fabricating group consciousness in ways that lay the foundations for the construction of nationalism in the later genre, the epic is an indispensable forerunner of national subjectivity.

In Spain, social groups who perceived that their interests were aligned with those of the Castilian monarchy now found it desirable to promote in heroic narrative the idea of a community, which they represented as sacred and universal. In an essay alluded to above, Maxime Chevalier explores the readership of the learned epic in the early modern period, concluding that the readers and writers of epic belonged to the same social group:

> The educated men of Habsburg Spain revere good letters, but they have their doubts about the value and interest of what we call "literature." Literature, if its aim is merely to entertain, has no justifi-

29. Anderson, *Imagined Communities*, 25.
30. Bakhtin, *Dialogic*, 30–31.

cation for many of them. From this point of view, they find the epic to
be a noble and reputable genre, when compared with a lyric poetry
that is frequently contemptible and hollow.[31]

The epic poems of this age glorified the warrior mentality, a belief sys-
tem that Chevalier calls "the warlike ideology" of gentlemen and nobles.
Quite a few of the writers of epic were soldiers. Among them were
Francisco Garrido de Villena, translator of Boiardo (*El verdadero suceso de la
famosa batalla de Roncesvalles*, 1555), Nicolás Espinosa (*La segunda parte de
Orlando*, 1555), Alonso de Ercilla (*La Araucana*, part 1, 1569), Luiz de
Camões (*Os Lusíadas*, 1572), Jerónimo de Urrea, translator of Ariosto (*El
victorioso Carlos V*, 1584), Juan Rufo Gutiérrez (*La Austriada*, 1584), Cristóbal
de Virués (*El Monserrate*, 1587), and Gaspar Pérez de Villagrá (*Historia de la
Nueva México*, 1610). Through the epic, these men fabricated an identity
that was in many ways a projection of themselves, here linked to a specif-
ic form of state. The epic promotes a body politic and a group subjectivity
that are unabashedly aristocratic; one should not expect to find any pre-
tense of democracy here. Instead, the discourses of epic empower an elite
to articulate its own centralist and expansionist aspirations, which it views
as harmonious with those of the state as a whole.

Like the nation, imperial monarchy is a discursive formation that the
writer of epic invokes through specific expressions (*énoncés*), such as the
appearance of the monarch in the text, expeditions of conquest, favorable
comparisons of Spanish heroes to their Roman counterparts, the represen-
tation of a united Christian self against an "other" usually depicted as
backward and heathen, the celebration of geographic knowledge resulting
from the discoveries, and admonitions against the excesses of conquest or
the lack of soldierly discipline. The fact that the epics did not always glo-
rify empire explicitly does not mean that the poets were not solidly behind
the imperial enterprise, or that other Spanish literary genres of the time
were more oppositional than the epic (though in some cases they undoubt-
edly were). What set the epic apart was that, for innate reasons, the poetic
universe that it figured forth appeared more inaccessible. Spanish theater
of the times displayed a wide variety of types, including serious characters
from different social groups and various kinds of female characters. The
heroic world of epic, on the other hand, positions its highborn characters
at a distance, always out of reach. The relationship of culturally or ethni-
cally identifiable subjects is almost always adversarial in the epic: with rare
and partial exceptions, the heroic poems of the Golden Age pit Spanish

31. Chevalier, *Lectura y lectores*, 123.

Christian caballeros against Amerindians, Muslims, or Jews. Thus all of these epics depend, to some degree, on an opposition, "Spain and her others," which remained in full force in sixteenth-century texts and has now been problematized in the work of José Rabasa and other scholars.[32] Through the absorption and neutralization of alterity, these epics attempt to paint a tidy picture of the ethnic purgation of a national space that they also constitute as thoroughly gendered. When the attempt fails, disruption tears open the poetic text, exposing the seams of the epic's dominant belief systems. To be sure, other discursive practices in Spain at the time were also hegemonic in varying degrees, but unlike these, the epic presumed to speak for the polity, which it attempted to represent as magnificent but somehow finished, untouchable, and closed to all but a noble few.

This book focuses on five epics published in Spain during the period 1569 to 1611, chosen in part because they are the poems most commented upon by critics of centuries past (starting with Alonso de Quijano's barber and his priest). In this sense, they might constitute an epic canon for the period, if we had one. Each chapter examines a cultural complex in which subject-fashioning depends on a complex scripting of otherness, but the "other" who opposes and at once defines Spanish heroism is different in each case. In chapter 1 it is the Amerindian. Here, discourse analysis is used to arrive at a complex paradigm of authorial subjectivity which can begin to account for opposing readings of Alonso de Ercilla's *La Araucana,* unquestionably the most important Spanish-language epic of its time. Chapter 2 begins with a close examination of poetic imitation in Juan Rufo's *La Austriada* that establishes a genetic link between Rufo's epic and *La Araucana.* Rufo's text, which criticizes the conduct of royal troops during the Alpujarras War, proves that, by itself, the censure of greed (a structural element in *La Araucana*) does not indicate an anti-imperialist stance. Rufo's ambivalent attitude toward an Islamic "other" also suggests the influence of Ercilla. Chapter 3 juxtaposes two readings of an epic of foundation that opens with a rape scene. In this case, the "other" is female. A philological reading of Cristóbal de Virués's *El Monserrate* complements and fleshes out another that is rooted in feminism. Chapter 4 identifies Diego de Hojeda's *La Christiada* as an evangelizing text that manifests an interdependent relationship between two apparently opposing inscriptions of identity: Christian hagiography and anti-Semitism. Chapter 5, on Lope de Vega's *Jerusalem conquered,* shows how the neutralization or elimination of female characters shores up a construct of heroic identity that is

32. José Rabasa, *Inventing America: Spanish Historiography and the Formation of Eurocentrism,* 6.

always already gendered. Since there is not a single avenue to the truth, it has not seemed advisable to use a single critical methodology here. Instead, several theoretical frameworks are used in combination to preserve the richness of epics that narrate the program of imperial monarchy but are, in themselves, very different. These parameters allow plenty of room for other scholarship on the five epic poems studied here.

A word about the need to cross academic boundaries is in order. Especially when dealing with the epics of the imperial age, it is impossible to avoid placing side by side texts that, in our time, are either disputed by distinct periods or fields or have been relegated to one or another of them. During the period of Spanish conquest and colonization of American lands, such a separation would perhaps have seemed artificial, especially in the case of epic, which deeply depends on ancient tradition, regardless of the place of composition. This has led to the inclusion here of Ercilla's *La Araucana*, which, at the very least, was a product of the poet's eight-year sojourn in American lands, and to that of Hojeda's *La Christiada*, composed in its entirety in Peru (though published in Seville, the birthplace of its author—a Dominican missionary who received his theological training in Lima). That said, it must not be supposed that a scholar trained in Golden Age studies can examine poems written in colonial Peru, for example, without encountering hidden stumbling blocks. This book has benefited from a full-hearted respect for scholarly work in the fields of both Golden Age and colonial Spanish American literatures and cultures, and from the educated opinion of specialists in both areas. It is hoped that the research has been thorough enough to overcome the most serious of the perplexities inherent in any study that ends up being transatlantic (a term that perhaps ought to inspire more caution than it has of late).

Imperial powers have always found it desirable to establish a construct of oneness and unanimity at home in the process of expansion and conquest abroad. Inside sixteenth-century Spain, the supporters of imperial monarchy had to do this under circumstances in which ethnic and regional differences made the creation of group identity particularly difficult. In the epic, these writers had a genre of great stature already equipped to suggest the real tensions that existed among different cultural groups in the peninsula, and certainly between a stylized image of themselves and recently conquered peoples in the periphery. Not all the texts examined here write identity in the same manner, nor do they uniformly reflect the cultural preoccupations at stake in their representations of the Spanish self and what they construct as its subalterns. As previously suggested, there are moments where the epics cannot successfully absorb alterity and conflict. But for reasons that are fundamental to the genre, the epic strains unceasingly to forge an overriding image of Spain that appears more unassailable and undivided than Spain and her empire ever were. While a similar foundational myth is certainly in evidence in other Golden Age genres, the master narrative of the program of imperial monarchy is to be found in the epic, a genre that has remained too long hidden from view.

1

Alonso de Ercilla's Fractured Subjectivity
Internal Contradictions in *La Araucana*

Of the five poems studied in this book, Alonso de Ercilla's *La Araucana* demonstrates the greatest tendency toward conflict and away from simple, unitary subjects. The poem, published in three parts (in 1569, 1578, and 1589), is a vast epic about the suppression of rebellion against the Spanish crown in distant Arauco (present-day Chile), in which campaign the poet himself took part. Because poetry, history, and autobiography converge in its pages, Ercilla's text is unrepresentative of its genre in some respects. The popularity of *La Araucana*, however (it was a Golden Age "best-seller"), lent instant prestige to this epic, which in some ways then set the paradigm for the Spanish heroic poems to follow.[1]

An issue that has characterized *Araucana* criticism since the nineteenth century is the question of "nationalist" readings. The idea of an "anti-imperialist," Chilean national interpretation standing in opposition to an older, pro-Habsburg "Spanish national" reading of Ercilla's text creates the impression of a divide in the scholarship surrounding this, the most-read Spanish-language epic of the period.[2] Both national readings, however, to the extent that they are really national at all, are grounded in textual dismemberment that is ideologically motivated. Furthermore, both interpretations ignore the complex, sometimes terrible contradictions of the text, contradictions born of the poet's own divided subjectivity. In other words, there is indeed a kind of divide in the *Araucana*, but it is not the one on which Ercilla scholarship has traditionally broken down. The lines of demarcation in the *Araucana* have to do, rather, with the way the dominant discourse of Ercilla's epic partially conceals the writer's other discourses, both intra- and extratextual. The argument elaborated in the following

1. See Keith Whinnom, "The Problem of the Best-seller in Spanish Golden-Age Literature."
2. Luis Íñigo Madrigal notes the tendency toward an "anti-imperialist" interpretation of the *Araucana* (*Historia de la literatura hispanoamericana*, 1:193), while Jaime Concha mentions the two "national" readings in "El otro Nuevo Mundo," an essay appearing in *Homenaje a Ercilla*, ed. Gastón Von Dem Bussche.

pages is that discrepant interpretations of the poem are conceivable in the first place because Ercilla's own split subjectivity creates a space in which many "misreadings" are plausible, even inevitable, particularly as the text enters into new transactions with a reading public that spans two continents and four centuries.

Nobility as Service

Because of the convention that military parity between the feuding parties is always desirable in epic, the absence of an identifiable and well-wrought Spanish hero has perplexed readers of the *Araucana* almost from the beginning. Cristóbal Suárez de Figueroa, an early biographer of García Hurtado de Mendoza, governor of Chile and leader of the Spanish troops in Arauco, criticized the poem for being "headless" (*acéfalo*). This biographer claimed that since Don García had banished Ercilla from Chile and jailed him, the author of *La Araucana* was too filled with resentment to treat the Spanish commander as he deserved:

> The advised harshness with which Don Alonso was treated made him try to bury the illustrious deeds of Don García in silence. He rendered the wars of Arauco in verse, always inserting in them a body without a head, that is, an army with no recollection of a general. Ungrateful for the many favors received from his [Don García's] hand, he left only a sketch of him, rather than painting him with the lively colors he deserved: as if it were possible to hide in this world the valor, virtue, providence, authority and good fortune of that gentleman who practiced deeds as well as words, and in whom both words and deeds were admirable.
>
> (El conveniente rigor con que Don Alonso fue tratado, causó el silencio en que procuró sepultar las ínclitas hazañas de D. García. Escribió en verso las guerras de Arauco, introduciendo siempre en ellas un cuerpo sin cabeza, esto es un ejército sin memoria de general. Ingrato a muchos favores que había recibido de su mano, le dejó en borrón, sin pintarle con los vivos colores que era justo: como si se pudieran ocultar en el mundo el valor, virtud, providencia, autoridad y buena dicha de aquel caballero, que acompañó siempre los dichos con los hechos, siendo en él admirables unos y otros.)[3]

On the other side, the principal Araucanian warriors stand out as individuals with unforgettable characteristics: the Achilleus-like Rengo is

---

3. Quoted by Antonio de Sancha, introduction to *La Araucana*, by Alonso de Ercilla, xx–xxi.

mighty and good-hearted but also contentious; Lautaro is an inspired ora-
tor and fighter whose false pride blinds him in the end; physical strength
and leadership grace Caupolicán until the conditions of his capture and
death turn him into an unmistakably pathetic figure. The reader can visu-
alize the scantily clothed bodies of the Araucanian fighters thanks to
descriptions that specifically mention robust arms, well-built muscles,
sturdy members, ferocious visages, curly hair, beautiful faces, sturdy
sinews, and so on. It must be said, however, that most of the graphic
images of Araucanian bodies come not from battle scenes, but from the
victory games, which are episodes full of strong Homeric overtones. There
are no such celebrations of battles won by the Spanish, and Ercilla might
have been a little leery of depicting his own compatriots in such starkly
pagan terms, anyway.

Whatever his reason, the poet chose not to round out the Spanish char-
acters in terms analogous to those used to render the Araucanian heroes.
Indeed, he seems to deliberately shy away from embodying the Spanish
heroic at all, which does not mean it is not present in the text. The closest
thing to a Christian hero is the character of Andrea the Genoese, described
as a "valiant bellicose lad" (*valiente mozo belicoso*) whose face is "fierce,
dirty and dusty, full of blood and stained with sweat" (fiero, sucio y
polvoroso, / lleno de sangre y de sudor teñido).[4] Andrea, said to be a
"giant in greatness and proportion," is not Spanish, but Italian, as his epi-
thet makes clear. In European texts of the time, it is not unusual to find
Spaniards in league with Italian troops in different parts of the
Mediterranean world. A case in point is the battle of Lepanto, but Spanish
epic of this period boasts other instances of Spaniards and Italians uniting
to fight Turks and Muslims, in general. In Cristóbal de Virués's *El
Monserrate*, for example, the hero sails to Italy, is carried to Africa by a
storm, and joins forces with Italians to defeat local warriors identified as
both African and Muslim. Ercilla's Andrea is neither a strategist nor a mil-
itary leader, but he is the only European the epic shows in physical terms
that are equivalent to some of the well-drawn Araucanian heroes (Tucapel,
for example), and he is the only one who relishes the prospect of fighting
Rengo. So Andrea stands out on the Spanish side for his physical prowess,
which Lerner refers to as his "legendary strength" (434 n. 35). To refer to
the Spaniards, the Ercillan text generally settles for a ritualistic affirmation
of a collective we (*nosotros*) and an occasional listing of surnames of brave
soldiers, such as in the catalogue of troops (25.26–27). Claiming that newer

---

4. All quotations of *La Araucana* are taken from the edition of Isaías Lerner
(Madrid: Cátedra, 1993), and appear hereafter in the text by canto, octave, and where
necessary, lines, in this case, 14.44.

technology (particularly the harquebus) encourages group heroism rather than individual heroic acts, Murrin calls heroism in the *Araucana* "anonymous," and he is undoubtedly correct that Spanish firearms (the Araucanians have none) directly influence both the odds and the way in which battles are fought, in the epic and in history.[5] But how is it that *La Araucana* can successfully invoke a Spanish hero that remains collective and nameless?

The lack of symmetry in the text has led the majority of critics to adopt one of two mutually exclusive positions. On one side are those who argue that the epic is pro-Spanish but aesthetically flawed by the absence of a champion for the Habsburg cause. In this spirit, Morínigo and Lerner— who are not necessarily champions of this position—remind us that critics have always complained about the *Araucana*'s missing hero. On the other side are the critics who consider Ercilla's poem a pro-Araucanian "epic of the defeated," which either lacks a dominant hero, or offers as its most important heroic figure Caupolicán. These are the positions of David Quint, whose reading ultimately positions him solidly within the camp of "anti-imperialist" readers of the poem, and José Durand, respectively.[6]

Although these interpretations reflect alternatives that are practically canonical in *La Araucana* scholarship, they cannot adequately account for Ercilla's poetic and political project because there are too many contradictions in the text to allow for an easy reduction of the poet's position. In the prologue, for example, Ercilla acknowledges that some might think he is more inclined toward the Araucanian side, but in the second and third parts of *La Araucana* he reverses the textual dynamics. Here, the Spaniards win battles that they never won in the first part; here, too, Ercilla promotes an increasingly panegyrical view of the entire Habsburg imperial program, in evidence in his own character's dream of the victory at St. Quentin and the prophetic vision of the battle of Lepanto. In a recent study of Ercilla's use of poetic imitation, Nicolopulos arrives at precisely this conclusion.[7] And if the poet ocasionally draws his reader's sympathetic gaze toward some of the Araucanian characters in the poem, he does not shrink from denigrating them at other points. Neither does he make any effort to conceal his enthusiasm for Spanish discoveries and military

5. Michael Murrin, *History and Warfare in Renaissance Epic*, 174.

6. See Marcos A. Morínigo and Isaías Lerner, introduction to *La Araucana*, by Ercilla, 63 and 78; David Quint, *Epic and Empire: Politics and Generic Form from Virgil to Milton*, 157–85; José Durand, "Caupolicán. Clave historial y épica de *La Araucana*," 368.

7. See James R. Nicolopulos, "Prophecy, Empire and Imitation in the *Araucana* in the Light of the *Lusíadas*," chaps. 4, 5.

exploits in the Old World and the New. Still, the lack of sharply drawn Spanish heroes in the epic creates serious textual rupture because it transgresses the reader's expectations of the genre.

García Hurtado de Mendoza was the logical choice for the figure of the Spanish hero since he was the commander of the king's troops in the Araucanian campaign. Indeed, *La Araucana* affirms Don García's role in the Chilean war, although it is true that Ercilla does not develop the character of the Spanish leader in the poem with the same enthusiasm he brings to the characterization of Lautaro or the early Caupolicán. Some critics have called Don García's lukewarm appearance in the epic an expression of Ercilla's resentment toward García Hurtado de Mendoza for imprisoning him and banishing him from Chile. Other scholars have found the character of Don García much more in evidence in the text. Writing in the eighteenth century, Antonio de Sancha notes that there was no way the Spanish commander could appear in part 1, which Sancha considered "the main part of the poem," because Don García had not yet arrived in Chile when the events narrated in part 1 took place. Sancha also notes that the Spanish military leader's name does, in fact, appear in the poem repeatedly. In the introduction to his 1993 edition of the poem, Lerner asserts that the figure of García Hurtado de Mendoza in the text is multifaceted due to Ercilla's decision to treat the Spanish commander with impartiality. Accepting Ercilla's complex text on its own terms, Lerner finds heroism, but also cruelty, in the individual deeds of courage or atrocity that stand out from the anonymous collective acts of Spanish soldiers in *La Araucana*.[8]

Part of Ercilla's problem was that the testimonial perspective of his narrative and his determination to recount very recent historical events did not allow him to create or recycle a purely literary hero. Golden Age epic boasts numerous examples of heroic characters reconfigured from the chronicles, from ballad collections (the *romancero*), and from medieval legends and hagiography. One thinks of Lope de Vega's Garcerán Manrique, for example (*Jerusalem conquered*), or Cristóbal de Virués's hermit, Juan Garín. Indeed, there was a veritable treasure trove of material of which sixteenth-century poets could avail themselves to remodel an old hero, if they were so inclined. But history, veracity, and testimony were all key elements of Ercilla's poetics. In the *Araucana*, he repeatedly affirms that he is sticking

---

8. Echoing Suárez de Figueroa's position, Quint writes that "Ercilla presumably could not stomach the idea of presenting his personal enemy, Mendoza, as a triumphant figure of royal authority and justice" (*Epic and Empire*, 172); also, see Sancha (introduction to *La Araucana*, by Ercilla, xxi–xxii) and Lerner (introduction to *La Araucana*, by Ercilla, 34).

close to historical truth as he witnessed it, frequently lamenting the dryness of the narrative that results from that decision. While it would be dangerous to take Ercilla's claim that his poem is nothing but the "bare truth" at face value, the poet's declared intention to give an accurate account of what happened in Arauco evidently placed very real constraints on what license he could take with what he and other veterans of the campaign knew had happened there. Thus, Alonso de Ercilla could not, as Virués and Lope would do, invent an exemplary Christian soldier to fight the Araucanians. Because Ercilla's historical method constrains him to tell the facts, Murrin writes that "the Indians at Purén probably have no names because Ercilla as an eyewitness could not find out who they were."[9] This is an oversimplification, however, since it is doubtful that the poet was ever in a position to really know any of the Indian warriors about whom he wrote. On his own Spanish side, all he could do was name his real comrades-in-arms at the appropriate moments. This he did in various places, moving some into the foreground, but he never turned any one of them into a hero larger than life.

However, there is another way of thinking about the absent Spanish hero, which is to suggest that the figure of the narrator and the character Ercilla are so dominant in the poem that they virtually preclude the possibility that a separate Spanish hero could command the poetic universe of the text without throwing it into serious imbalance.[10] This does not necessarily mean that Ercilla made a conscious decision to exclude from his epic any heroic figure that would rise above the rest of the Spanish troops so as to avoid diminishing his own presence in the text, though that could be true. What it does mean is that Ercilla's own position as a soldier of the Spanish crown is profoundly implicated in his narrative, and that his decision to write about real soldiers he knew on the Chilean campaign made it difficult for him to see them as anything but what they were: his peers. Ercilla could make heroes of the Araucanians much more easily. The poet's representations of the Araucanian people, in general, and his sympathetic portrayals of the women of Arauco, in particular (which establish gender as an important classification within the larger category of the Amerindian "other" represented in *La Araucana*), are well-studied aspects of the epic. As Pastor has shown, Ercilla attempted to represent the Araucanian warriors using conventions that made them more easily assimilable to the terms of

9. Murrin, *History and Warfare,* 174.
10. For alternative views on Ercilla's presence in his poem, see Juan Bautista Avalle-Arce, "El poeta en su poema (El caso Ercilla)"; Beatriz Pastor, *Discursos narrativos de la Conquista: Mitificación y emergencia,* 424–32; and Frank Pierce, *Alonso de Ercilla y Zúñiga,* 62–69.

Western epic tradition.[11] Nonetheless, their perceived radical difference allowed for aggrandizement of the principal Amerindian characters in a way that would have been inaccessible to Ercilla's comrades-in-arms, who share an equal standing with the figure of the poet in the text. The Amerindian could also be represented according to strategies considered beyond acceptable bounds for the representation of high-ranking Europeans. Writing of Shakespearean practice, Greenblatt observes that the vulnerable lower classes, "who may at most times be represented almost without restraint," fall in the category of "things indifferent (*adiaphora*): there for the taking." In Spain, comparisons between the customs of domestic lower classes and those of American Indians were already being made. Precisely because they were perceived as "there for the taking," inhabitants of the New World were depicted by writers in ways unsuitable for Europeans.[12] A case in point is the scene in which Fresia, wife of Caupolicán, throws her infant child at the feet of its captured father, exclaiming that she will not raise "the infamous child of an infamous father" (33.82). The baby is given to a new mother, which means, among other things, that the child of Caupolicán lives and that he can grow to take his father's place—a touch of romance that holds out the hope of future rebellion among the Araucanians. It is difficult to imagine Golden Age poets writing of similar defiant acts by Spanish mothers. In general, Ercilla had freer rein to fictionalize the Araucanians than to turn his comrades, or himself, into figures of mythical proportions.

As both narrator and character, Ercilla intrudes into his narrative at every turn, but he is no more a hero than any other Spanish soldier in the Araucanian war, and his character cannot fill the heroic void on the Spanish side of the text. The crucial mitigating circumstance, however, is that throughout the poem the character Ercilla and the authorial voice appear always and everywhere connected to the figure of the monarch, and this fact lends an aura of prestige to the poet's own character that conditions the entire epic. The illuminating presence of Philip II permeates *La Araucana* to

11. For a sampling of views on the problem of Westernizing representations of the Amerindian in *La Araucana*, see Pastor, *Discursos narrativos*, 382–403; Francisco Javier Cevallos, "Don Alonso de Ercilla and the American Indian: History and Myth"; and Murrin, *History and Warfare*, 101. For Ercilla's sympathetic (and literary) treatment of Araucanian women, see José Toribio Medina, "Las mujeres de *La Araucana* de Ercilla," and especially Lía Schwartz Lerner, "Tradición literaria y heroínas indias en *La Araucana*."

12. For European attitudes toward the vulnerable classes, see Greenblatt, *Shakespearean Negotiations*, 9, and Julio Caro Baroja, "Religion, World Views, Social Classes, and Honor during the Sixteenth and Seventeenth Centuries in Spain," in *Honor and Grace in Anthropology*, ed. J. G. Peristiany and Julian Pitt-Rivers, 95.

a greater extent than most Ercilla scholars seem to have recognized. An exception can be found in the article of Albarracín Sarmiento, who distinguishes between narrative and metanarrative levels in *La Araucana*, analyzing aspects of the connection between Ercilla and Philip II on each level. In truth, it is impossible to grasp the inner workings of Ercilla's text without appreciating Philip II's appearance there as implied addressee, or reader. For Lerner, Ercilla's dedication of the poem to Philip II was an acknowledgment of this, "a corroboration of the central idea of his poem: the sovereign would be the best reader of the enterprise that best defined the purpose of his reign."[13] By inscribing the monarch into his text in this way, the poet is able to identify his poem as a tribute to his king, and he can invoke the eminence of monarchic presence at will across the trajectory of the poem simply by using the device of apostrophe. In so doing, he exhibits a confidence verging on complicity with the royal person, one that authorizes both his values and his perspective as narrator.

But this is not just an ingenious way to manipulate the text. The concept of "nobility as service" was as old as the aristocracy itself. Domínguez Ortiz sees the positioning of noblemen in the administrative apparatus as a natural outgrowth of the old notion that the nobility had certain obligations that counterbalanced its privileges:

> The nobility was considered the nursery of high-level administration. Different strains of thought contributed to this belief: the prejudice according to which noblemen were the noblest, most faithful and intelligent servants on whom the Monarchy could count; the fact that their social situation and economic means could afford them an education which was unattainable by most plebeians; the nobility's aversion to putting themselves at the service of anyone who did not have their status; the tradition of nobility as service, a kind of cross entry to their privileges, preferably military service but also service on a council, according to a tradition of remote origin.[14]

The discourse of service reinforces rather than contradicts the traditional discourse of blood, which, as Mariscal points out, by the second half of the sixteenth century was no longer able to constitute subjects without the aid of other discursive formations.[15] An aristocratic background and

---

13. Lerner, introduction to *La Araucana*, by Ercilla, 13. See also Carlos Albarracín Sarmiento, "El poeta y su Rey en *La Araucana*."

14. Antonio Domínguez Ortiz, *Instituciones y sociedad en la España de los Austrias*, 20.

15. See George Mariscal, *Contradictory Subjects: Quevedo, Cervantes, and Seventeenth-Century Spanish Culture*, 50–51. I have been particularly influenced by the

compelling biographical reasons led Ercilla to frame his relationship to Philip II in the terms of service. The poet had been Philip's page and had spent seven impressionable years in the future king's company. A careful reading of *La Araucana* hints that Ercilla wishes his readers to see an especially strong bond between himself and the monarch. There is also extratextual evidence that suggests the significance of this connection.

Among the preliminaries of the first edition of part 1, there is a letter to the king that reads as follows:

> Sacred Catholic Royal Majesty: Since in the first years of my childhood I began to serve your Majesty, which was at the time that you first went to Flanders [1548/1549], as I grew older, the inclination and desire to serve which I have demonstrated everywhere I have gone (which by now has been to many and different places) always grew stronger in me; being your Majesty's page in England, many years after my father, servant of your Majesty and of your council, was dead, and also my mother, head of the ladies-in-waiting of the Empress Doña María, seeing myself orphaned of both parents and such a young boy, and since the news of Francisco Hernández's rebellion in Peru had just arrived, with the will to serve your Majesty that I had always had and with your license and grace, I was disposed to undertake such a long journey; and so I traveled to that realm, in which I was present for everything I write about which the Viceroy did for the pacification of the land. And judging the labors of that campaign to be small, with the same desire to serve your Majesty which I always had, knowing that the native people of Chile were in rebellion against the Royal Crown, I determined that I would travel to those provinces; and when I had arrived, having seen the remarkable things and wars of the state of Arauco, and participated in them to the extent that my insufficient strength would allow, believing that I still had not achieved that which I desired, I also decided to spend the poor talent which God had given me on something that could serve your Majesty, in order that nothing would remain which I had not offered you. And so in the midst of weapons and in the short space that they gave me to do so, I wrote this book, so that you may take it under your protection, which is what will make it flourish. May our Lord keep the Sacred Catholic Royal person of your Majesty, with increase of greater kingdoms and domains. In Madrid on the 2 of March, 1569.
> Sacred Catholic Royal Majesty.
> Your Majesty's servant,
> who kisses your royal hands.
> Don Alonso de Ercilla

---

work of Mariscal for my understanding of competing discourses and fractured subjects in early modern Spain.

(S.C.R.M. Como en los primeros años de mi niñez, yo comenzase a servir a vuesa Magestad, que fue cuando pasó la primera vez a Flandes, siempre con la edad creció en mí aquella inclinación y deseo de servir que en todas partes por donde anduve, después acá que han sido muchas y diversas he mostrado, que siendo page de V.M. en Inglaterra, después de muchos años que mi padre criado de V.M. y de su consejo era muerto, y asimismo mi madre guarda mayor de las Damas de la Emperatriz doña María, viéndome huérfano de padres, y tan mozo, llegando a la sazón la nueva de la rebelión de Francisco Hernández en el Perú, con la voluntad que siempre tuve de servir a V.M. y con su licencia y gracia me dispuse a tan largo camino, y así pasé en aquel reino, donde me hallé en todo lo que escribo, que el Visorrey hizo para el allanamiento de la tierra. Y estimando en poco el trabajo de aquella jornada, con la codicia que de servir a V.M. tenía, sabiendo que los naturales de Chile estaban alterados contra la Corona Real, determiné de pasar en aquellas provincias, y llegado a ellas, visto las cosas notables, y guerras del estado de Arauco, haciendo en ellas lo que mis flacas fuerzas pudieron, pareciéndome que aún no cumplía con lo que deseaba, quise también el pobre talento que Dios me dio gastarle en algo que pudiese servir a V.M. porque no me quedase cosa por ofrecerle. Y así entre las mismas armas, en el poco tiempo que dieron lugar a ello escribí este libro, el cual V.M. reciba debajo de su amparo, que es lo que le ha de valer. Cuya S.C.R. persona de V.M. nuestro Señor guarde, con acrecentamiento de mayores reinos y señoríos. En Madrid a dos de Marzo de 1569.
    S.C.R.M.
    Criado de V.M.
    Que sus Reales manos besa.
    Don Alonso de Ercilla)

It is hard to know how much of this letter is heartfelt nostalgia for a past bond, and how much is eloquently expressed self-interest. The document reads like a record of services rendered (*hoja de servicios*), but it starts from a position of acute vulnerability on Ercilla's part. It emphasizes the poet's feelings of abandonment and youthful preoccupation with his orphaned state, sentiments mitigated only by an advantageous situation in the royal household. The letter also bespeaks a strong desire (*codicia*) to serve the monarch and an inclination to turn to him for protection. These are not passing concerns, for they crop up in numerous ways throughout the epic itself, which Ercilla composed over a span of more than twenty years. What is distinctive about the letter is its strikingly personal tone. Beginning with the 1578 (Zaragoza) edition of the second part, Ercilla replaced the letter with a brief and somewhat perfunctory dedication to the king. The 1569 letter, which details key aspects of Ercilla's association with Philip II, never appeared again. Judging from its contents, the author of *La Araucana* invested a great deal in his ties to the monarch. Even so, it is impossible to tell whether the poet's allegiance to Philip was more than just "very rhetorical and conformist, in keeping with tradition," as Alegría claims.[16] The appeals Ercilla makes to the monarch throughout the epic have a highly rhetorical function, and they serve to move the discourse of service to the foreground in his epic. This discourse has a dual function: it partially safeguards the Spanish heroic from taint of unsavory events in the Araucanian war, and it places a buffer around Ercilla's own character. By constantly reaffirming the connection between himself and Philip II, the writer cloaks his own character in the prestige of closeness to royalty.

When the poet introduces the king into his text, he is not engaging in an empty gesture. On the contrary, the figure of the monarch in literature of the period usually casts a shadow of austerity across the page. When the king comes on stage as a character in Golden Age theater, for example, he imposes automatic constraints on the demeanor and behavior of surrounding characters. Guillén de Castro's *Las mocedades del Cid*, for example, shows that it was forbidden for a character to unsheathe his sword in the monarch's presence. As Dian Fox has shown, the political philosophy that Golden Age Spain inherited from ancient Greece attributed many virtues to the king, the most important of which was the quality of justice.[17] But justice, as Ercilla's text makes clear, is not an abstract idea; the monarch or his representatives (in the case of *La Araucana*, the viceroy) must mete out justice in a real world where some subjects deserve clemency, while others have earned harshness. What Ercilla's epic teaches us about justice is that in concrete circumstances of rebellion against the crown, exemplary punishment must be applied sooner, rather than later, so as to avoid continued sedition. It is surely no coincidence that both cantos 1 and 2 end by lamenting the fact that Valdivia, here depicted as remiss in his duties, did not take stricter measures against the rebellious Araucanians from the beginning.

Apart from the complex notion of monarchic justice, however, the king's appearance in Golden Age literature is often tantamount to an almost divine presence in the text. It is a commonplace, for example, that the monarch possessed powers that no one else held, not even members of the highest nobility. The title and themes of plays such as Rojas Zorrilla's *Del Rey abajo, ninguno* (*No one of lower rank than the king*), Lope de Vega's *El*

16. Fernando Alegría, "Ercilla y sus críticos," in Alegría's *La poesía chilena del siglo 16 al 19,* 54.

17. See Dian Fox, *Kings in Calderón: A Study in Characterization and Political Theory,* 8. It is worth noting that Philip II forbade the portrayal of any monarch on stage, which suggests his extreme sensitivity to such portrayals. See Geoffrey Parker, *Philip II,* 51.

mejor alcalde el Rey (*The best mayor is the king*), and Vélez de Guevara's *Más pesa el Rey que la sangre* (*The king carries more weight than does lineage*) are illustrative of this point. Legal constraints, decorum, awe, and fear all operated in the texts of the period to construct the king as a terrible, god-like figure who embodied a type of social control that limited the options available to his subjects.

Albarracín Sarmiento writes that the monarch's presence is in evidence in the battle scenes of *La Araucana* through specific emblems and attributes (the royal flag and standard, the king's piety, clemency, and prudence).[18] In truth, the attributes and objects that Albarracín Sarmiento mentions appear in many other scenes as well. Indeed, there is much more of Philip than this in *La Araucana*. Ercilla's text tells us that the monarch's voice or his name alone was enough to make traitors shudder:

> for when the King's voice is heard
> there is no sound so hard or rough to the ear,
> whose name alone has strength enough
> to crush and oppress the bones of the listener.
>
> (pues que cuando la voz del Rey se siente
> no hay són tan duro y áspero al oído
> que tiene solo en nombre fuerza tanta
> que los huesos le oprime y le quebranta.)
> (12.93.5–8)

Previous scholars have noticed the abundance of apostrophes to Philip II in *La Araucana*. They have even counted them: Pierce calculates that there are approximately fifty, while Lerner makes out thirty-three instances where the direct address is explicit, not implied. This critical mass of apostrophic utterances alerts us to a striking difference between Ercilla's text and other Golden Age epics, none of which exhibit such sustained use of this figure of speech. *La Araucana* is also at odds with ancient epic in this regard. Because each occurrence of apostrophe interrupts the referential function generally associated with the third-person focus of epic poetry, the frequency of these appeals already signals a distinctive eagerness on the poet's part to lure the monarch's gaze toward his poem.[19] Based on their discrete functions in the text and on a discernible pattern of occurrence, these apostrophic sentences are by no means random. Rather, they create the effect of forging a tight, constant link between the narrator and the figure of the monarch.

18. Albarracín Sarmiento, "El poeta y su Rey," 109.
19. See Lerner, introduction to *La Araucana*, by Ercilla, 24 n. 21; Pierce, *Alonso de Ercilla*, 57–58; Roman Jakobson, *Selected Writings*, 3:26.

A close reading of Ercilla's epic shows that not all instances of direct address to the sovereign belong to the same category. Each time that the narrator's voice addresses the regal "Lord" (*Señor*) who seems to govern this text, it is modulated in a slightly different way according to what is at stake. The apostrophic utterances that stand out most clearly in the poem are rhetorical. They correspond to a function of language focused on the addressee that Jakobson calls the supplicatory conative function.[20] The tone of these addresses is already detectable in the 1569 letter that Ercilla wrote to Philip II. Included in this category are the apostrophes that adorn the text at major turning points in the poem, but also ones used to certify the truth of the narration. In general, the function of these addresses is thus to validate the narrative and to mark the way for the reader.

The occasion of greatest intensification of apostrophe occurs at the moment when Ercilla narrates his sojourn in England at the king's side and his journey to Peru (cantos 12–13), where Hurtado de Mendoza had recently quashed the rebellion of Francisco Hernández de Girón. This is a decisive moment in the narrative, for it is here that Ercilla takes leave of Philip II. He then repositions his character in the western hemisphere by inserting himself into the epic as eyewitness and participant in the events of the subduing of the Peruvian rebellion, then the Araucanian war. The figure of the poet addresses the king concerning specific aspects of this situation that are pivotal both in his life and in his text, a text that he now claims will take on greater authority since he is physically present in Arauco. To certify the truth of events he has already narrated that occurred before his arrival in American lands, he tells Philip that he has listened to both sides, then included only those things on which everyone agreed (12.69). The authorial voice appeals to the monarch for indulgence because of his youth, adducing the rightness of his cause, his zeal, and his eagerness as grounds to excuse any errors in what he writes (12.74). The poet's inexperience, very considerable compared to his accomplishments, also appeared as an important consideration in the letter to the king cited above. In canto 12, Ercilla surveys the landscape of treason that Hurtado de Mendoza encountered on his arrival in Peru, and affirms the viceroy's prudence, his warranted severity, and his clemency, all characteristics normally associated with the monarch in whose name Hurtado de Mendoza acts (13.5). Nonetheless, Ercilla refuses to condemn those who were punished for the revolt, stating that judgment is the king's alone ("de vos solo es el juzgarlos," 12.82).

Affirming Philip's power and sovereignty, the authorial voice then states his obligation to the king and reflects back on his trip to England with the royal court:

20. Jakobson, *Selected Writings*, 3:23.

> For I was in your service in England,
> not having been armed a knight,
> when news came of the wrong committed
> in your disservice by those of Arauco . . .
>
> (Que estando en Inglaterra en el oficio
> que aun la espada no me era permitida,
> llegó allí la maldad en deservicio
> vuestro, por los de Arauco cometida . . .)
> (13.29.3.6)

This memory establishes a temporal link between the past and the present and a spatial link between England (Europe) and America, each metonymically embodied in the persons of the king and his subject and former page. The stanza's opening phrase, "I also with them" (*yo con ellos también*), announces Ercilla's will to submerge himself in the sea of Spanish soldiers fighting in Arauco.

However, he immediately undercuts the fleeting wish for anonymous stewardship by asserting his record of long-standing service to the crown. This recollection of nearness and dedication to the king during his adolescence, already visible in the dedicatory letter, creates the effect of setting Ercilla apart from the nameless mass of royal troops, none of whom had a personal connection of this type with the royal household. At a time when very few people had direct access to the monarch, Alonso de Ercilla and two other pages gave up coveted posts in Philip's entourage—posts that also guaranteed them a measure of material comfort at court—to join Hurtado de Mendoza's party.[21] The circumstances of their decision are unknown. Did they belong to a faction that did not enjoy favor at the time? Had they been tantalized by stories of easily acquired wealth in Peru? These questions have no answer. What is immediately important is that in this passage, Ercilla establishes his own figure in the text as polyvalent: he is both ordinary (one soldier among many in the royal troops), and exceptional (former page and member of the king's retinue), a circumstance that allows him to invoke proximity to or distance from his comrades-in-arms on the Araucanian campaign. For example, when he writes "where the king is absent, affronts are present in abundance" (adonde falta el rey sobran agravios, 4.5), though Ercilla the character is as distant from his king as anyone else in the American colonies, his words constitute a warning whose

---

21. See Madrigal, *Historia de la literatura*, 1:189. On Philip II's inaccessibility in his own court, see Fernando Bouza Alvarez's analysis of the monarch as *"Roi casanier"* in "La majestad de Felipe II. Construcción del mito real," in *La corte de Felipe II*, ed. José Martínez Millán.

truth is presumed to be universal and general. The poet's courtly grooming, however, makes him appear different from the rest; the admonishment certainly does not extend to him. Ercilla's sustained "dialogue" with the king, revealed in the apostrophes to Philip II and his memories of an elite background, induce the reader to judge him far more capable of discerning right from wrong than many of his compatriots.

Drawing attention to his service to the crown, therefore, achieves the purpose of surrounding the figure of Ercilla with a halo of exceptionality. Since he positions himself within a courtly imaginary that includes the king, the poet is able to take the moral high ground when confronted with unpalatable events taking place around him in these lands so far away from Spain. So it is that Ercilla finds fault with the mode of Caupolicán's execution. In a self-serving disclaimer, immediately upon narrating the gruesome death to the tiniest detail, Ercilla hastens to reassure his king that if the poet had been present, none of it would have happened:

> It seems to me that even the most cruel
> and hardened listener is moved
> when this monstrous case is told,
> for which, my Lord, I was not present,
> since I had gone off on a new conquest
> of far-away and unknown peoples;
> if I had been there at the time,
> the brutal execution would have been suspended.

> (Paréceme que siento enternecido
> al más cruel y endurecido oyente
> deste bárbaro caso referido
> al cual, Señor, no estuve yo presente,
> que a la nueva conquista había partido
> de la remota y nunca vista gente;
> que si yo a la sazón allí estuviera,
> la cruda ejecución se suspendiera.)
> (34.31)

It is significant that Ercilla added this strophe in the 1589–1590 edition.[22] The writer, who apparently cannot bear his own terrible complicity in a conquest that inevitably leads to events such as the one he has just recounted, tries to soften or whitewash the record for his listener by distancing himself from a character like the "black Wolof" (*negro gelofo*) whom the Spaniards forced to impale Caupolicán and, indeed, from the whole execution. Instead,

22. Lerner, *La Araucana*, by Ercilla, 904 n. 43.

he says he was elsewhere, involved in a "new conquest" to the south, the material successes of which the poet celebrates with evident relish:

> I shall not be able to embellish our pride,
>   our young and lively spirits,
>   our hope of goods and wealth,
>   our vain plots and speeches.
> Hills, mountains, crags and uneven terrain,
>   all were easy and flat roads to us,
>   and excessive danger or work
> no longer dared to stand in our way.
>
> (No sabré encarecer nuestra altiveza,
>   los ánimos briosos y lozanos,
>   la esperanza de bienes y riqueza,
>   las vanas trazas y discursos vanos.
> El cerro, el monte, el risco y la aspereza
>   eran caminos fáciles y llanos,
>   y el peligro y trabajo exorbitante
>   no osaban ya ponérsenos delante.)
> (35.28)

Ercilla depicts himself as a beneficiary of the conquest in these verses, which show him in a jolly mood and far from the scene of Caupolicán's death. That the poet should want to separate himself from such an appalling situation is understandable: impalement is a particularly brutal form of execution, but on a symbolic level, this is also a rape scene, a fact that adds an extra measure of humiliation to defeat and death. For Ercilla, these are the "inhumane deeds that take the shine off the grand Spanish victory" (actos inhumanos, / iban la gran vitoria deslustrando, 26.7.3–4), a victory he simultaneously celebrates in his verses about the voyage to the south. He responds in exactly the same way to Galbarino's death (canto 26).

Thus, the poet is at one and the same time a participant and a spectator, one who is just as capable of making pronouncements about the conduct of his fellow Spaniards as he is about that of the foe. Beatriz Pastor's analysis of Ercilla's distancing mechanisms, which she refers to as "different degrees of distance of that poet-soldier, who is the narrator, with respect to particular events in an action in which he finds himself doubly implicated," is correct. But Pastor's view of this verbal behavior of Ercilla's is overly generous, for the poet's veiled criticisms are convenient attempts on his part to salvage his own image, now compromised by his historical complicity with a Spanish war in Arauco that grows more and more brutal, rather than a principled protest against official policy.[23]

23. Pastor, *Discursos narrativos*, 425–27.

The constant reminder of Ercilla's patrician past (as well as his father's and mother's) also serves to bridge the vast gap that separates his character, in the epic but also in history, from the monarch. Whether he is in Spain, England, Peru, or Chile, service to the crown is the one thing that in the poet's case remains equally compelling, when all else seems unstable and ephemeral. The act of memory, therefore, is crucial to Ercilla's sense of connectedness to the king and to his own desired identity. But it is through apostrophe, a figure that inherently implies both a presence and an absence, that he has immediate access to the monarch from a distance.[24] Through direct address or appeal, the poet carries the monarch with him to America, as it were. Even if it is on the level of a trope that governs his text, the figure of Ercilla becomes the effective link to the past and the conductor of monarchic presence into Arauco. By constantly invoking Philip II wherever he goes, Ercilla also represents himself as a higher caliber of Spaniard.

Some instances of direct address seem less momentous in character and tone than the type of apostrophe discussed here. Sometimes apostrophic phrases fill a need for clarification or further explanation on the narrator's part; thus, they are primarily metatextual in nature. An example of this kind of apostrophe is the clarification Ercilla offers after Marcos Véaz holds talks with Lautaro: "His intention, Lord, was to make Véaz believe that their feigned hunger was real" (Era, Señor, su intento que pensase / ser la necesidad fingida, cierta, 12.29.1–2). There are other instances when the apostrophe to the king comes at the beginning or the end of an episode. In such cases, it serves as a signpost that marks either a shift in the direction of the narrative or the introduction of a new section. An example of this type of address occurs when Ercilla jettisons a plan to narrate first the Araucanian council, then European events, in favor of recounting Don García's expedition to the south.

> But if you do not tire, Lord,
> before I tell you what Colocolo said,
> I want to take a long and different road
> and return the enterprise to our own pole.
> For though I propose to tell you many things,
> the subject I now take up is by itself enough
> to lift my sunken, tired voice above
> topics to this point unavoidable.
>
> But if you give me leave I should like
> (so that I could tell this at a better time)

---

24. See Jonathan Culler, "Apostrophe," in *The Pursuit of Signs: Semiotics, Literature, Deconstruction,* 150. I owe this reference to Robert ter Horst.

to catch up with Don García, if I could,
though the course is long and uneven . . .

(Pero si no os cansáis, Señor, primero
que os diga lo que dijo Colocolo,
tomar otro camino largo quiero
y volver el designio a nuestro polo.
Que aunque a deciros mucho me profiero,
el sujeto que tomo basta solo
a levantar mi baja voz cansada
de materia hasta aquí necesitada.

Mas si me dais licencia yo querría
(para que más a tiempo esto refiera)
alcanzar, si pudiese, a don García
aunque es diversa y larga la carrera . . .)
(34.44–45.1–4)

In this particular instance, the apostrophe facilitates two abrupt shifts in the plot line; without it, the reader would be quite lost. At times, however, the narrator seems to address his king just to make sure that he is still "listening," that he is following, that he is still there. A case in point is the passage where Lautaro sets free a Spanish horse as proof that he has been in Villagrán's camp ("He had taken ten horses, Lord, in the skirmish and previous revolt" [Diez caballos, Señor, había ganado / en la refriega y última revuelta], 11.51.1–2). In cases like this, the apostrophe serves not so much a rhetorical function as a phatic one; it insures that the thread of communication between poet and monarch is not broken, and that the channel of imagined exchange is still open.

These and many other instances of apostrophe to the monarch throughout the cantos of *La Araucana* emphasize a textual bond between Ercilla and Philip II that is meant to appear unbreakable. They also help to establish the discourse of service as the dominant one in the epic, one that does not fade but resurfaces all through the poem. This does not mean that Ercilla's constant mobilization of the discourse of service is selfless, or that the utterances this discourse comprises should be interpreted as transparent. On the contrary, it was customary for Spaniards "on the make" in Peru to use such utterances to ingratiate themselves with the court in the hope of obtaining material gain. Sixteenth-century letters from the Spanish Indies give ample proof of this.[25] The discourse of service, however, does create a bias in the text. The significance of the link between the monarch and the poet throughout the three parts of the *Araucana* is that it places the

25. See *Letters and People of the Spanish Indies: Sixteenth Century*, ed. James Lockhart and Enrique Otte.

text into a default pro-Habsburg position, and this partially makes up for the lack of a clearly defined Spanish hero in the epic. In view of all Ercilla's appeals to Philip II everywhere, there is simply not much space left, nor perhaps is there a burning need, to develop larger-than-life heroic figures on the Spanish side.

The frequently rhetorical affirmation of service that Ercilla chooses to privilege in his text belongs to a discursive formation learned during his youth in the household of the future Philip II. The idea of nobility as service binds the vassal to his lord, but it also constrains the lord to reward his faithful servant, a fact not lost on Ercilla. The discourse of service appears more intensely toward the poem's end, and its status in the text is reaffirmed, finally, by the introduction of the monarch as character in the thirty-seventh and final canto, which narrates Philip II's annexation of Portugal as a legally justified fait accompli.

Vassalage is by no means the only discourse that constitutes subjectivity in *La Araucana*. If it were, such widely divergent readings of this epic would not have been thinkable in the first place. The discourse of service, however, cannot fairly be opposed to nineteenth-century nationalist or "anti-imperialist" discourses that would not yet have been available to a sixteenth-century Spaniard like Ercilla. If other discourses could subtly challenge vassalage (a profoundly aristocratic discourse), these would have to be modernist discourses that, in one way or another, threatened the underpinnings of the aristocratic worldview as a whole, of which vassalage was an intrinsic part.

To emphasize the discourse of vassalage is to acknowledge a priority immanent in the text. It is not to detract from everything else that the poet has inscribed there: the vast American geography, the occasionally stunning representations of Araucanian heroes, a textualization of the poet's own idealized dealings with the Araucanian widows, and the foregrounding of Spanish discoveries. The discourse of service in the *Araucana* has a strategic importance in that it prevents the narrative from ever straying too far from the watchful eyes of Philip II, whose gaze Ercilla has deliberately written into his text in order to control a story that belongs to a far-away place. Seen in this way, the monarch's presence in *La Araucana* suggests that the rules that govern sociopolitical life in Arauco should be the same ones that obtain in the home country. Ercilla seems to suggest that like Francisco de Vitoria, he considers the American Indians to be "subject to the same laws of intellectual change, progress and decline as other men are."[26]

---

26. Anthony Pagden, *The Fall of Natural Man: The American Indian and the Origins of Comparative Ethnology*, 99.

Ercilla's poem, however, shows evidence of other discourses, ones that serve to strengthen the discourse of service and, occasionally, to undercut it. By focusing on the discourse of blood and that of virtue, but also on traces of a newer, economic discourse in the text, one can shed light on Ercilla's divided subjectivity and thereby understand what it is in *La Araucana* that makes viable readings that are at variance with one another. The idea that Ercilla's sense of self was split is not entirely new; Pastor also describes Ercilla's consciousness as "profoundly divided." These pages, however, are heading in a different direction from the one that leads Pastor to read *La Araucana* as "the first Spanish American literary expression of a consciousness that comes to terms with the fact of its own alienation."[27] By looking at Ercilla's distinct discourses, it becomes possible to delve deeper into the things in his epic that have been variously interpreted for so long.

"Viper or Scorpion Indian:" Dissension and the Discourse of Blood

The ideology of blood was for centuries the dominant discursive formation by which the Spanish nobility constituted its own identity and, inversely, that of groups it excluded from its ranks, as George Mariscal has brilliantly argued. It was almost inevitable that Spanish imperial monarchy, emerging on the heels of the recently concluded *Reconquista*, should transfer discriminatory domestic cultural practices onto the peoples of its new American territories. There was, as is well known, much discussion and debate within Spain about the Amerindian's nature and his rights.[28] Especially in his discussion of just war (canto 37), Ercilla shows himself to be conversant with some issues and theories of these debates. And, as suggested above, the poet showcases the Araucanian heroes (in particular, Lautaro, but also, especially early on, Caupolicán) in a way that makes patent his admiration for them. But the Araucanians were racially different from sixteenth-century Spanish aristocrats and Ercilla, as a member of the latter group, could not apprehend racial difference in total isolation from the discourse of blood, a discourse that surreptitiously winds its way into *La Araucana* as a tacit means of justifying the very war that repulses the writer at its most violent moments.

Ercilla does not invoke the discourse of blood overtly to put the Araucanians "in their place" on the losing end of a war of conquest. However, by ascribing to the Araucanian people political forms and social

27. Pastor, *Discursos narrativos*, 424, 440.
28. Mariscal, *Contradictory Subjects*, 45. The best-known examples of peninsular debate on the nature of the American Indian are Francisco de Vitoria's reflections on the subject (delivered in 1539), and the Las Casas-Sepúlveda debates of 1550.

habits that could only be interpreted as "barbaric" from a sixteenth-century European perspective, the poet manages to suggest racial inferiority without the use of blood or lineage, per se. At the same time that he arouses the reader's enthusiasm for the patriotic character of the Araucanian people through speeches that call for the foreigners' expulsion, Ercilla implicitly condemns it as inferior by mobilizing an old hierarchical opposition, civilization versus barbarism, and locating the Araucanians on the lower side of it by dint of their alleged inability to achieve or hold unity within their ranks. Even so, the poet's stance toward the American Indian remains ambivalent.

Quint writes that dissension is one of those characteristics that, in the imperial ideology of epic, has traditionally been displaced from within the ranks of a supposedly unified Western self onto an "othered" opponent.[29] *La Araucana* ascribes discord to the Araucanians on such a sustained basis that it appears to be an intrinsic characteristic, one that is constitutive of identity. The problem of disunity opens out in two directions in the epic: first, it textualizes a faulty social organization or political structure; second, it represents the Araucanians as torn by strife within their own ranks and consequently as an eminently defeatable opponent.

Siding with such advocates of the rights of the Amerindian as Vitoria and Bartolomé de Las Casas, Ercilla represents Araucanian society as civilized by virtue of its adherence to a social structure that shows both a type of ruling elite (the caciques and their chosen leader, Caupolicán), and a warrior elite, though in fact these functions are carried out by the same group in the epic. The existence of a bellicose ruling circle proves that, whatever other signs of backwardness the Araucanians may demonstrate, they are in possession of an ordered and hierarchical social body. Aristotle's theory of natural slavery, therefore, does not apply to them and it cannot be invoked to justify their enslavement. Thus, Ercilla's poetic representation of the Araucanian leaders suggests he is in the camp of those who do not oppose the grant of land and Indians known as the *encomienda*, but do oppose the de facto slavery that was practiced on some *encomiendas*. The poet, who begins the *Araucana* with the selection of a new Araucanian cacique and frequently details the Indians' bravery in battle, shows himself to be much closer to the position of Vitoria and the "School of Salamanca" than to that of Spaniards who had openly affirmed the right of Spain to enslave the Amerindians, such as Bernardo de Mesa, Gil Gregorio, Juan López de Palacios Rubios, and Matías de Paz.[30]

29. See David Quint, "Epic and Empire," 7.
30. See Pagden, *Fall of Natural Man*, 72, 48, 50–54.

The Araucanians' unwillingness to submit to government by a king, however ("No king has ever subjugated these proud, free people" [No ha habido rey jamás que sujetase / esta soberbia gente libertada], 1.47.1–2), as well as what Ercilla calls their lawlessness and devil-worship ("They are a people without god or law, though they honor the one who was thrown out of heaven" [Gente es sin Dios ni ley, aunque respeta / aquel que fue del cielo derribado], 1.40.1–2), indicate that their social hierarchy and mores are imperfect or, at best, that they remain in a state of becoming. While most modern commentators have interpreted the line about Araucanian lack of submission in positive terms as an expression of the right to self-determination, it is not at all clear that a sixteenth-century Spaniard could have intended them to encode subversion. On the contrary, the notion of subjecting oneself to a king (literally, making oneself his subject) would have had a positive value from Ercilla's perspective, not only because of the author's background, but because he would have assumed monarchy to be a higher form of government than rule by a warrior elite. Pagden shows that in Aristotelian terms, the more complex a society was, the more civilized it was considered to be.[31] Ercilla gives the Araucanians sixteen caciques, but no king; he gives them warriors, but no legitimating spiritual end for the wars they make. The epic suggests that Araucanian society is intricate enough to make enslavement (or enslavement on the *encomienda*) unjustified, but still far from what it ought to be by European standards. Borrowing a Spanish proverb, Ercilla "gives with one hand and takes back with the other."

According to *La Araucana*, internal strife and bickering among the Araucanians (which Alegría refers to as "intestine struggles")[32] constitute a graver problem still, because they augur time and again the inevitability of the conquest. Discord marks numerous encounters between the Araucanian leaders, and always characterizes their dealings at turning points in the text. At the beginning of part 2, the Araucanian caciques meet to discuss the recent arrival of the Spaniards near Penco and to devise a strategy for countering the enemy presence. Caupolicán urges war, arguing that only by doing battle with the invaders can the Araucanians achieve immortality (16.42–45). Peteguelén, on the other hand, advocates a two-pronged strategy: he wants to overtly negotiate with the Spaniards while covertly gathering troops to match their numbers (16.46–49). The irate Tucapel will not hear of this:

> Understand that as long as I have
> strength in my arm and a voice in the senate,
> no matter what Peteguelén says,

31. Ibid., 73.
32. Alegría, "Ercilla y críticos," 54.

this matter will be settled by arms.
He who proposes a different road
will have to open it through my side,
since my iron-clad mace, not speeches,
will give you causes and reasons.

(Pues entended que mientras yo tuviere
fuerza en el brazo y voz en el senado,
diga Peteguelén lo que quisiere,
que esto ha de ser por armas sentenciado.
Y quien otro camino pretendiere
primero le abrirá por mi costado,
que esta ferrada maza y no oraciones
les ha de dar las causas y razones.)
(16.52)

Tucapel, who values deeds over words and arms over reason (he earlier killed the soothsayer Puchecalco for prophesying the defeat of Arauco), quickly enmeshes the other caciques in heated argument, to the point that Caupolicán tires of his troublemaking. His quickness to anger and inability to master his passions place Tucapel dangerously close to the Aristotelian category of the "natural slave," who has the faculty of reason but lacks the power to deliberate.[33] Only Colocolo saves the situation by issuing a stern warning to the senate. He states that pride will surely be the downfall of Arauco, then soberly assesses the weakness of the present Araucanian position, urging the caciques, especially Tucapel, to stop fighting amongst themselves when the enemy is nearby:

For surely it is a lack of spirit, and
a clear indication of disguised weakness,
to turn the sword against ourselves
with the enemy right in front of us,
instead of receiving, with unfailing courage,
the hard blows of irate fortune,
which a strong breast resists,
not wanting to have it all result in death.

However, since such strength resides in you
that sometimes, since it is so great, I condemn it,
and since, not this land, but the whole
universe is full of your deeds,
let fury and civil war surely cease,
and for the common good consider it is right

33. See Pagden, *Fall of Natural Man*, 42.

not to break up brotherhood in bungling ways,
for we are members of a single body.

(Que es, cierto, falta de ánimo, y bastante
indicio de flaqueza disfrazada,
teniendo al enemigo tan delante
revolver contra sí la propia espada,
por no esperar con ánimo constante
los duros golpes de fortuna airada,
a los cuales resiste el pecho fuerte
que no quiere acabarlo con la muerte.

Pero pues tanto esfuerzo en vos se encierra
que a veces, por ser tanto, lo condeno,
y de vuestras hazañas, no esta tierra
mas todo el universo anda ya lleno,
cese, cese el furor y civil guerra
y por el bien común tened por bueno
no romper la hermandad con torpes modos
pues que miembros de un cuerpo somos todos.)
(16.70–71)

Colocolo's famous speech brings a temporary end to the Araucanian quarrels, but it also establishes a direct link between discord and defeat. This connection, which Ercilla reaffirms throughout the epic, casts a shadow of doom over the Araucanian side.

Abruptly interrupted by the end of part 2, the duel between Rengo and Tucapel is another major textual site of Araucanian discord. Arguing that Ercilla deliberately avoids endings in his epic because he writes against a historical closure achieved by conquest, David Quint offers the suspended duel as an example of a "nonending ending" and as evidence of "an epic that deliberately falls apart in order to defeat narrative incorporation of a violence that exceeds explanatory or ideological structure."[34] The very elements to which Quint points as symptoms of the *Araucana*'s fragmentation and incompletion, however, can as easily be interpreted as evidence of Ercilla's efforts to achieve unity and closure in a long narrative poem whose composition was an arduous labor. The suspended duel between Rengo and Tucapel is a literary device employed to effect a linkage between parts 2 and 3 of *La Araucana*. It is not exactly an

34. Quint holds that against Virgilian epic, which has a closed form, Lucan and his followers—one of whom is Ercilla—oppose "a narrative of historical contingency that has no end in sight." He takes the invasion of Portugal at the end of part three as further proof of Ercilla's failure to find a narrative ending for his poem, of his "imitating and overturning epic models of closure." See *Epic and Empire*, 136, 164, 168.

"unending ending," therefore, but a bridge between contiguous sequences of the same text. Literary models for this type of bridging mechanism are to be found in numerous Italian *romanzi*. Ercilla knew them well, and in fact, he had already used one such device (the unresolved shipwreck) to bind together parts 1 and 2. Once the poet had decided to publish his poem in more than one section, there may have been no device available to him that could have forged a tighter link between its parts.

That Ercilla intended the figure of Rengo to serve as a kind of connecting thread seems clear. The duel with Tucapel activates the memory of an earlier fight between Rengo and Andrea the Genoese at Mataquito (canto 15). Mataquito is a bloodbath and a story of Amerindian betrayal of their own (nor is it the only such betrayal in *La Araucana*). At Mataquito, an Indian leads Villagrán to Lautaro's fort in the early morning while the Araucanians sleep. The Spaniards attack, killing Lautaro and all the Araucanian warriors present except Mallén, who commits suicide, preferring death to captivity. The reader does not learn of Rengo's survival until the first book of part 2. Because in each case Rengo lives and reappears in the poem's following installment, Quint interprets him as an Antaeus figure recycled from the *Pharsalia*, a character that "rises up again and again to oppose its would-be conquerors."[35] There is indeed something Antaeus-like about Rengo, something larger than life, but Quint's view of him is too benign, for when Ercilla fixes the reader's gaze on Rengo, he turns it away from the many Araucanian dead at Mataquito. This displacement, coupled with the time that elapsed before the publication of part 2, would have virtually eclipsed the memory of the massacre for contemporary readers. Rather than defeating the narrative incorporation of violence, Rengo's reappearance actually makes us forget some of the horror Ercilla had previously written into his epic. By inducing us to focus on the lone survivor instead of the many dead, the text elides some of its own violence, then ironically reinscribes it again and again because Rengo cannot stay out of trouble.

Ercilla's Rengo is a bit of a hothead who would just as soon fight his own kind as the Spaniards. Thus he embodies the dissension that plagues the Araucanians throughout Ercilla's epic, pitting them against one another and making them more vulnerable to Spanish attack and subjugation. Rengo is also a connecting element in a narrative that sometimes threatens to wander. Ercilla stages the character's repeated returns to create a unified plot line, but they also constitute a diversionary tactic that helps to contain

35. Ibid., 165.

and absorb Spanish atrocities in the text. By exemplifying Araucanian rivalry and contentiousness, Rengo also manages to foreshadow an unhappy outcome for the Araucanian side.

There are many more instances of Araucanian discord in the epic, but it will suffice to mention the one that Ercilla uses to finish off his war narrative: the renewed strife among the caciques after the execution of Caupolicán.

> Some with rabid thirst for vengeance
> over the affront and dishonor received,
> others desirous of the leader's office
> and already aspiring to his staff,
> instead of allowing delay to calm
> the spirits of the stirred up people,
> added fuel to the fire of war
> inciting all the land to fury.

> (Unos con sed rabiosa de venganza
> por la afrenta y oprobio recebido,
> otros con la codicia y esperanza
> del oficio y bastón ya pretendido,
> antes que sosegase la tardanza
> el ánimo del pueblo removido,
> daban calor y fuerzas a la guerra
> incitando a furor toda la tierra.)
> (34.36)

One cannot fail to notice that Ercilla finishes the war story much the way he began it, with strife and ambition tearing apart the caciques' singleness of purpose. To remedy the same tired situation, Colocolo calls a meeting to choose a new leader, which brings the narrative full circle. According to this account, the Araucanian leaders prove to be not only inharmonious and individualistic (in the sense of putting self-interest before the common good), but—in the terms of sixteenth-century Europe—politically backward, as well. Reading *La Araucana* all the way through, one gets the impression, an impression Ercilla surely intended to create, that each time they need new leadership, the Araucanians must go through this rivalry and conflict all over again because their social organization allows for neither succession nor continuity. *La Araucana* suggests that discord is a condition intrinsic to a social structure that the text compares unfavorably to monarchy. In a move that almost makes us forget that a conquest had taken place, the epic also implies that this tendency toward internal strife was the real cause of the Araucanians' undoing.

"Wily, Deceitful Barbarian:" Inverting the Discourse of Virtue

The discourse of virtue is one of the newer discourses marshaled into the service of the discourse of blood after the mid-sixteenth century.[36] It can, but does not always, serve as a counterdiscourse to the ideology of blood. Invoking the superiority of virtuous deeds, writers such as Teresa de Jesús and Miguel de Cervantes radically rejected the notion of a subjectivity founded on lineage alone. Virtue, however, is still an aristocratic discourse, and with the passing of time it became harder for the discourse of blood to do without it: a man continued to be his lineage, but increasingly he was also his works.

Like the other discourses mentioned here, virtue is "a divided and contradictory sign in itself," in Mariscal's words. It need not be construed affirmatively, therefore; it can be used negatively to compose subjects whose identity is thereby perceived as a lack. Subjects without virtue are undeserving of esteem, and sometimes utterly despicable. When Ercilla makes the Araucanians of his poem act repeatedly in ways that are traitorous and deceitful, he inverts the discourse of virtue and turns it against the Amerindian, whom he represents as double-dealing and treacherous. The Araucanians, who elsewhere behave according to a peculiarly Spanish honor code, as Pastor has shown, here oppose everything for which chivalry and fair play stand.[37]

The notion that "all is fair in war" does not have much currency in the early modern period. On the contrary, the codes of chivalry inherited from the Middle Ages stipulated fair play, and what would today be called a "level playing field." Before the introduction of firearms, any deviation from this ideal was considered ignoble and unacceptable. As Murrin has shown, the harquebus changed all that. Condemnation of firepower abounds in Golden Age literature; Don Quijote deplored "the appalling fury of these bedeviled instruments of artillery, whose inventor, in my opinion, is in hell receiving the reward for his diabolical invention, which made it possible for an infamous coward to take the life of a worthy knight" (la espantable furia de aquestos endemoniados instrumentos de la artillería, a cuyo inventor tengo para mí que en el infierno se le está dando el premio de su diabólica invención, con la cual dio causa que un infame y cobarde quite la vida a un valeroso caballero, *Don Quijote* 1.38). But the poets of epic were not all so quick to dismiss the new technology, and Ercilla includes it not only in the battle of Lepanto but in most of the battles fought in Arauco against an enemy who did not have it. It is Murrin's

36. Mariscal, *Contradictory Subjects*, 51.
37. Ibid., 46; Pastor, *Discursos narrativos*, 382.

argument that Ariosto and Ercilla both use enemy fraud to resolve the evident inequities caused by the ungentlemanly advantage of firearms. But unlike Ariosto, Ercilla does not link the charge of fraud to the gun; since he is not ready to surrender the chivalric code, he makes both sides engage in fraud, actually inventing Araucanian fraud, "to spread around the guilt."[38]

Murrin points out that the apologia for firepower reflects a modernist ideology that is conspicuous in Ercilla's epic. The problem of fraud in *La Araucana*, however, goes beyond the confines of Murrin's argument because, if Ercilla does not link the accusation of fraud to the gun, he does indeed link fraud to the Amerindian, generally.[39] Ercilla introduces treachery into his narrative at numerous points, and the Araucanian side commits almost every instance of betrayal and deceit. When the *yanacona* Andresillo betrays the Araucanian spy, Pran, at Cañete, some guilt may indeed be shared, but throughout the poem Ercilla assigns by far the greatest part of it to the Araucanians.

Betrayal is one of the main themes of *La Araucana*, yet among the critics, Jaime Concha alone mentions "the crime of betrayal as one of the most perfidious evils," in an analogy he makes between Caupolicán's death and that of Christ. Time and again the epic shows that duplicity and sedition carry a high price. Hurtado de Mendoza's harsh repression of the Peruvian colonists who had participated in Girón's rebellion against the Spanish crown leaves little doubt about the attitude of sixteenth-century Spaniards in this matter. Treason, after all, is only an extreme form of betrayal, one that in sixteenth-century Europe was punishable by death. By the time he arrives in Arauco, the figure of the poet has already recounted how the rebellion in Peru ended in execution or exile of the perpetrators. This may seem like an excessive form of punishment, but it was meant to set terror in the hearts of other would-be traitors. The Ercillan text insists over and over that exemplary punishment (*castigo ejemplar*) is a good thing, especially when it is timely enough to preclude the growth of greater sedition. Cantos 1 and 2 both end in condemnation of Valdivia for not taking early action to punish the Araucanians for "breaking faith" with the crown. Valdivia himself declares, "you see that faith is broken and war has broken out, the treaties are altogether in shambles" (veis quebrada la fe, rota la guerra, / los pactos van del todo en rompimiento, 3.11.5–6). There is nothing in *La Araucana* to make us think that Amerindians who rebel will be treated any differently from the Spaniards

38. Murrin, *History and Warfare,* 145–46, 159.

39. For the occasionally positive assessment of firearms in epic, see Murrin, *History and Warfare,* 138–59.

who followed Girón. In fact, the opprobrium of Galbarino's mutilation (canto 22), the hanging of twelve Araucanian leaders "to threaten and frighten the people" (para amenaza y miedo de las gentes, canto 26.22.6), and the supreme degradation of Caupolicán's impalement (canto 34) all show that Indian treatment at the hands of the Spaniards is worse than what happened to the rebels in Peru. This may be because, as Caro Baroja points out, while rebellions such as those of Girón or Aguirre ultimately ended up strengthening the monarchy, unrest among the Amerindians was a potential threat to Spanish dominion in America altogether.[40]

Even though the stakes are very high, however, Ercilla makes the Amerindians of *La Araucana* engage in trickery and double-dealing on a regular basis. The Spaniards, on the other hand, behave in a deliberately treacherous fashion only once, at the battle of Cañete, and then only in response to Araucanian foul play. Some instances of Araucanian deceit belong to the category of ruses used against the enemy in war. Lautaro, depicted as a sort of wily Odysseus, tries to trap the Spaniards in a fort, returning and securing the doors to do battle with them there (11.56). Since the Araucanians turn to come back too soon, the plot is spoiled and Lautaro infuriated. In the same canto, the Araucanian leader pretends to withdraw from the fort, which he has no intention of surrendering (11.75). This time the plan succeeds, and the Spaniards suffer heavy losses. Later, in a parley with Marcos Véaz, Lautaro claims that he has no food for his people and that they are hungry. His plan, which Villagrán sees through, is to get the Spaniards to distribute food to the enemy and at that very moment, attack (12.29). The Spaniards realize that Lautaro's "ingenious shrewdness" (*ingeniosa astucia*) and "latest deceit" (*nuevo engaño*) put them in constant danger, so they withdraw under cover of night, which frustrates Lautaro's next trick: to flood the plain if the Spaniards attack (12.35). Even Colocolo devises trickery of this type, sending Millalauco to the Spaniards supposedly with tidings of peace, but really on a reconnaissance mission (16.77–82). These ruses usually come to naught, which could be Ercilla's way of affirming Spanish sagacity over Araucanian ingeniousness. They certainly do not have the same far-reaching repercussions as the grand Amerindian betrayals of Amerindians that Ercilla includes in his epic, but what is notable about them is that they are all on the Araucanian side. For the most part, Ercilla does not endow the Spanish soldiers with the same craftiness he ascribes to Lautaro. An exception is the battle at Purén, where the poet's own character suggests that the Spaniards with-

---

40. See Concha, "Otro Nuevo Mundo," 64; Parker, *Philip II*, 99; and Caro Baroja, "Religion, World Views," 100.

draw to a nearby hill while the Araucanians are busy looting (28.63–67). There, they have a good position from which to make the enemy think Spanish numbers are greater than they are, and they devastate the Araucanians.[41]

The treachery that Ercilla has American Indians commit against one another in *La Araucana* is one of the most tragic aspects of the epic, yet it is one of those issues that most critics avoid. With the exception of Concha noted above, there is virtually no commentary on the problem of betrayal in *La Araucana*. When we stop to consider, however, that treachery played a part in the death of both great Araucanian heroes, Lautaro and Caupolicán, the pall of silence that covers this topic is particularly difficult to understand.

It is Francisco de Villagrán who attacks Lautaro's fort at Mataquito, in a bloody battle that leads to the chief's death and that of all the great Araucanian warriors who accompanied him. What is often forgotten about Mataquito is that Villagrán would not have known how to get there if a "neighboring Indian" (*indio comarcano*) had not taken him there, surely knowing what would happen to the Indians inside the fort. This Indian is one of many looters ("people greedy for coveted loot" [gente codiciosa del robo deseado"], 12.58) who regularly go to Lautaro's fort to rob him. The neighboring Indians belonged to different tribes, so one could easily argue that they were under no obligation to show any kind of loyalty to Lautaro, especially when Lautaro himself had marched toward Maule with a band of 600 of the toughest soldiers, committing atrocities against the Indians in his path (11.34–38). That there was strife among the various Amerindian tribes and that it benefited the Spaniards is a matter of historical fact. The Spaniards would not have been able to carry out the conquest without help from their Indian allies, as Murrin's statistics indicate. Ercilla tells us that 400 "neighboring friends" fought with the Spaniards at Mataquito. It is nevertheless deeply disturbing that an anonymous *indio comarcano* should be the one to lead the Spaniards to Lautaro and to help them take his life. The Araucanian chief dies when an arrow from an unidentified source pierces his heart (14.16–7). As Murrin writes, "Missile exchanges are inherently anonymous. No one knows, for example, who killed Lautaro at Mataquito . . . Probably an allied Indian shot the youth."[42] It could be argued that the neighboring Indians were allies of the Spaniards, not of the Araucanians, and that therefore it makes little difference whether a Spaniard or one of them killed Lautaro. It does appear to have made a dif-

41. See Murrin, *History and Warfare*, 161.
42. Ibid., 163, 174.

ference to the poet, however, in that guilt for the death could be partially displaced from Villagrán and his troops onto another Indian. Because that displacement is so easily effected, the picture Ercilla paints of Amerindian treachery against Amerindians is a profoundly unsettling one.

The betrayal of Caupolicán is even more sinister than the treachery that leads to Lautaro's death, for there can be little doubt that the traitor is a member of the chief's own tribe and that Caupolicán knows him. Described as a nameless Indian prisoner, "a man daring according to the evidence of his spirit, with ready hands and light feet" (hombre en las muestras de ánimo atrevido, / suelto de manos y de pies ligero, 033.56.3–4), the Indian decides to turn over Caupolicán in exchange for "promises and gifts" (*promesas y dádivas*). Concha identifies the Indian as Andresillo, the double-agent that sold out the Araucanians at Cañete.[43] There is, however, no indication in the text that Caupolicán's traitor is Andresillo, and in fact, the anonymity of the betrayal makes it even more heinous. The unnamed Indian takes the Spaniards almost all the way to Caupolicán's hideout, then panics:

> "I will not take a step further, nor can I
> continue down this road I undertook,
> for the deed is great and the fear terrible
> which halts my cowardly step, imagining
> the horrible expression of Caupolicán
> the great, turned in anger against me,
> when he finds out that I alone am
> the traitorous soldier who betrayed him."

> ("Yo no paso adelante, ni es posible
> seguir este camino comenzado,
> que el hecho es grande y el temor terrible
> que me detiene el paso acobardado,
> imaginando aquel aspecto horrible
> del gran Caupolicán contra mí airado,
> cuando venga a saber que solo he sido
> el soldado traidor que le ha vendido.")
> (33.61)

When the traitor starts to talk about the error of his ways ("*mi gran yerro*" 33.62.8) and the risk he is taking, the Spaniards tie him to a tree and proceed without him. After capturing Caupolicán, the Spaniards free the traitor on their way back to camp, but Ercilla does not give the Araucanian chief an opportunity to confront the man who has betrayed him. When they arrive at the plaza with the prisoner, there is applause. None of the

---

43. Concha, "Otro Nuevo Mundo," 64.

Indians present is willing to identify Caupolicán in public, but later, in private and reassured of his certain death, they all confirm his identity.

The arrest and imprisonment of Caupolicán, to say nothing of his execution, are much more pathetic than Lautaro's rapid and honorable death, even if the latter died at the hands of a neighboring Indian. The possibilities for guilt displacement, however, are similar in both cases. The poet of *La Araucana* recounts both deaths (that of Caupolicán to the last excruciating particular), without implicating himself in either case. According to Ercilla's account, the Spaniards as a group, though they are the primary beneficiaries of these deaths, never need bear the onus of the betrayals. By deploying an inverted discourse of virtue against the Araucanian and the Amerindian, generally, Ercilla problematizes his own magnificent representations of the Amerindian "other." This manner of subtracting oppositionality from the very Indian heroes toward whom the poet so often seems to want to draw the reader's sympathies indicates a division not only in the way Ercilla viewed the American Indian, but in his understanding of his own role as a servant of the Spanish crown in the context of a war of conquest.

Personal Advancement: Service's Other Side

The discourse of personal advancement or individual economic progress is based on modernist conceptions of the self and on new economic orders that in the late sixteenth century were only coming into being, and that the aristocracy did not openly welcome. And yet, the seeds of the idea of personal advancement already exist within the discourse of service. Vassalage implied that the servant of the crown should be rewarded for deeds rendered in the monarch's name. Domínguez Ortiz makes it clear that this reward, which took the form of royal favor (*merced regia*), was not a metaphor or an ethereal thing. On the contrary, the *merced regia* was something that aristocrats in the service of the Spanish crown expected to receive and took very seriously:

> Since booty taken in war, a source of wealth in previous times, no longer bore fruit, and few dared to undertake commercial or industrial enterprises, because of the habitual prejudices as well as the lack of vocation and aptitude, the high aristocracy relied, above all, on *mercedes regias* to obtain the funds necessary for maintaining its rank. The Spanish Crown hardly ever made outright gifts of large sums to courtiers, as was customary in France. Our aristocrats did not ask for money, but rather lucrative positions, *encomiendas* and financial assistance. Certain positions were considered onerous, because they cost the winner more money than they produced; embassies, for example. Others were desirable, not only because of the authority they brought with them, but the

benefits; in the first place, the American viceroyalties; afterward, those of Italy; the peninsular ones were far less esteemed.[44]

Ercilla uses the discourse of service not only to validate his long poem, but also to control a narrative that occasionally threatens to ramble. But though the discourse of vassalage is very strong in *La Araucana*, the epic genre, as a whole, does not easily admit self-serving motives or petitions of earned royal favor. If the idea of material gain appears in this genre, it can only do so as a metaphor or an allusion to conquered lands or booty justly won in battle. In contrast to the novel, the epic rarely expresses the idea of wealth as a goal in itself, for reasons that appear to be intrinsic to the genre. For the epic hero, personal prosperity is not the most important thing, because he moves in a world of collective or group motives. As Greene writes:

> Epic awe, as distinguished from religious or mythic awe, springs from the realization that a man can commit an extraordinary act while still remaining limited . . . The hero must be acting for the community . . . What he does must be dangerous, not only for other people but for him. It must involve a test. Moreover it must make a difference; it must change in some manner the hero's situation or the community's.[45]

At least as far back as Virgil, perhaps even in Homer, the hero's deeds are not, as a rule, guided by the motive of profit; he always acts for the common (public) good, for which he may risk everything. And it is the collective that stands to benefit from the hero's efforts and achievements. The poetic universe of the epic, for reasons that have to do with its fundamental raison d'être, is in perpetual tension with the idea of progress expressed in material terms. It is true that in *El Cantar de Mío Cid*, the hero sends gifts to Alphonse VI of Castile, who has banished him. However, this is a case of riches taken as war booty and conquered lands, offered by the "good vassal" as a gift to his king with a secondary motive: to "buy back" his own honor. This type of offering falls within the norms of epic because it suggests that the hero, offended by his king, has the moral authority that Alphonse VI lacks.

In addition to the altruism that generally characterizes the epic hero, there is a moral austerity traditionally associated with the genre. Even in primary epic, the censure of greed serves as a rejection of accumulated

44. Antonio Domínguez Ortiz, *La sociedad española en el siglo 17*, 1:242–43.
45. Thomas M. Greene, *The Descent from Heaven: A Study in Epic Continuity*, 15.

wealth. Writing in very different contexts, Lucan, Ercilla, Camões, Virués, Rufo, Hojeda and others denounce the love of money as a cause of war. For these writers, greed is an unacceptable motive for "just war." Indeed, Ercilla expresses this idea quite directly:

> And since the weight and heavy burden of war
> hang on the king, as he is the head,
> and the occurring damage or evil is his responsibility,
> all of this he carries on his shoulders alone.
> He must consider well what he undertakes,
> and before he gives free rein to his fury,
> must justify the arms which he has gotten ready,
> never to be motivated by greed or ambition.

> (Y pues del rey como cabeza pende
> el peso de la guerra y grave carga,
> y cuanto daño y mal della depende
> todo sobre sus hombros solo carga.
> Debe mucho mirar lo que pretende,
> y antes que dé al furor la rienda larga,
> justificar sus armas prevenidas,
> no por codicia y ambición movidas.)
> (37.13)

Similarly, greed constitutes a dangerous pretext for lack of military discipline, which in the epic is signed negatively. Especially in Renaissance epic, true spiritual wealth can generally be found in opposition to false, worldly riches, which lead inevitably to decadence. In the codes of Western epic, as Quint argues, contact with Eastern opulence produces a gradual corrosion of the warrior's will, and can eventually lead to effeminacy.[46]

In the epic of Spain's imperial age, therefore, a king's man must not adduce reasons of personal profit for the projects he undertakes, which does not mean that he does not have them. In the epic, soldiers do not get rich except by fortunes of war or conquest, but they do acquire valor and honor. There is an abundance of epics dedicated to the monarch, to another member of the royal family or a distinguished figure at the court, but never do these texts show a sense of entitlement to material compensation, even in cases where the epic was requisitioned by a royal patron, like Rufo's *La Austriada*. They all insist that they are redeeming the glories of a heroic Spain previously forgotten by her poets, and they all ask for ostensibly little in exchange for rescuing the luminous national past.

---

46. See Quint, *Epic and Empire*, 24.

Though the peculiar blend of history, autobiography, and poetry in its pages makes *La Araucana* atypical in some respects, the hero's apparent selflessness remains faithful to the spirit of the ancient genre. Rather than summon a personal motive for going to distant Arauco, the figure of the poet constantly insists that it is royal service that has carried him to the end of the globe. Let us take a closer look at an octave quoted only in part above. When the poet inscribes his own character into the narrative, the royal troops are leaving Lima to put down Araucanian insurgency in Chile:

> I also with them, who in your service
> began and shall end my life,
> for I was in your service in England,
> not having been armed a knight,
> when news came of the wrong committed
> in your disservice by those of Arauco,
> and the great shamelessness of those
> who were disobedient to the Royal Crown.

> (Yo con ellos también, que en el servicio
> vuestro empecé y acabaré la vida,
> que estando en Inglaterra en el oficio
> que aun la espada no me era permitida,
> llegó allí la maldad en deservicio
> vuestro, por los de Arauco cometida,
> y la gran desvergüenza de la gente
> a la Real Corona inobediente.)
> (13.29)

Ercilla uses several oppositions to contrast his own obsequious attitude toward the crown with the purported disloyalty of the Araucanians who are in rebellion against the king of Spain. In this way, the text incorporates a value system founded on one basic criterion: exemplarity of the subject of the Spanish crown. On the one hand, the epic accounts for services rendered to the monarch in contrast to the "disservice" (*deservicio*) committed by the rebellious Indians. On the other, it registers the writer's hope for compensation that the "good vassal" may expect or hope to receive in payment for his service. All through the thirty-seven cantos of *La Araucana*, the oppositions service/disservice and favor/disfavor constitute more than just privileged themes. In fact, they point to the existence of an economy of service and compensation that informs the entire Ercillan epic. Due to its insistent presence, this textual economy would appear to suggest a sense of very real preoccupation on the part of the historical poet, the courtier Ercilla, who may have hoped for more tangible compensation from the king than the incorporeal prizes of valor and honor.

What, exactly, did Ercilla hope to obtain from the king in payment for his service record as soldier, discoverer, and poet? First of all, he wanted for his poem the authority that would issue from royal favor. When he dedicates the epic to Philip II, the authorial voice asks explicitly for the monarch's blessing for his "needy" poem (1.3). This is not surprising, since this type of request constitutes a topic in the rhetoric and in the discourses of power of the times. In this, however, Ercilla's epic is much more persistent than other texts of its kind. When in the next octave the poet reemphasizes the same point, it is to ask the king's protection for a text that he apparently considers to be more vulnerable than most. Ercilla mobilizes the "affected-modesty topic" as a strategy for finding in the monarch a refuge for his poem, which according to the poet contains "something hidden" (*algo escondido*). The mention of hidden messages in his text invites conjecture about what they might be, but finally the matter remains shrouded in mystery.

The petitions for royal favor can probably be explained as a rhetorical motif that was very frequent in many literary types of Renaissance Spain. They intensify during the narration of the Battle of St. Quentin (canto 18), a triumphal moment of Philip II's reign (1557). This is a locus in which the textual economy of service and favor suddenly becomes palpable through phrases such as the following: "but the great desire to serve you always, which has always pulled me in this direction" (mas de serviros siempre el gran deseo / que siempre me ha tirado a este camino, 18.2.5–6); "[your favor] is that which I request and which can enrich my poor understanding" ([vuestro favor] es el que agora pido y el que puede / enriquecer mi pobre entendimiento, 18.3.3–4); "if, on your account, Lord, I am granted that which you do not deny anyone" (que si por vos, Señor, se me concede / lo que a nadie negáis, 18.3.4–5); and finally,

> Trusting in your generosity,
> because the reason for which I ask it is just,
> I hope, Lord, to be heard,
> for that alone is enough to make me favored . . .

> (Y de vuestra largueza confiado
> por la justa razón con que lo pido,
> espero que, Señor, seré escuchado,
> que basta para ser favorecido . . .)
> (18.4.1–4)

It is in the poem's final canto, however, that the poet's aspirations seem to come to a head. Ercilla textualizes this situation precisely in the terms of service to the king and royal favor, dialogically positioned against the concepts of disfavor and poverty or misery (*miseria*). This part of the epic seems to point in the direction of a not-so-veiled skepticism about the whole value system, vassalage, that has served as the ideological foundation of the text. Calling attention to the credentials that authorize him to expect royal compensation, the narrator emphatically enumerates all the voyages he has carried out for the purpose of enlarging the crown's territories. This passage solders together in one thematic nucleus the motifs of expansionism, service to the king, and the expectation of compensation:

> I traveled so many lands, I crossed
> so many nations toward the frozen north,
> also conquering the unknown antipodes
> in the lower Antarctic regions!
> I changed climates and constellations,
> swimming gulfs not navigable,
> extending your crown, Lord,
> almost to the frigid southern zone.

> (¡Cuántas tierras corrí, cuántas naciones
> hacia el helado norte atravesando,
> y en las bajas antárticas regiones
> el antípoda ignoto conquistando!
> Climas pasé, mudé constelaciones
> golfos innavegables navegando
> estendiendo, Señor, vuestra corona
> hasta casi la austral frígida zona.)
> (37.66)

In these words there still pulsates the spirit of *Plus ultra* ("Onward and upward") that typified imperial expansion during Charles V's reign. Suddenly, however, the poem changes direction, and what stands out at the end of the text is a pained expression of exhaustion, apparent resignation and failure:

> But even if the determination of my star
> has thus left me cast aside and downhearted,
> in the end you will see that I have run
> the difficult race on a straight path;
> and though my misfortune increasingly impels me,
> the reward resides in having deserved it,
> and honors consist not in having them,
> but only in striving to deserve them.

> The cowardly disfavor which has me
> cornered in the greatest poverty/misery,
> suspends my hand and halts it,
> forcing me to stop my pen here.
> So I bring this to an end, since

another talent, another voice
and accent, can better sing the innumerable
sum of your deeds and high thoughts.

(Mas ya que de mi estrella la porfía
me tenga así arrojado y abatido,
verán al fin que por derecha vía
la carrera difícil he corrido;
y aunque más inste la desdicha mía,
el premio está en haberle merecido
y las honras consisten, no en tenerlas,
sino en sólo arribar a merecerlas.

Que el disfavor cobarde que me tiene
arrinconado en la miseria suma,
me suspende la mano y la detiene
haciéndome que pare aquí la pluma.
Así doy punto en esto pues conviene
para la grande innumerable suma
de vuestros hechos y altos pensamientos
otro ingenio, otra voz y otros acentos.)
(37.72–73)

There is an unmistakable echo of Garcilaso de la Vega's "First Eclogue" here, though the intentionality of the Ercillan text is quite different from the postponement of epic that appears in the earlier poet's dedication to Don Pedro de Toledo. Showing the same apparent abnegation projected throughout *La Araucana*, the epic's final octaves allude to the satisfaction Ercilla derives from knowing himself worthy of honors never received. But what weighs most heavily in these verses are the twin themes of *disfavor* and *miseria*, which blend together with the poetic figure of the little boat that never makes it to port, a modernist metaphor for spiritual life that, according to Caro Baroja, originates with a Golden Age merchant class engaged in maritime commerce with America and Asia. These lines emit an unmistakable feeling of disenchantment for which Ercilla has not prepared the reader, who continues to search out viable interpretations. The most logical thing is to construe these verses as a rhetorical device that articulates the theme of vanity in worldly things with which the poem closes; this is Lerner's position.[47] But given the persistent tone of bitterness in these final words of *La Araucana*, one may harbor doubts about whether or not the courtier Ercilla expected more real, concrete compensations from the king in exchange for his long, apparently selfless demonstrations of loyalty and service.

47. Caro Baroja, "Religion, World Views," 96–97; Lerner, introduction to *La Araucana*, by Ercilla, 18.

We know that the poet asked for the equivalent of an *encomienda* from the king while he was still in America. On leaving Chile, Ercilla wrote a letter to Philip II soliciting the favor (*merced*) of "a distribution of land and Indians here in Peru, with which I could maintain myself in the manner befitting a servant of Your Majesty . . ." (un repartimiento aquí en el Perú conque me pueda sustentar conforme a criado de Vuestra Magestad . . .). According to Medina, Philip II approved this request.[48] It made no difference, however, because the grant of an *encomienda* came not from the crown, but from the governor or viceroy, and the viceroy of Peru had not given Ercilla a warm welcome. Much more to the point, however, Ercilla returned from Chile to Peru in 1559, and the distribution of Peru in grants (*encomiendas* or *repartimientos*) had been completed much earlier. The lion's share of the valuable *encomiendas* were already held by conquistadores who had seniority in the conquest of Peru. By the 1560s it was extremely difficult to claim such a grant because everything was already taken, and neither Ercilla's high birth nor his past ties with Philip II could change that.[49] How much of the poet's disenchantment at the end of *La Araucana* is a rhetorical construct, then, and how much of it is real disappointment at not having been handed a plum in payment for his career of service? The fact that other courtiers, such as Don Juan de Silva, Conde de Portalegre, complained bitterly of the very same thing makes it even harder to interpret Ercilla's plaintive verses.[50]

In spite of the distinctly aristocratic thinking that permeates the poem, there are clear divisions in Ercilla the subject that are not so different in kind from those that arise in writers that come along just a bit later, "contradictory subjects," in Mariscal's terms, such as Cervantes and Quevedo. Medina describes how, after his return to Spain, Ercilla remained close to the court, carrying out assignments and receiving favors in return. However, the Chilean biographer also has a chapter that elucidates Ercilla's extensive financial and commercial dealings. The image that

48. The request for a *repartimiento* is partially reproduced in Morínigo and Lerner's edition of *La Araucana*, 2:254. For the details of Philip II's letter to the viceroy, ordering him to provide for Ercilla "if any *repartimientos* were vacant," see José Toribio Medina, *Vida de Ercilla*, 83–86.

49. For a history that offers a real Peruvian background against which to measure Ercilla's utterances about service and favor, as well as his request for a *repartimiento*, see James Lockhart, *Spanish Peru, 1532–1560: A Social History*, chaps. 1–3.

50. See Fernando Bouza Álvarez, "Corte es decepción: Don Juan de Silva, Conde de Portalegre," in *La corte de Felipe II*. I owe this reference to Geoffrey Parker. In this vein, Elizabeth R. Wright mentions cases of melancholy at the court of Philip III and even deaths attributed to "sadness over insufficient royal prizes." See her "The Poet as Pilgrim: Lope de Vega and the Court of Philip III, 1598–1609," 271.

emerges from Medina's meticulous research into this aspect of Ercilla's life is that of a considerably wealthy man constantly buying and selling all kinds of valuable objects (imported furniture, plates and cups of gold and silver, a carriage trimmed in velvet and gold), at the same time that he lent money to anyone who wanted to borrow it, regardless of their social background. "This intense activity," writes Lerner, "is nothing if not an early sign of a well-defined consciousness of a new economic order, which valued finance activity and the acquisition of money over the possession of lands and titles."[51]

It may still surprise as much as it surprised Medina to find Ercilla involved in usury at the same time that he composed the verses lamenting his *miseria* at the end of *La Araucana*. When the subject is truly fractured, however, new-fashioned consciousness cannot exist separately from the ensemble of beliefs and values that previously constituted subjectivity and that still remain in force. Precisely because subjectivity does not come about in a void, but rather in the context of social organisms, Mariscal argues that "the concept of subjectivity as the intersection of multiple subject positions is impossible to understand without first understanding 'society' as a configuration of different group interests and investments."[52]

The social organism that served as Alonso de Ercilla's first place of apprenticeship was none other than the court of the future king of Spain, the "pious and prudent" Philip II. The aristocratic discourses of blood and virtue that he absorbed in this place certainly retained their original effectiveness for him until the end, even though during his later years he became involved in a decidedly modern and unaristocratic activity: financial speculation. In the Spain of this period, the category of economic class became a more influential factor in the constitution of subjects, but in the end, as Mariscal explains, "any form of subjectivity constituted through economic categories bore an inherent negative connotation."[53] Ercilla, therefore, would have been obliged to dissimulate his enthusiasm for financial activity, and he certainly would not have allowed any of it to creep into his epic poem. At the same time, traditional discursive practices persisted, and in some cases they articulated a powerful residual ideology. Such, it would seem, is the case of Alonso de Ercilla: exemplary vassal who probably never received from his king the favor, the reward or recognition that he thought he deserved after long and laborious battles and journeys.

51. On Ercilla's financial activities, see Medina, *Vida de Ercilla*, 169–85; and Lerner, introduction to *La Araucana*, by Ercilla, 18.

52. Mariscal, *Contradictory Subjects*, 35–36.

53. The aristocracy's rejection of new financial activities such as speculation and brokerage was particularly harsh. See Mariscal, 74–89.

This is the image of himself that he projects at the end of his epic, and it is the image that four centuries of readers have received. On the other hand, the internal conflict alluded to here helps to explain the exceedingly melancholy tone of the ending of his poem, as well as his determination to surround himself with the comforts of wealth, regardless of whether or not the crown gave him his due.

The discourses of blood and virtue, the exaltation of expansionism, and the enthusiasm for individual advancement, all sign *La Araucana* in a way that is deeply contradictory, thereby undercutting the discourse of vassalage that governs the epic. Blood and virtue, construed negatively and applied to the Araucanians to indicate their inharmonious social structure and treacherous nature, have a severely deleterious effect on the representation of the Amerindian in the poem. If Ercilla had shown Araucanian social hierarchy as backward according to European standards, while proving that Araucanian character was consistently innocent or virtuous, the representation of American Indians in *La Araucana* would be indisputably positive. By linking blood to a lack of virtue (bad behavior, bad moral choices), the writer silently clinches their fate, while he simultaneously glorifies them at other moments.

In the same vein, when he exploits the theme of royal favor so insistently, he engages in a deft, subtle interrogation of the very discourse of vassalage that he has used everywhere to secure his narrative. In consonance with the demands of the genre, the latter discourse strives to retain control of the text, but it is a discourse under siege. This situation creates a peculiar tension in the epic of Ercilla that is not common to other Spanish epics of the period, a tension strong enough to open up the *Araucana* to diverse and opposing interpretations. When each of these discourses—service, virtue, economic gain—is already divided in itself, and when there are so many contradictory strains operating at the same time in the text, the viability of incompatible misreadings increases. Because it deliberately sheds light on their inevitability, this reading of *La Araucana* cannot resolve any of the contradictions previously at work in the critical tradition of the Ercillan epic. It shall stand as one more willful misreading, but one that refuses to mutilate the text.[54]

---

54. I use the term *misreading* loosely but certainly following in Bloom's footsteps.

2

Writing after Ercilla
Juan Rufo's *La Austriada*

It is difficult for modern readers to fully appreciate the prestige that was accorded *La Araucana* from its first appearance. The publication of parts 1 (1569) and 2 (1578) generated an enthusiasm that opened up new ways of thinking about epic, and both parts were reprinted numerous times. Contrary to what twentieth-century readers might expect, the complexities and internal divisions of Ercilla's poem do not appear to have daunted writers determined to compose epics that were openly laudatory of Habsburg accomplishment and dominion. It is impossible to know whether they even noticed them. One such triumphalist epic was Juan Rufo's *La Austriada* (1584), a work commissioned by Philip II's sister María, Holy Roman empress, which received a subvention of five hundred ducats from the monarch, himself.[1] Rufo's epic, a celebration of the life of Don John of Austria (Philip's half brother) consists of two loosely connected parts: the first eighteen cantos cover Don John's campaign against the rebellious Moriscos (recently converted Moors) in the Alpujarra, and the last six narrate military actions against the Turks in the Mediterranean, culminating in the great naval battle of Lepanto (1571). Rufo depicts the foe in both parts of his poem as one and the same. In this, contemporary and modern histories of the Morisco insurrection prove him right to a certain extent, even though his poetic vision sometimes blurs important distinctions between the Moriscos, themselves, and the Ottoman Turks who watched the Alpujarra rebellion with interest and expectation from outside Spain. In these pages, I will argue that Ercilla's influence on Rufo leads the latter poet to compete with the artistry of *La Araucana* in an effort to capture for his own text some of the prestige of the Ercillan epic and that, mutatis mutandis, Rufo's attitude toward Spain's internal Muslim

1. Although the publication date for the poem is usually given as 1584, Rufo signed the prologue in 1582, there making the claim that he had been working on his text for ten years. For Philip II's subvention of *La Austriada*, see Geoffrey Parker, *Philip II*, 51.

"other" is as ambivalent as Ercilla's disposition toward the Araucanians. This tells us, perhaps, as much about Ercilla's text, or about its early reception in Spain, as it does about *La Austriada*. Rufo's epic has, to be sure, a single hero and a group of commanding officers that metonymically represents the imperial monarchy.[2] But it also has in common with *La Araucana* a tendency to speak about the enemy with occasional sympathy, while deeds of the Christian side are muted or narrated with reserve. In both texts, therefore, a collective "Spanish" subjectivity seems to emerge surreptitiously and by way of constant juxtaposition to an "othered" enemy about whom the epics are comparatively eloquent.

When Rufo undertook to write an epic in homage to Don John of Austria some time around 1572, he had an object of encomium that was in some ways intrinsically superior to the one Ercilla confronted. In contrast to the pieces of Ercilla's narrative, the war stories of *La Austriada* blend together harmoniously by virtue of a strong hero who is present throughout. Unlike the Araucanian resistance, which continued sporadically into the nineteenth century, both armed conflicts in Rufo's narration were finished: the rebellion in the Alpujarra had long since been suppressed and the battle of Lepanto decisively won. Finally, Don John was deceased. His death of typhoid in 1578, probably the event that spurred Philip's sister to solicit the poem, precluded the possibility of further developments in the hero's story.[3]

Despite these inherent advantages, however, Rufo had to contend with one obstacle that for Ercilla was not an impediment: the specter of *La Araucana*, itself, which must have appeared insurmountable to any Iberian writer of epic in the 1580s. How was it possible to write epic after the *Araucana* without either falling into servile imitation of Ercilla, or constantly dodging his shadow? Rufo's text shows signs of both these tendencies. *La Austriada* shows, in other words, signs of that "anxiety of influence" which Harold Bloom articulated. Bloom's theory of poetry, informed by Freudian thinking about generational conflict, suggests how poets engage the work of a powerful predecessor in the endeavor to emerge as "strong poets," themselves. In the early modern period, however, the relationship between one generation of poets and the next is not always antagonistic; as Colombí-Monguió remarks, this relationship was sometimes (though certainly not always) conceptualized as one of continuity and filial veneration, rather than Oedipal antagonism.[4] Moreover, Bloom's theory comes out of English poetry. It might be dangerous, therefore, to apply his ideas to the Spanish

2. For the role of the officers in Rufo's epic, see Michael Murrin, *History and Warfare in Renaissance Epic*, 179–96.
3. Parker, *Philip II*, 136.
4. See Harold Bloom, introduction to *The Anxiety of Influence: A Theory of Poetry;*

Renaissance without any qualification. Nonetheless, the phrase "anxiety of influence" seems to define well the attitude and method of a sixteenth-century poet like Juan Rufo, plotting out his royal octaves in the large shadow cast by Alonso de Ercilla. The question of whether Rufo ever became a "strong poet," in Bloom's terms, is perhaps moot: the Golden Age curriculum and canon are quite forceful in their rejection of learned epic as a whole, and it would be difficult to argue Rufo's poetic prowess in the face of the virtually total marginalization of his poem. However, it is one thing to argue that *La Austriada* is an overall match for *La Araucana;* it is quite another to demonstrate Rufo's success as a poetic rival to Ercilla in weighty themes and decisive episodes of his epic.

The Renaissance, of course, had its own theory of poetry and specific categories of poetic imitation. That some of these seem to loosely overlap with those of Bloom suggests that, though the attitude of the times toward imitation has changed, the problem of influence spans the trajectory of Western poetic production. Renaissance *imitatio* comprised a fairly precise taxonomy of imitative strategies. First expounded in *De imitatione libri tres* (1545), Bartolomeo Ricci's categories, which range from "following" the precursor text in servile fashion (*sequi*), to full-blown challenges to it (*aemulatio*), are more accessible since the 1980s thanks to the work of George W. Pigman. Of the kinds of imitation Pigman identifies ("transformative," "dissimulative," and "eristic"), dissimulative imitation may well be the most challenging for the reader, who must discern the subtext despite the poet's ingenious attempts to hide it. In these circumstances, only cultured readers were likely to identify classical or Petrarchan subtexts, particularly if several of them were recombined in the new text, as was often the case with Garcilaso de la Vega's Italianate poems, for example. For the poets, themselves, the greatest challenge was *aemulatio* (Pigman's "eristic imitation"), which was the intentional striving to outdo a precursor by besting his text. Colombí-Monguió cautions that because it is so difficult to prove poetic intention, the best the critic can often do is construe *aemulatio* in the results of the imitative attempt.[5]

Thomas M. Greene expounds Renaissance imitative strategies using a classification that includes "sacramental" or "reproductive" imitations, ones

---

and Alicia de Colombí-Monguió, *Petrarquismo peruano: Diego Dávalos y Figueroa y la poesía de la Miscelánea Austral,* 139.

5. See G. W. Pigman III, "Versions of Imitation in the Renaissance"; and Colombí-Monguió, *Petrarguismo peruano,* 192–93. I have been particularly influenced by the work of Colombí-Monguió for my understanding of the way Ricci's categories apply to Golden Age lyric, and by that of James Robert Nicolopulos for the ramifications of imitation in Hispanic epic. See his fine "Prophecy, Empire and Imitation in the Araucana in the Light of the *Lusíadas*" (Ph.D. diss., Berkeley: University of California,

that behold the precursor text with awe, rendering it again and again without attempting to change it; "eclectic" imitation, which mixes allusions to numerous subtexts together in an apparently random way in the new poem; "heuristic" imitations, which announce their subtext but then move away from it, as if to foreground their difference from it; and finally, "dialectical" imitation, which simultaneously acknowledges "two eras or two civilizations at a profound level," and may lead to parody of the subtext, but always involves tension with it. For Greene, the problem of anachronism is intrinsically important to both heuristic and dialectical imitations, because these were the two imitative strategies that humanists used to "reanimate" a text that belonged to the precious lost past of antiquity. Only those new texts that succeeded in bringing the ancient model to life in a new time qualify as what Greene calls "necromantic" imitations.[6]

Given the broad gamut of imitative strategies and possible combinations thereof, Renaissance writers, even to compete with one another, often attempted to revive classical texts in their own writing. However, it was possible for writers of the same generation to engage in poetic rivalry without ever attempting a truly necromantic imitation. The most esteemed imitation, however, would be the one that attempted the greatest challenge: to outdo a contemporary by digging into the past and reviving—in the terms of the present—a prestigious but long-silenced text, competing with eminences of classical antiquity in the process. The first part of this chapter will examine Juan Rufo's poetic rivalry with Ercilla, evident in two elements of his epic: the first, thematic (the censure of greed), and the second, episodic (the battle of Lepanto). The condemnation of greed is an utterance that has sometimes been used to partially ground a belated "anti-imperialist" reading of *La Araucana* that would have been anachronistic by sixteenth-century standards. The prophecy of the naval battle at Lepanto, on the other hand, has been referred to as proof of *La Araucana's* pro-Habsburg unity. Both are sites of intense critical scrutiny and poetic rivalry. Because they show Rufo's repeated endeavor to spar with the successful Ercilla of *La Araucana* parts 1 and 2, the theme of greed and the victory at Lepanto are important passageways to the politics and the poetics of *La Austriada*. Various concepts from the mix of imitative possibilities outlined above inform the following analysis of poetic imitation in *La Austriada*.

1992, forthcoming as a book at Pennsylvania State University Press). Two other studies are fundamental as a reminder of the extent to which imitation structured all Renaissance Hispanic poetics: Anne J. Cruz, *Imitación y transformación: el petrarquismo en la poesía de Boscán y Garcilaso de la Vega;* and Ignacio Navarrete, *Orphans of Petrarch: Poetry and Theory in the Spanish Renaissance.*
   6. Thomas M. Greene, *The Light in Troy*, 38–40, 46, 37.

Ercilla, Rufo, and the Condemnation of Greed

Critics said that Oliver Stone's *Wall Street* was a cinematographic emblem of U.S. values of the 1980s. The unforgettable words of character Gordon Gekko—"greed is good"—allegedly typified the attitude of a young generation interested only in the proverbial "bottom line," but from a historical perspective, Gekko's affirmation indicates a radical shift in thought within Western culture, where traditional values have opposed the exaltation of riches for their own sake. More familiar to those of us who work in Renaissance literature is the Horatian *aurea mediocritas* topic, which, in the literature of antiquity, is always accompanied by the censure of greed. In Horace, too, one finds the indictment of seafaring for self-serving motives, and the critique of money's abuse, generally. What was essentially a moral criticism in Horace is resemanticized in the historical codes of epic as the condemnation of greed for its power to turn soldiers and leaders (such as Valdivia in *La Araucana*) into adventurers, thereby breaking faith with the higher duty of their calling. Virgil coined the phrase "accursed hunger for gold" (*Auri sacra fames*), which resonates throughout Renaissance epic as the reproof of greed for riches.[7]

It is in Lucan's *Pharsalia* or *De bello civili* that the critique of greed is contextualized in such a way that it goes beyond the parameters of a moral preoccupation, in other words, in such a way that it ceases to be a topos. Jaime Concha argues that it is Ercilla's *La Araucana* that grounds the topic in historical reality when he writes that "with the Spanish conquest, greed, a theological and moral topic in the Middle Ages, becomes a decisive sociohistorical fact, the repercussions of which *La Araucana* depicts with all its implications."[8] But much earlier, the *Pharsalia* had linked greed and war in explicit denunciation. Lucan tells us that conquering peoples carry within themselves the "seeds of war" (suberant sed publica belli / semina, quae populos semper mersere potentes): prosperity, excess wealth, booty captured in battle, greed, extravagance.[9] These hidden causes invariably give rise to the blight of political corruption, usury, and interest, practices that transform the lives of those peoples and eventually lead to their ruin.

---

7. All quotations of the *Aeneid* are taken from the Loeb Classical Library and appear in my text by book and line, in this case 3.57. The English translations are taken from the corresponding page of this edition. Quotations and translations of the *Georgics* are also taken from this edition.

8. Jaime Concha, "El otro Nuevo Mundo," 35, in *Homenaje a Ercilla*, ed. Gastón Von Dem Bussche.

9. All quotations from the *Pharsalia* appear by number of book and verse, in this case, 1.158–82. In the *Pharsalia*, war of imperial conquest is inseparable from civil war.

If the condemnation of greed as one of the first causes of war is already present in the *Pharsalia*, in Renaissance epic this utterance abounds and takes on more elaborate formulations. Camões reactivates the ancient topos in the harsh warning that the "old man of Belem" issues to the adventurers who take to the sea to search for treasures abroad (4.94–104). But it is in *La Araucana* that the topic of greed takes on its canonical profile, according to which it characteristically appears in later Spanish epic. Alonso de Ercilla takes up the Lucanean formulation of the complaint of greed and endows it with new historical specificity that is unmistakable, concentrating his attention on the topic in such a sustained way that he turns it into a structural principle of his own epic. From Valdivia's defeat (canto 2) until the voyage to the south (cantos 34–36), Ercilla stresses the importance of this theme time and again, occasionally to suggest that greed can make a soldier forget his duty, at other times, to accuse his compatriots of having introduced the insatiable hunger for riches into a world previously pristine and free of moral blemish. The Araucanian leaders are aware of the foe's weakness for gold: Colocolo wants to take advantage of that character defect to seduce and deceive the Spaniards (16.76–77), while Galbarino attempts to uncover the real motives for the conquistadores' arrival in Arauco:

> And it is a pretext, a vain illusion,
> to try to show that their main intent
> was to spread the Christian religion,
> when their motive is pure self-interest;
> their resolution stems from greed,
> everything else is deceit,
> for we see that, more than other peoples,
> they are adulterers, thieves, and arrogant men.

> (Y es un color, es apariencia vana
> querer mostrar que el principal intento
> fue el extender la religión cristiana
> siendo el puro interés su fundamento;
> su pretensión de la codicia mana,
> que todo lo demás es fingimiento
> pues los vemos que son más que otras gentes
> adúlteros, ladrones, insolentes.)[10]

Coincidentally, the Moriscos accuse the Spaniards of some of these same transgressions (theft and adultery, among others) in Hurtado de

---

Just as Ercilla would do later, Lucan textualizes the censure of greed from the perspective of an elite, in this case, the senatorial class. I owe this point to Isaías Lerner.

10. All quotations of *La Araucana* are taken from the edition of Isaías Lerner (Madrid: Cátedra, 1993), and appear hereafter in the text by canto, octave, and where necessary, lines, in this case, 23.13.

Mendoza's *Guerra de Granada* (*War of Granada*), one of the main sources for Juan Rufo's poem.[11]

Ercilla's foregrounding of the problem of greed does not mean that he considers it to be a uniquely Spanish defect. On the contrary, battles in *La Araucana* always end with the spoliation of the loser's camp, no matter who the victor is, and Ercilla represents Araucanian pillage in terms no less harsh than those he uses to depict its Spanish equivalent. When the Araucanians defeat the Spaniards at Penco (Concepción), Ercilla dedicates twenty octaves to the description of the plundering and ruin of the city. The codes the poet employs to create an image of Araucanian greed belong to the same kind of discourse he uses in other instances to reprove Spanish cupidity:

> For one of them, it is not enough to rob
> the house which offers certain fortune,
> because insatiable, thirsty desire
> makes him imagine another richer in booty;
> making greedy and foolish calculations,
> he looks for the uncertain one, leaving the certain,
> and, arriving at his bed after sundown,
> because he searched for much, he is left with nothing.
>
> (Alguno de robar no se contenta
> la casa que le da cierta ventura,
> que la insaciable voluntad sedienta
> otra de mayor presa le figura;
> haciendo codiciosa y necia cuenta
> busca la incierta y deja la segura
> y llegando, el sol puesto, a la posada,
> se queda, por buscar mucho, sin nada.)
> (7.51)

For Ercilla, greed typifies no particular ethnic group or nationality. If all men are potentially rapacious, in the conqueror, by dint of his having conquered, greed becomes manifest, real and concrete. So it is that *La Araucana* is overwhelmingly predisposed to the characterization of Spaniards as actively greedy. But the disparaging representation of the Araucanians at Penco is not only a response to the aesthetic need for epic parity between Araucanians and Spaniards. It also shows that Ercilla is

---

11. All quotations of Diego Hurtado de Mendoza's *Guerra de Granada hecha por el rey D. Felipe II contra los Moriscos de aquel reino, sus rebeldes* are taken from the facsimile of the Barcelona edition of 1842 (Chiclana: Lipper, 1990), and appear hereafter in the text by abbreviated title and page, in this case, 18.

determined to judge both parties by the same exacting standard. Just as the poet makes both sides engage in fraud, however unequally, he makes them both greedy, whether there is historical basis for this or not.

La Araucana is enormously complex, and its discourses encode all sorts of ambiguities. And—though its exegetes might wish otherwise—it is, above all, poetry. The text of Ercilla articulates the condemnation of the *encomienda*, emphasized in recent years by *Araucana* criticism, only in an indirect and implied way.[12] There is a single allusion—subtle, to be sure— to slavery: "Self-interest and malice grew at someone else's expense, sweat, and harm" (Crecían los intereses y malicia / a costa del sudor y daño ajeno, 1.68). For sixteenth-century peninsular readers who did not have all the facts about the harsh sociohistorical realities of the conquest and colonization of America, greed in *La Araucana* almost comes across as an allegorical figure: a sinister but inescapable invading force that accompanies the Spaniards onto American soil, immediately infecting the Amerindian peoples. Whatever else it is in the Ercillan epic, greed is a flaw whose condemnation had a strong rhetorical tradition behind it.[13]

It is in the followers and imitators of Ercilla that one detects the impact of *La Araucana*, partly because of the reverberation of its themes. In several important aspects, the influence of Ercilla is evident in the text of Juan Rufo. One such aspect is the censure of greed. Rufo had access, as mentioned earlier, to the first two parts of Ercilla's epic, and he almost certainly composed the verses of his *Austriada* under the influence of the extraordinarily popular first editions of *La Araucana*. However, Juan Rufo's subject matter is very different from Ercilla's. Here, it is not a matter of conquest somewhere beyond the sea, but rather, of an internal war: the peculiarly violent uprising of the Moriscos in the realm of Granada between the years 1568 and 1570. Why would Rufo apply the censure of greed, a vice that Ercilla portrayed as inextricably bound up with wars of conquest, to the dirty little war in the Alpujarra?

The answer to this question lies in the conditions that characterized the crisis Philip II faced in the turbulent Andalusia of those years. According to Fernand Braudel, the rebellion in the Alpujarra started as a

12. See, for example, Beatriz Pastor, *Discursos narrativos de la Conquista: Mitificación y emergencia*, 403–11. Jaime Concha also alludes to a conflict of interests between *encomenderos*, Church, and monarch during the conquest. See his "Otro Nuevo Mundo," 67; and José Durand, "El chapetón Ercilla y la honra araucana."

13. For the rhetorical tradition of the condemnation of greed, see María Rosa Lida de Malkiel, *Juan de Mena: poeta del prerrenacimiento español*, 498–99. I owe this reference to Isaías Lerner.

minor incident, but it erupted "with a violence out of all proportion to the real importance of what was, at the beginning at any rate, a second- or even third-rate military operation." Due largely to reasons of a geopolitical nature (the real threat of Ottoman supremacy in the area and the deployment of a limited number of troops and Spanish galleys in Flanders and Italy), the rebellion of the Moriscos of Granada aroused great interest in the outside world and sparked hopes among the Moriscos of other regions of Spain. The rugged mountain terrain, the impossibility of blockading the coastline where ships from Algiers and Barbary arrived carrying "men, munitions and weapons . . . artillery and rations, rice, grain, or flour" for the insurgent Moriscos, the religious fervor on both sides—all of these factors helped to prolong the conflict. Don John of Austria, in official communications to Philip II, complains of the soldiers' demoralization, of desertion, indiscipline, and of the lure of plunder that turned the conflict into a "spontaneous private war," in Braudel's words.[14] This is the situation that Don John, hero of Rufo's poem, confronted when he took command of his troops in Granada on Easter Sunday in 1569, an event that Rufo narrates in language that draws a parallel between Don John's reception in Granada and Christ's triumphal entry into Jerusalem on Palm Sunday (canto 6). This real disarray among Don John's soldiers explains much of Juan Rufo's insistence on the problem of greed in *La Austriada*.

Like Ercilla, Juan Rufo prizes historical truth, and in *La Austriada* he figures forth a male world of soldiers like the one with which he is familiar. Almost completely ignoring gender as a category of fictional representation, Rufo thoroughly rejects the influence of Ariosto. This is one aspect in which he partially differs from the poet whose work has influenced him in so many other ways. For example, Rufo begins to introduce a love story between a Morisco named Zaide and a slave named Haxa (canto 9), thinks better of it, and never mentions the lovers again. In general, his epic follows the historical facts, as recorded by Hurtado de Mendoza and others.

The narrative shows numerous signs of a serious morale problem among the hero's troops. In the first battle, the army of the marquis of Mondéjar, captain general of Granada, pursues the soldiers of the newly elected Morisco king (*rey chico*), Abenhumeya. The latter take shelter in the mountains to the southeast of Granada, where Mondéjar's troops are put to it to catch them. The marquis's soldiers are inexperienced and unfamiliar with "the arduous and noble trade of the soldier, crucible of

14. Fernand Braudel, *The Mediterranean and the Mediterranean World in the Age of Philip II*, 2:1060, 1065, 1063, 1069.

true honor and valor" (el arduo y noble oficio de soldado, / Crisol de la fineza verdadero).[15] They do not withdraw when they are supposed to, but at other times, they take flight. After a spirited harangue from their leader, the troops return to combat. When they win, they reward themselves with the spoils of the battle: "certain Morisco women and children who were hiding in the bushes" (ciertas moriscas y criaturas / Que estaban entre grandes espesuras, 3.103.7–8).

Juan Rufo is not being inconsistent when he weighs up the motives of the Spanish soldiers. The temptation to loot was just as real in the Alpujarra as in the campaign of Arauco, maybe more so, because the Morisco women regularly adorned themselves with many different kinds of gold jewelry, which, as Caro Baroja observes, "aroused even more greed and caused even greater acts of violence and barbarism on the part of the Castilian soldiers when the Granada Moriscos were defeated." In both armed conflicts, official policy did not allow greed as a motive for just war, and in both, pillage of the enemy camp was the usual practice. But inside Spain this reality could seem more shocking because it was impossible to adduce arguments such as the monarch's distance to explain the excesses committed by those who fought in his name. The taking of "human booty" on both sides certainly falls within the category of excess: Caro Baroja recounts that at Sorbas (Almería), it was common practice for the Moriscos to trade a Christian prisoner to the Algerians in exchange for a musket, and that the royal council and the court (*audiencia*) of Granada ruled that Moriscos could be sold as slaves "for having called out to Mohammed and having declared that they were Moors." In the Alpujarra, Morisco prisoners were coveted because they could be sold both in and outside of Spain. According to Braudel, "Every city in Spain was crammed with Morisco slaves for sale: boatloads were sent off to Italy."[16] No less than in the *Araucana*, therefore, the complaint of greed in *La Austriada* has a basis in historical reality.

Juan Rufo says nothing about the destiny of these "human spoils," but there are textual indications that the author was well aware that they were being led into captivity. The taking of Morisco prisoners, usually

15. All quotations of *La Austriada* are taken from the edition of Don Cayetano Rosell, Biblioteca de Autores Españoles 29 (Madrid: Rivadeneyra, 1854). Rosell does not number the octaves. I have made my own numbering of the stanzas, excluding from my count an octave that summarizes the plot, which appears above the text proper at the beginning of each book. Hereafter, in the text the canto number will be indicated first, followed by octave, and where appropriate, lines, in this case 3.79.5–6.

16. Julio Caro Baroja, *Los moriscos del Reino de Granada: Ensayo de historia social*, 126, 188, 198; Braudel, *Mediterranean World*, 2:1069.

women and children, is a frequent occurrence in *La Austriada*. One of the most wrenching episodes in this respect is the sack of Válor, a wealthy village that was supposed to be off limits to the soldiers because it was protected by Mondéjar. In his prose text, Hurtado de Mendoza describes the troops of Antonio de Ávila and Alvaro de Flores as "men risen up without pay, without the sound of drums, sent in by the council [*concejo*], who consider thievery to be their salary, and greed to be their commanding officer" (hombres levantados sin pagas, sin el son de la caja, concejiles; que tienen el robo por sueldo, y la codicia por superior" [*War of Granada*, 60]). According to Rufo's account, these same soldiers, frustrated in their mission to capture Abenhumeya, rebel and decide to lay waste the village.

> You should have seen gluttonous delusion
> unleash her insatiable hunger
> for untarnished silver, fine gold,
> and silk, highly esteemed in some places,
> forgiving neither woolen cloth, wax, linen,
> nor any other piece of cheap jewelry whatsoever;
> so much so that he who comes out breathless
> and most weighted down, judges himself most honorable.
>
> They take as captives most of the Moriscas
> of the village, but not tied up, which is
> the customary manner of leading them away,
> nor pressing them with hard handcuffs;
> rather, oh treachery unworthy of blemish!,
> they are burdened with the weapons of their captors,
> who handed them over to them because the weight
> robbed them of their strength, and also of their minds.
>
> (Viérades el goloso desatino
> Desenfrenar su hambre insaciable
> Tras la cendrada plata, el oro fino,
> Y la seda, que en parte es estimable,
> Sin perdonar a paño, cera o lino,
> O a cualquiera otra alhaja miserable;
> Tanto, que aquel se juzga más honrado
> Que sale sin aliento y más cargado.
>
> Todas las más moriscas de la villa
> Llevan captivas, pero no ligadas,
> Como ya se acostumbra de trailla,
> O con duras esposas apretadas;
> Antes, ¡oh engaño indigno de mancilla!
> Con armas de sus dueños van cargadas,
> Los cuales se las daban porque el peso
> Las fuerzas les quitaba, y aun el seso.)
> (6.15–16)

At the end of the pathetic scene, in which the Moriscas do not wear hand-cuffs because they need free hands to carry the weapons of their captors, the narrator declares that this surely must be "the world-upside-down" (*el mundo al revés*). The ancient topos of the world-upside-down, common in the Middle Ages and refashioned by the Baroque, was a protest against social disorder and marginalization in both Golden Age and colonial Spanish American texts.[17] Rufo's narrator describes this   situation as "disorder and madness" (*desorden y locura*), "unjust error" (*injusto error*, 6.17.7). The discourse the poet uses to denounce the soldiers' greed is the same one noted earlier in Ercilla: "gluttonous delusion," "insatiable hunger" (*goloso desatino, hambre insaciable*). Hunger for gold incites the soldiers to go against their own values: according to the code of chivalry, honor stands apart from, and usually in opposition to, spoils. This is what Rufo means when he refers to the plundering of the village and degradation of the Morisco prisoners as a world-upside-down.

The opposition between false or apparent honor and long-established values of good soldiering appears explicitly in many other passages of *La Austriada*. In one instance, the Moriscos "feign to flee, leaving behind great spoils" (fingen huir dejando gran despojo) to deceive and devastate the enemy. The Castilian soldiers, "lacking prudence and blinded with such a rich prize in sight" (faltos de prudencia, / y ciegos con tan rica presa al ojo, 12.56.3–4), begin carrying off women, children, baggage, jewels, and Morisco clothing. At this moment, the enemy returns "and wounds the Christians in such manner as to make a great mound of their bodies" (y hiere de manera en el cristiano, / que hace de sus cuerpos gran ribazo, 12.57.5–6). Once order is restored, Luis Fajardo, the marquis of Los Vélez, reprimands the soldiers for their greed, which he describes as a scandal "that offends the heroic suppositions of soldiering" (que ofende / la heroica presunción de la milicia, 12.60.3–4).

In these examples, greed always appears in combination with attitudes that are deemed highly unacceptable in just war, such as cowardice, disobedience, and disorder. In other words, *La Austriada* repeatedly poses the same problems of hunger for riches, demoralization, and indiscipline that Braudel documents in his analysis of the War of Granada, which he calls "an incoherent, disappointing conflict, a mountain war, full of surprises, difficulties and sometimes atrocious cruelty."[18] In a manner reminiscent of the way the codes of just war function in Ercilla, *La Austriada* affirms time and again that wealth is nothing more than apparent honor; it is not the kind of honor that counts. For Juan Rufo, greed constitutes an obstacle to genuine martial values: heroism, honor, and royal service.

17. Rolena Adorno, *Guaman Poma: Writing and Resistance in Colonial Peru*, 164 n. 18.
18. Braudel, *Mediterranean World*, 2:1062.

Rufo takes advantage of poetic license to tell us that there are instances when hunger for material things can cost a man his life. As if to emphasize that this is not mere metaphor, the epic recounts how the victorious soldiers at Lepanto threw themselves into the sea to pluck gold, silk, and pearls from the bodies of the fallen, drowning in the process (canto 24). There is nothing like this in the Lepanto episode of *La Araucana*, nor in Ercilla's main source for the naval battle, Fernando de Herrera's *Relación de la Guerra de Chipre y Suceso de la batalla naval de Lepanto* (*Account of the war of Cyprus and occurrence of the battle of Lepanto*). Rufo pilfers the image of those who drown for greed from *Pharsalia* 3.674–75, where fighters at the naval battle of Massilia (Marseilles) grab hold of the bodies of the dead and steal their weapons before they can sink to the bottom. But Ercilla also ponders the end to which rapaciousness can lead in literal terms when he recounts the death of Valdivia, brought on precisely because the captain general of Chile had taken a detour from the "profitable road" (*camino provechoso*) in search of a gold mine. With these words, the author of *La Araucana* condemns the moral flaw that was Valdivia's undoing:

> Incurable illness! Oh great fatigue,
> nourished with much indulgence!
> Common vice and sticky birdlime,
> desire without reason unbridled,
> enemy of the public good or profit,
> thirsty beast, dropsical and swollen,
> beginning and end of all our evils!
> oh insatiable greed of mortal men!

> (¡Oh incurable mal! ¡oh gran fatiga,
> con tanta diligencia alimentada!
> ¡Vicio común y pegajosa liga,
> voluntad sin razón desenfrenada,
> del provecho y bien público enemiga,
> sedienta bestia, hidrópica, hinchada,
> principio y fin de todos nuestros males!
> ¡oh insaciable codicia de mortales!)
> (3.1)

Juan Rufo's *Austriada*, in turn, textualizes greed at Lepanto in the following manner:

> Oh loathsome inebriation, hungry gluttony,
> odious ingratitude, incurable illness,
> useless beast, dropsical, thirsty,
> unbearable uneasiness and craving;
> misery which feeds on hunger,

> contrary to what is just and reasonable,
> with false appearances of wealth,
> and essence of coarsest poverty!

> (¡Oh infame embriaguez, gula hambrienta,
> Odiosa ingratitud, mal incurable,
> Inútil bestia, hidrópica, sedienta,
> Desasosiego y ansia intolerable;
> Miseria que de hambre se alimenta,
> Contraria de lo justo y razonable,
> Con falsas apariencias de riqueza,
> Y esencia de asperísima pobreza!)
> (24.90)

Both Ercilla and Rufo are imitating a strophe from a Horatian ode on money and its abuse:

> By indulgence the dreadful dropsy grows apace, nor can the sufferer banish thirst, unless the cause of the malady has first departed from the veins and the watery languor from the pale body.

> (Crescit indulgens sibi dirus hydrops,
> nec sitim pellit, nisi causa morbi
> fugerit venis et aquosus albo
> corpore languor.)[19]

The language of the two octaves, Ercilla's and Rufo's, contains common elements, and the semantic fields are roughly the same. Ercilla waits until line six to use the metaphor of greed as thirst, playing instead with different meanings of *mal* (illness or vice, which appears in his text as "common vice and sticky birdlime" [vicio común y pegajosa liga]). He retains the Horatian image of dropsy (edema) that "grows" (*alimentada*) by indulgence, and he loosely holds on to Horace's distinction between the greedy ruler ("del provecho y bien público enemiga") and the successful leader who can remain indifferent to riches. The concept of self-will run riot (*voluntad sin razón desenfrenada*) is Ercilla's own addition. By combining possible registers of the word *mal*, and by exploring the reach of the concept of insatiability, which Horace opposes to the common good, Ercilla loosely glosses the idea of thirst for riches but does not radically depart from Horace.

La Austriada shows direct influence from the surface text (Ercilla), as well as from Horace and Lucan. Rufo departs from Herrera more than Ercilla does here, and he exploits the opposition between greed and reason

19. All quotations from Horace appear in the text by ode and line numbers, in this case, book 2.2.13–16. English translations are taken from the corresponding page in the Loeb Classical Library edition.

much more than does Ercilla, but this is absolutely consistent with his way of treating the theme of hunger and thirst for riches throughout the twenty-four cantos of his poem. In *La Austriada*, no case of pillage appears in isolation from a problem of military indiscipline, expressed as disorder, fury, or abandon (*desasosiego y ansia intolerable*)—in other words, as appetite or unreasonableness (everything that opposes "the just and reasonable"). Juan Rufo's text also insists much more than *La Araucana* on the opposition between apparent riches (gold and worldly possessions, to which he refers as "falsas apariencias de riqueza"), and true wealth (heroism, honor, duty). Both Ercilla and Rufo preserve much of the Horatian subtext, but the main thrust of Rufo's imitation seems to come from the Ercillan notion of unbridled desire. Swerving from the the Ercillan text, Rufo reads that "unbridled" state in a way that permits him to use it as the foundation for his own opposition of greed or unreasonable appetite versus the idea of reasoned order and military discipline. Order and discipline are concepts that have a deep ideological connection with the martial values that Rufo promotes throughout his epic, and indeed, with the preservation of political power in the state. The double strategy of embracing what is, in Bloom's terms, the "family" of his precursor (Horace through Ercilla), then distancing himself from both subtexts, places Rufo squarely in Greene's category of "heuristic" imitation. Because he also draws on Lucan where Ercilla does not, Rufo's imitation is more eclectic than the one in the *Araucana*. Ercilla's imitation of Horace seems more "sacramental" than necromantic, even though he has added an element (the opposition between reason and appetite) that later proves crucial to Rufo's own reworking of Horace. But neither poet's best work is offered in these imitations.

Even though there is an obvious affinity between the two epics in their treatment of greed, there is also divergence. This was perhaps inevitable because, in spite of the fact that Rufo learned the poetic importance of greed from Ercilla, these were two writers with very different trajectories. Furthermore, *La Austriada* plays several subtexts against one another that Ercilla does not need or chooses to avoid (Hurtado de Mendoza and, for the Lepanto section, Paruta and Lucan). Those differences can perhaps explain why one does not perceive in Rufo the disenchantment one feels in the last cantos of *La Araucana*, but rather the optimism of a soldier who has triumphed at Lepanto and who still believes that soldiering is the "crucible of true honor and valor."

Outwriting Ercilla: Juan Rufo's Battle of Lepanto

David Quint's book on *Epic and Empire* reminds us of an important link Spanish epic poets perceived between the naval battles of Lepanto and

Actium.[20] *La Austriada* is an example of a text that plays on this link to create the image of Spain as a new Rome. But the battle of Lepanto does not appear until the end of Rufo's epic, of which the first eighteen cantos narrate the campaign against the rebels in the Alpujarra. The skirmishing between Christians and Moriscos in the blue-gray mountain villages of Rufo's native Andalusia comprise some of the most haunting episodes of *La Austriada*, this despite the fact that Rufo himself fought in the naval battle against the Ottoman Turks. So why, exactly, is Lepanto here?

The reason is surely none other than the same one Alonso de Ercilla gives for inserting the battle of Lepanto into the second part of *La Araucana*. In the cave of the magician Fitón, the figure of the poet contemplates a globe that is both a repository of the past and a compendium of the future (canto 24). When pressed to reveal the outcome of Spain's military enterprise in Arauco, the magician replies that this American war has already given the poet ample material for descriptions of land combat, and that what he really needs is a good sea battle:

> You need only a naval battle
> with which to authorize your story,
> and you shall write of matters of war,
> war at sea as well on land.
>
> (Sólo te falta una naval batalla,
> con que será tu historia autorizada,
> y escribirás las cosas de la guerra
> así de mar también como de tierra.)
> (23.73.5–8)

As Lerner explains, in the Golden Age, the phrase *great naval battle* (*gran batalla naval*) was a code name for Lepanto. Golden Age writers used these words so freely that by the seventeenth century, Francisco de Quevedo was able to make a pun with them. In his picaresque novel, *La vida del Buscón*, Quevedo combines the phrase with the word for turnip (*nabo*), to refer to turnip fights between delinquent adolescents as "*batallas nabales*" (book 1, chapter 3; book 3, chapter 2). For the learned reader of epic, the mere mention of the words *naval batalla* would automatically mobilize the whole paradigm of decisive imperial battles at sea. Through Fitón, Ercilla makes the claim that Lepanto "authorizes" the rest of the story; it legitimates and brings luster to an epic whose American events must have seemed remote to many Spanish readers. The force of the connection may no longer be so obvious, but to a writer like Ercilla, the

---

20. David Quint, *Epic and Empire: Politics and Generic Form from Virgil to Milton*, 158.

inclusion of such a battle would immediately conjure echoes of the confrontation at Actium. On the one hand, there is the connection between Augustus and Charles V's title of Holy Roman emperor, which Quint adduces.[21] On the other, there is Ercilla's personal *aemulatio:* to "authorize" his poem with Lepanto is to constitute himself as the Spanish imperial poet or new Virgil. Lepanto thus brings to the sixteenth-century text the full weight of the *translatio imperii* project, both in its political and its literary ramifications.

Juan Rufo certainly understood the importance of this aspect of Ercilla's poetics, but that would not be extraordinary in a context where poetic imitation was such a widespread practice. For the epic, *imitatio* meant imitation of Virgil, but also of Lucan. An obvious model for a naval battle was the iconographic representation of Actium on Aeneas's shield (*Aeneid* book 8). Following Virgil's ekphrastic passage about the adorned shield, poets like Ercilla and Virués carefully frame the battle of Lepanto by enclosing verbal pictures of it in a globe or in descriptions of carvings on the walls of a ship (*Monserrate* canto 4). Juan Rufo, on the other hand, includes the sea battle in the first narrative, much as Lucan had done with Caesar's naval attack against Marseilles in *Pharsalia* book 3. But *imitatio* did not necessarily prescribe subservience to a sole model. Eclectic imitations included elements from several different subtexts blended together in the new poem. Indeed, by the time Juan Rufo wrote his version of Lepanto, there were already important encomia on the naval victory in vernacular tongues to place alongside the well-established sea battles of Roman precursors. The poet of *La Austriada* thus had access to a variety of stories on which he could draw to figure forth his Lepanto.

Mary Gaylord [Randel] has suggested that the influence of Herrera's *Account of the war of Cyprus* is evident in *La Austriada,* and that Rufo may have read Paolo Paruta's *Historia vinetiana* (1605), as well. The text of Herrera, published in Seville in 1572, was one of the first accounts of the battle of Lepanto to appear in Spain. For his part, Alonso de Ercilla had ample time to peruse Herrera's *Account of the war of Cyprus* as he worked on the second part of his epic. Lerner states unequivocally that Ercilla's Lepanto narrative is based on the text of Herrera.[22] In fact, the version of Lepanto that probably had the greatest impact on the Spanish literary world of the moment was Ercilla's own, published in 1578. At this time, Juan Rufo had already made considerable progress on his long poem about the achievements of the hero of Lepanto. Rufo's dependence on *La*

Araucana part 1 for his treatment of the condemnation of greed surfaces throughout his own epic, most notably at the end of the Lepanto episode (canto 24). There can be little doubt, however, that Rufo also read Ercilla's second part before finishing his own poem, both because of its prestige and because, despite real differences, the similarities between his poetic project and Ercilla's would have attracted him to it quite naturally.

Yet the connection between Rufo and Ercilla remains largely unexamined. One reason for this could be that the influence of Hurtado de Mendoza's *War of Granada* has dominated criticism of *La Austriada* at the expense of other sources. Rufo's borrowings from Hurtado de Mendoza are practically undisputed nowadays. Gaylord [Randal] agrees, in the end, with Díaz-Plaja and others that Rufo borrowed from Hurtado de Mendoza, not the other way around.[23] There is, however, no sea battle in the *War of Granada*. One must look for influences on Rufo's Lepanto section in encomiastic texts that deal with Lepanto itself or with ancient naval battles. In many ways, the plot line of Rufo's Lepanto story is close to that of Herrera's *Account of the war of Cyprus*, while his peculiar rendering of the battle shows numerous points of contact with classical poets. For various reasons, the writers of sixteenth-century epic construct Lepanto as the point on which all of history converges. Whenever the naval battle between the Christian Holy League and the Ottoman Turks appears in a literary text, it is accompanied by intense poetic imitation and literary rivalry. In the following pages, I will argue that in the Lepanto section of *La Austriada*, Juan Rufo sets out to do more than echo the poet of *La Araucana*, and that one of his goals is to take advantage of the great models of sea battles by the poets of imperial Rome to surpass Ercilla's version of Lepanto.

From Rufo's perspective, such a task might have seemed feasible. For one thing, Ercilla's Lepanto was a digression from the war of Arauco, so he could not afford to enlarge it too much at the expense of his first narrative. He gave it one canto and probably worried that even that was too much of a distraction from the main plot. Juan Rufo, on the other hand, perceived the Lepanto victory as being of a piece with the rest of his epic. Not only was the hero the same as that of the first eighteen cantos, but the enemy and the cause were for him, as for other Spaniards of the time, so deeply interconnected as to be virtually identical.[24] Rufo not only explicitly links the military of the Moriscos with that of the Turks in various passages of the Alpujarra war narrative, he also engages in a generalized representation of "barbaric Muslims" that has the effect of col-

---

23. Gaylord [Randel], *Historical Prose of Herrera*, 100 n. 33.
24. Albert Mas, *Les Turcs dans la Littérature Espagnole du Siècle d'Or: Recherches sur l'évolution d'un thème littéraire*, 1:199.

lapsing both groups into one entity. The battle of Lepanto was a corner-stone in the effort to secure Christian hegemony over Islam in the Mediterranean world; it was this aspect that allowed Juan Rufo to easily blend it into the first part of his epic. So, while Rufo surely realized that Ercilla was a literary rival to be reckoned with, he might well have thought that the poet of *La Araucana* was not in a position to compete with him in his own Mediterranean domain. Moreover, whereas the space Ercilla dedicated to Lepanto was, of necessity, limited, Rufo could afford to structure his exposition of the background and military prepa-rations over four cantos, reserving the final two for the battle proper. Since he had twice the space Ercilla did in which to present the con-frontation itself, the Andalusian poet could gloss brief passages from *Araucana* canto 24 at length, or narrate any aspect of the sea battle in a leisurely manner. Thus Rufo probably thought his version of Lepanto would easily outstrip Ercilla's.

The plot line of the battle in Herrera, Ercilla, and Rufo includes the following parts: the approach of the two armadas, the epic harangues of Don John and Alí-Bajá, the encounter of the lead ships, the capture of the ships of the Order of Malta and slaughter of their crew, the seizure of the Ottoman lead ship and raising of the cross on its mast, the pursuit of Luchalí (Ochalí), and the flight of the surviving Turks. But Herrera and Rufo examine elements that Ercilla does not include, some of which are literary and derive from ancient epic, such as the intervention of Discord (*Aeneid* 8.702), Alí-Bajá's consultation of a soothsayer, shifts in the wind and their effect on the outcome of the battle (*Aeneid* 8.682 and *Pharsalia* 3.523), Alí-Bajá's promise to free Christian slaves if he wins, and the death of Alí-Bajá and surrender of his two children.

Interspersed among the main points of the plot are octaves that vividly describe the fighting, and the sights, sounds, and smells of war. These descriptions offer evidence that Rufo includes poetic objects and specific phrases he finds in Ercilla's version of the battle. This is not a case of sustained imitation, but rather the preservation of discrete lexical items or important allusions from Ercilla that Rufo marshals at several points on the more extended trajectory of his own battle narrative. For example, when the two armadas clash in *La Araucana*, Ercilla writes that the fire and smoke and clanging of swords at Lepanto are greater even than those at Troy in its hour of destruction (24.42). For his part, Rufo pauses in the middle of his own battle narrative to invoke the presence of Aeneas by alluding to the Trojan hero's shield:

> Come hither, mythical wars,
> waged between gods and giants,

with horrific enchanted lances,
which outstrip natural strength,
bring on scaly cuirasses
with breastplates and shields of diamonds,
and the very same arms which the burning
furnace of Vulcan forged for the Trojan.

For we will wage another true battle here
among men, with unenchanted weapons,
in which a hundred thousand extremes will be seen,
whose legacy to the world will be eternal horror;
on winning, we will celebrate unprecedented glory,
if such a great thing can fit into verse or prose,
a truth at once completely pure and simple,
which if it were fiction, would still be fantastic.

(Vengan aquí las guerras fabulosas,
Trabadas entre dioses y gigantes,
Las encantadas lanzas espantosas,
A fuerza natural sobrepujantes,
Y salgan las corazas escamosas
Con los petos y escudos de diamantes,
Y aquellas mismas armas que al Troyano
Forjó la ardiente fragua de Vulcano.

Que otra batalla cierta aquí daremos
Entre hombres, y con armas sin encanto,
En la cual se verán cien mil extremos
Que al mundo dejarán eterno espanto;
Nueva gloria en vencer celebraremos,
Si en verso o prosa puede caber tanto,
Una verdad purísima y sencilla,
Que a ser ficción, aun fuera maravilla.)
(23.27–28)

Declaring a *verista* poetics worthy of Ercilla himself, Rufo insists that these are real military events that supersede classical battles between giants and gods, even though the men who fight at Lepanto are unassisted mortals. Rufo favorably compares Don John to Aeneas here, and implies a second comparison between himself and Virgil. But this passage is fundamentally an attempt to hold at bay critics who would fault him for following historical sources too closely and dispensing with the superhuman machinery of ancient epic.

Surrounding this fragment there are various octaves of battle description that use the following vocabulary items, which appear first in Ercilla: bullet, cannons, a great crash, confusion, fire, a clashing of swords, furor, to thunder, to shudder, to stir or spin around (*bala, cañones, estruendo, confusión, tiro, golpear de las espadas, furor; tronar, estremecerse, revolverse*). This could be mere coincidence, since many of these are stock lexical items for sixteenth-century sea battles. On the other hand, there is evidence of a more specific Ercillan subtext. When the two armadas clash, Rufo says that the elements "were stirred in new confusion" (en nueva confusión se revolvieron, 23.26.4), which appears to be an adjustment of Ercilla's "all was in a spinning confusion" (todo en revuelta confusión hacía, 24.41.7), used to describe the sound of the crashing of ships and of firepower. Rufo's "The sea turns to red blood" (El mar en roja sangre se convierte, 23.41.6) recalls Ercilla's "the sea suddenly covered with blood" (la mar de sangre súbito cubierta, 24.49.7), but also Lucan's "Their blood foamed deep upon the wave" (Cruor altus in unda / spumat, *Pharsalia*, 3.572–73), and the Virgilian verse, "Neptune's fields redden with strange slaughter" (arva nova Neptunia caede rubescunt, *Aeneid* 8.695). When he broaches the weighty subject of fires at sea ("With flames which, in the face of the waves, defended the natural power they had been given" [Con llamas que a las aguas defendían / el natural poder que les fue dado, 24.84.3–4]), Rufo attempts to outdo Ercilla at imitating an outstanding passage of Lucan's battle before Marseilles (3.680–90). The Ercillan passage reads, "it seemed that, not only did the sea burn, and the ground sink, but that high heaven came down to earth" (no sólo arder el mar, hundirse el suelo, / pero venirse abajo el alto cielo, 24.42.6–8). These borrowings show a close reading of *La Araucana* and perhaps a desire to challenge Ercilla. But they are not yet a full-fledged, aggressive *aemulatio* of the surface text, such as one might expect to find in a battle scene as prestigious as this one. For that, one must look to one of the most serious confrontations of the episode.

A crucial moment in all Lepanto narratives is the encounter of the two lead ships (in Spanish, *nave capitana* or *galera real*). The galley bearing Don John of Austria and that of Alí-Bajá, commander of the Ottoman armada, pursue one another, then are positioned face to face. Quickly, other ships from both armadas intervene, but for a brief moment, the two ships oppose one another unaccompanied. Ercilla narrates the confrontation in a single octave and with little embellishment:

> Gallant Don John, recognizing
> the enemy lead ship at the front of the formation,
> and sharply cleaving the churning water,
> breaks through the burning flames;
> but the Turkish ship comes out to meet him
> with impelling impetus, where both equally
> charge at one another with furious clashes,
> breaking both iron-clad cutwaters.
>
> (El gallardo don Juan, reconocida
> la enemiga real que iba en la frente,

hendiendo recio el agua rebatida
rompe por medio de la llama ardiente;
mas la turca, con ímpetu impelida
le sale a recebir, donde igualmente
se embisten con furiosos encontrones
rompiendo los herrados espolones.)
(24.43)

The next octave brings seven Turkish galleys to the aid of Alí-Bajá. Here again Ercilla uses the verb *to charge* (*embestir*) for the action of the Ottoman ships against the hero's galley. There is alliteration, to be sure, and a metonymic relationship between galley and captain that seems to personify the ships. Otherwise, Ercilla's narrative of the encounter is straightforward and his language relatively simple. The verb *embestir* also appears in the narrative of Herrera, but there, too, the story unfolds largely free of poetic adornment.[25]

However, where there had been only a suggestion of metaphor in Ercilla and Herrera, *La Austriada* boasts an elaborate cluster of similes when the armadas clash. Juan Rufo likens the two lead ships to horses ready to attack, scraping the earth with their hooves and stirring up a cloud of dust.

As spirited stallions, perhaps,
swiftly measuring the dusty corral
with their shod hooves,
their owners unaware of any danger,
and heading furiously toward a collision,
they crash, tearing apart their mighty chests;
thus the two powerful lead ships hurled themselves
at one another, terrible and horrifying.

(Como tal vez caballos animosos
Con las herradas uñas van midiendo
Velozmente los sitios polvorosos,
Sus dueños el peligro no sabiendo,
Y al encuentro recíproco furiosos
Llegan, los fuertes pechos deshaciendo;
Así las dos galeras poderosas
Terribles se embistieron y espantosas.)
(23.34)

He then compares the maneuvers and speed of the galleys to furious blazing comets and arrows in flight.

---

25. Fernando de Herrera, *Relación de la guerra de Chipre y suceso de la batalla naval de Lepanto*, 357.

> At the sound of trumpets and bugles,
> the other ships lunge forward, enraged,
> with the fury characteristic of rushing comets,
> which leave behind them fiery lines;
> arrows do not fly through the air
> in a swifter course, having been shot,
> than that of the armadas closing in, on whom depends
> the good or ill fortune of the enterprise undertaken.

> (Al son de los clarines y trompetas
> Se embisten las demás embravecidas,
> Con la furia que suelen ir cometas,
> Dejando tras sí rayas encendidas;
> No pasan por el aire las saetas
> En curso más veloz, siendo impelidas,
> Que cierran las armadas, de quien pende
> El bien y el mal del hecho que se emprende.)
> (23.35)

Finally, the poet of *La Austriada* represents the two galleys as bulls in mating season, stomping and groaning:

> As brave bulls that have sired,
> wounded by that sickness they call rut,
> are wont to bellow through forests and valleys,
> scraping the hard ground with their hooves;
> and summoned by their own sign,
> they enter the contest without hesitation,
> whereby it is established in war
> which will be the victor, which the vanquished;
> Such was the hardfought collision and intense brutality
> with which the two lead ships ran into each other.

> (Como toros valientes madrigados,
> Heridos de aquel mal que llaman celo,
> Suelen bramar por selvas y collados,
> Con las uñas rayendo el duro suelo;
> Y de su misma seña convocados,
> Vienen a la contienda sin recelo,
> Donde queda por guerra establecido
> Cuál será vencedor y cuál vencido;
> Tal fue el reñido encuentro y fuerte saña
> Con que las dos reales se encontraron.)
> (23.37–38)

Rufo takes the verb *embestir* that already appeared in Herrera and Ercilla and deliberately attaches it to two referents (horse and bull) that seem filled with connotations of maleness, sexuality, and brute force. The poet assigns these attributes to the lead ships, but by the same metonymic steps noted in the Ercilla passage above, they are displaced onto the ships' captains, constructing a sexualized, masculine pair of foes ready to engage in combat. This is a far cry from Ercilla's "gallant Don John."

And no wonder. For Rufo, in his attempt to best Ercilla, has turned to Virgil, who was for Spanish epic poets of the time the greatest precursor of them all. This with an important caveat: it is Ercilla who ushers into Spanish epic the image of the bull, especially the fighting bull (*toro de lidia*). The image of the bull appears at least six times in *La Araucana*, and Lerner calls Ercilla's use of this image "early." When the bull appears in classical literature, it is usually within the context of animal husbandry. Pliny discusses the attributes of the bull (*taurus*) when he is discussing varieties of oxen.[26] The bull that Ercilla has in mind (and certainly the one that Rufo intends) is the fighting bull known in Spain. The bulls that appear in *La Araucana* are generally of this variety, and in one case, Ercilla compares Rengo to a bull watching over cows and calves, using language remarkably similar to Rufo's ("like the jealous bull who has sired, and follows the slow-paced cows" [como el celoso toro madrigado / que la tarda vacada va siguiendo, 22.44.5–6]). It is precisely this small surface debt to Ercilla that gives away a deeper imitation in both texts, one that Ercilla dissimulated, but that Rufo decided to flaunt as proof of thoroughgoing *aemulatio*.

In order to model such an important passage as the clashing of the two armadas, Rufo required a similar momentous occasion from classical epic; nothing else would endow his text with the necessary prestige. Indeed, the final battle of the *Aeneid* pits the hero, Aeneas, against his enemy, Turnus, with the exact same simile of two bulls ready to lunge at one another ("as . . . when two bulls charge, brow to brow, in mortal battle" [cum duo conversis inimica in proelia tauri / frontibus incurrunt, 12.716–17]). As Bloom would say, Rufo has "daemonized" Ercilla's text by reaching past it "to a range of being just beyond that precursor."[27] His procedure is clear: to pick up what were vivid images of bulls in Ercilla and infuse all the prestige and weight of Virgil's epic into his own rendering of them, thereby vouchsafing the accolade for his own text while implying that there was nothing so unique about Ercilla's.

But this still does not account for the reproductive aspect of the bull image (the *celos* of the *toro madrigado*), either in Ercilla or in Rufo. It is an

26. For the early appearance of the fighting bull in Ercilla, see Lerner, *La Araucana*, by Ercilla, 349 n. 91. For the use of the word *taurus* to denote the bull of Indian oxen, see Pliny, *Natural History*, book 8, section 70.122–29. I refer to the English translation on the corresponding page of the Loeb Classical Library edition.

27. Bloom, *Anxiety of Influence*, 15.

image that connects not with the epic Virgil, but with the more agricultural facet of the Roman poet's work. Most surely, in the *Georgics* lies the key to the puzzle of both images, that of Ercilla and especially that of Rufo. In book three, Virgil writes that to increase the strength of the male, whether bovine or equine, one must isolate him:

Therefore men banish the bull to lonely pastures afar, beyond a mountain barrier and across broad rivers, or keep him well mewed beside full mangers. For the sight of the female slowly inflames and wastes his strength . . .

> (Atque ideo tauros procul atque in sola relegant
> pascua, post montem oppositum et trans flumina lata,
> aut intus clausos satura ad praesepia servant.
> carpit enim viris paulatim uritque videndo
> femina . . .)
> (3.212–16)

By separating the bull from the rest of the herd, as Virgil explains, there comes a moment when his strength is so great that he "tests himself, and, learning to throw wrath into his horns, charges a tree's trunk; he lashes the winds with blows, and paws the sand in prelude for the fray" (ventosque lacessit / ictibus, et sparsa ad pugnam proludit harena, 3.233–34). In these verses there lies a substantial part of the Virgilian subtext for the image of the "toro madrigado," but there is more.

Virgil continues to detail the mating season of all living things:

> Yea, every single race on earth, man and beast,
> the tribes of the sea, cattle and birds brilliant of hue,
> rush into fires of passion: all feel the same Love.

> (Omne adeo genus in terris hominumque ferarumque,
> et genus aequoreum, pecudes pictaeque volucres,
> in furias ignemque ruunt: amor omnibus idem.)
> (3.242–44)

As for the steed, the mare's scent makes him quickly forget the rider's rein and the lash:

See you not how a trembling thrills through the steed's whole frame, if the scent has but brought him the familiar breezes? No longer now can the rider's rein or the cruel lash stay his course, nor rocks and hollow cliffs, nay, nor opposing rivers, that tear up mountains and hurl them down the wave.

> (Nonne vides, ut tota tremor pertemptet equorum
> corpora, si tantum notas odor attulit auras?
> ac neque eos iam frena virum neque verbera saeva,

non scopuli rupesque cavae atque obiecta retardant
flumina correptosque unda torquentia montis.)
(3.250–54)

This, then, is the precursor text for Rufo's steeds, who are anxious to mate and ready to charge, "their owners unaware of any danger." Rufo has deliberately recast them in the protective role of the *toro madrigado*, the bull who has inseminated a cow and expects issue. It is the bull who has sired that becomes fiercest of all. Ercilla's text, in the brief comparison of Rengo and the bull, hints at the possibilities of the Virgilian subtext but quickly moves on, so that only the most skilled reader will catch him in his dissimulative imitation. Rufo, on the other hand, openly exploits the imagery of several Virgilian subtexts together in a gorgeous, multilayered simile for the lead ships that is not meant to conceal the subtexts, but to parade them. Ercilla is the innovator in Spanish epic images of bulls, and he is a furtive imitator of Virgil, at least here. But Rufo takes up the challenge of Lepanto, zealously embracing Ercilla's family of precursors to produce a dazzling heuristic imitation of Virgil's *Georgics*, now combined with the forceful hand-to-hand combat of the heroes at the finish of the *Aeneid*. Rufo, at least in this successful necromantic imitation, has gone far beyond the suggestion of the Ercillan text, and he makes no attempt to conceal his triumph.

There are many other similarities in the two passages about the encounter of the lead ships, but they are small lexical coincidences compared to the painstaking elaboration of the *toro madrigado* simile. Ercilla's influence on the Lepanto section of Rufo's epic is, it would seem, beyond question. The later poet selects an important fragment in Ercilla where the language is particularly dense, then digs deep into the cherished poetic past to find a way to overturn the *Araucana's* Lepanto passage. Delving deeper and expanding as he imitates, the author of *La Austriada* builds the similes of his own text on poetic reiterations present but embryonic in Ercilla. The new text is less hurried; Rufo allows us to partake of his poetic vision in a way that Ercilla does not. Finally, the similes Rufo creates here are more consciously literary than anything in the Ercillan subtext. Their function was undoubtedly to align the new work with the foundational texts of Western epic tradition, so rich in similes of this type. If thereby Rufo could outclass Ercilla, then the prestige of *La Araucana* would be his.

It would take far more than high-sounding language and well-wrought similes, however, to beat Ercilla at his own game. *La Araucana* had some advantages that Rufo's text could not match: the fascination with America; a proximity to the events that Rufo was not able to impart to his own text, despite his firsthand experience at Lepanto; and Ercilla's brilliant conjugation of the influence of Ariosto and Camões, among others. But one knows the importance of a work by its imitators. And Juan Rufo was certainly a much better imitator of Ercilla than received critical tradition has taught us.

Textual Disruption: The Relocation of the Moriscos of Granada

We have focused thus far on the influence of *La Araucana* on Juan Rufo's poetic decisions, an influence that is particularly evident in Rufo's imitational strategies and in the priority of his themes. The many contradictions of Ercilla's text did not foreclose on representational or other possibilities for those who came after the great soldier-poet. On the contrary, the success of *La Araucana* authorized an epic writing of identity that was, in some respects, highly ambiguous. Even an overtly triumphalist epic whose subject was the glories of Hapsburg power, such as *La Austriada*, could exhibit a surprisingly complex, ambivalent attitude toward the enemy. Ercilla's discussion of greed, which rules out the hunger for riches as a justification for war, connects with the general concern for discrimination between just and unjust wars, expressed not only in the epic, but also in theological debates during the Golden Age. Rufo's epic reflects this concern by adducing two conditions that mitigate the infamy of war: the objective of peace and the just cause of religion or "intact faith in God" (*la fe entera de Dios*, 9.4.8). But though he affirms that in the War of Granada, religious right is on Philip's side, Rufo's narrator is not oblivious to suffering within the opposing camp. To some extent, then, it seems that the inherently contradictory text of Alonso de Ercilla actually paved the way for later epic writers to express a degree of sympathy for an enemy that was still represented as a despised and feared "other."

It is one thing, however, for a sixteenth-century Spaniard to sympathize with the American Indian, as Ercilla sometimes does, and quite another to show sympathy with the plight of the Morisco, even though the completion of the Reconquest gave rise to objective similarities between the Morisco condition and that of Indians who endured de facto slavery on the American *encomiendas*.[28] Inasmuch as the Moriscos were considered a subspecies of Moor, Christian Spain could apply to his ethnic group an older, already institutionalized racial discourse that was based on events as early as the Arab invasion of Spain (A.D. 711), and as late as the *Reconquista*. Indeed, seen in the context of the recently concluded Reconquest, the War of Granada appeared to bring with it an imminent threat of new invasion and a return to the attenuated military campaign against Islam at home.

---

28. Caro Baroja, *Moriscos del Reino de Granada*, 8.

The Moriscos, however, were not just a "kind of Moor"; their predicament was culturally and historically specific. The Moriscos were a hybrid people who belonged to two cultures. Their identity was assumed to be based primarily on religion, but it was made manifest in easily recognizable signs, such as language and dress. Had Morisco identity been constituted only, or predominantly, through religion, the forced conversion would have eradicated the assumed basis for difference. It did not. In the first place, most Christians did not believe in the sincerity of the conversion. As much as twenty years after the Morisco uprising in the Alpujarras, Bernardino de Escalante, soldier, scholar, and commissioner of the Inquisition in Galicia and later in Seville, was still warning Philip II that the Spanish Moriscos were "for the most part, apostate Moors" (por la mayor parte moros apóstatas). To the extent that the conversion was perceived as inauthentic, it was thought to cover up a more familiar, marked identity, that of the Moor. Second, the external manifestations of cultural difference did not simply disappear with the forced conversion from Islam. Speech, clothing, mixed names (such as Diego López Abenabó and Francisco Núñez Muley), and simultaneous participation in public (Christian) and private (Muslim) religious ceremonies continued to signal "Moorishness" as well as a hybridity that, like any other hybridity in Christian Spain at this time, was largely deprecatory.[29]

Signed negatively in this way, Morisco difference derived from a thoroughly racialized dominant discourse that eventually used hybridity as a justification for Morisco deterritorialization, or exclusion from the body politic. Hurtado de Mendoza, for example, writes of the Morisco situation in terms of the negation of identity proper. In the *War of Granada*, Fernando de Válor, an erstwhile Morisco alderman (*regidor*) of Granada, says the Moriscos are "treated and thought of as Moors among the Christians, and thus despised, while we are taken for Christians among the Moors, thus no one believes or helps us. While we are excluded in this way from public life and conversation, they command us not to speak our language; at the same time, we do not understand that of Castile . . ." (tratados y tenidos como moros entre los cristianos para ser menospreciados, y como cristianos entre los moros para no ser creídos ni ayudados. Excluidos de la vida y conversación de personas, mándannos que no hablemos nuestra lengua; y no entendemos la castellana . . . , 16). Hurtado de Mendoza's text cannot arrive at a more positive conception of hybridity, as an "in-between" identity that manages to assimilate two cultures at the same

---

29. See Bernardino de Escalante, *Discursos de Bernardino de Escalante al Rey y sus Ministros, 1585–1605*, 196–200; and Caro Baroja, *Moriscos del Reino de Granada*, 105.

time, because it formulates Morisco identity in terms of exclusion: Christians scorn the converts, Moors no longer trust them, and they find themselves on the outside of all political and social discourse. Válor, whose personal experience is representative of that of his group, denounces the precarious Morisco situation, but we do well to remember that the point of view expressed here is that of the dominant culture.[30]

It is no accident that the external markers of identity were the very things that the 1567 edict (*pragmática*) attacked. This measure imposed eleven prohibitions on the Morisco population of Granada to bring the converts under stricter control, and to eradicate outward signs of their previous cultural identity. It was forbidden to speak, read, or write in Arabic for three years; all contracts written in that language were annulled. Similarly, all books written in Arabic were to be brought to the superior court (*Chancillería*) for examination. Moriscos were to dress in the Castilian manner (*a la castellana*), and the women were to unveil their faces. Religious ceremonies were to follow Christian customs, and Morisco songs and instruments were outlawed. The Moriscos were not to celebrate Fridays, nor were they to use Moorish names or surnames. The women were forbidden to color themselves with henna. It was forbidden to bathe in artificial baths, and those public baths already in existence were to be destroyed. Turks, Moors, and Berbers who lived in Spain as slaves (*gazíes*) were to be expelled, and the Moriscos were prohibited from holding *gaci* slaves. Finally, licenses for black slaves were to be reviewed. These prohibitions, which touched almost every aspect of Morisco life, came at a time when Granada was becoming increasingly Christianized.[31] Caro Baroja's analysis of the gradual loss of Morisco voice and power at all levels of society in the region makes it very clear how radically the area had changed during the first half of the sixteenth century. The Moriscos' control over their lives was steadily diminishing. The *pragmática* of 1567 exacerbated this sad situation, and it was the

---

30. The issue of hybridity has been theorized and debated in recent years. See especially Stuart Hall, *Questions of Cultural Identity*. The idea of deterritorialization as dispossession and exclusion from the body politic is theorized in the well-known essay by Deleuze and Guattari, "What is a Minor Literature?" and in Rafael Pérez-Torres, *Movements in Chicano Poetry: Against Myths, Margins*. This concept informs the writing of many U.S. Latino/a writers, such as Ana Castillo ("A Countryless Woman," in *Massacre of the Dreamers*), and Gloria Anzaldúa (*Borderlands/La Frontera: The New Mestiza*).

31. The stipulations of the 1567 *pragmática* were actually formulated in November 1566. See Caro Baroja, *Moriscos del Reino de Granada*, 152–53. On the prolonged tensions between Moriscos and Christians in the area, see Louis Cardaillac, *Moriscos y cristianos: Un enfrentamiento polémico, 1492–1640*.

resulting frustration and swelling sense of impotence and suppressed rage that finally led to armed Morisco rebellion. From the Christian point of view, the uprising fulfilled the threat of a return to *Reconquista* times.

Juan Rufo's narrative follows the events so closely that in some parts, *La Austriada* reads like a rhymed chronicle. After the Moriscos kill 248 Christians at the battle of Órgiva, John of Austria realizes the gravity of the situation and calls for deportations from the Morisco locality of Granada, the Albaicín, which he dubs the "root" of the problem.

> The fact that Ventomiz is in rebellion
> without having been forced into such an insult,
> is a clear and manifest indication
> that the whole realm is corrupt;
> and since this assumption is firm,
> the danger must be averted
> by curing the root, which is in Granada, and which
> has taken over even to the deepest abyss.

> I will request that my lord and brother,
> if you are in agreement, transplant
> the Albaicín throughout all Iberian realms
> that do not border on the Atlantic Ocean;
> to remove these goblins from our path
> will be a genuine benefit,
> for they are a false key into my secrets,
> and the cause of a thousand other deleterious effects.

> (De haberse Ventomiz en arma puesto,
> Sin ser a tal insulto compelido,
> Resulta indicio claro y manifiesto
> De que está todo el reino corrompido;
> Y siendo aqueste firme presupuesto,
> Debe ser el peligro prevenido,
> Curando la raíz, que está en Granada,
> Hasta el más hondo abismo apoderada.

> Pedir a mi señor y hermano quiero,
> Con vuestro parescer, que se trasplante
> El Albaicín por todo el reino ibero
> Que no confina con el mar de Atlante;
> Y será beneficio verdadero
> Quitarnos estos trasgos de delante,
> Que llave falsa son de mis secretos,
> Y causa de otros mil malos efetos.)
> (7.88–89)

Behind this move to expel the enemy from within the city walls lies the conception of the Moriscos as unfit to live within the city (*polis*), which identifies them as a fundamentally barbaric group. But the decision to compel a major human migration also contains the notion of the enemy as a pollutant that must be purged or expulsed from the political body. The evacuation of the Albaicín (June 23, 1569) and the relocation or redistribution (*repartimiento*) of the Moriscos of Granada throughout lower Andalusia and Castile led first to heightened hostility (or the perceived threat thereof) throughout the peninsula, and eventually to the total expulsion of the Moriscos from Spain, as mandated in a series of regional edicts. Expulsion was, of course, already an accepted method of removing groups perceived to "contaminate" the body politic. By the time Juan Rufo composed his epic, Christian Spain perceived both the Jews and the Moriscos as internal enemies whose very proximity caused unease. The traditional stereotypes of Jews and Moriscos as a "fifth column" or as parasites on the body are deeply entrenched in Spanish culture.[32] Seen in this context, the evacuation of the Albaicín (canto 10) serves as a link between the 1492 expulsion of the Spanish Jews and the later Morisco deportations; the latter Rufo textualizes as an extirpation of untrustworthy or infirm parts of the political body.

There is something strange about the evacuation narrative in *La Austriada*. The narrator recounts a heartrending scene of families being led away and groups of Moriscos with their hands tied together. Thus, *La Austriada* figures forth the dispossession of the self and elimination of an objectified "other" in the most literal, graphic terms.

> Armed skirmishes and surprise attacks, meanwhile,
> occur in Granada as frequently as every few hours;
> but now, according to a just and holy proclamation,
> the city's Albaicín was being depopulated;
> no pen could dare to explain the weeping
> which, during the ill-fated migration,
> those unhappy people displayed outwardly,
> since part of it they dissimulated.
>
> With a well-armed guard all around them,
> in a long procession and with slow steps,
> they were taken to the royal hospital,
> to make plans for their removal . . .

32. Caro Baroja is inconsistent about the date of the evacuation (*Moriscos del Reino de Granada*, 200, 205), but virtually all sources indicate that it occurred after Don John took command (April 13, 1569). Braudel writes that the Morisco expulsion from Granada city took place in December 1569 (*Mediterranean World*, 2:1066), and massive deportations from the realm began in 1570 (2:1072). On the use of negative stereotypes of Jews, see Paul Julian Smith's provocative essay, "*La Celestina*, Castro, and the Conversos," in *Representing the Other: "Race," Text, and Gender in Spanish and Spanish American Narrative*.

Thus proceeding, in perfect imitation of
a miserable example of vanquished people,
so much so, that the scene could move to compassion
the hardest of hearts . . .

Under the supervision of armed guards and captains,
their hands tightly bound together with ropes,
they were transported to various places,
suffering the most cruel misfortunes;
and when our opponents were transported from this place,
the faithful remained behind in Granada,
with less fear of uprisings,
but without comfort in their lodgings.

(Las armas y rebatos entre tanto
Por horas menudean en Granada;
Mas ya por un edito justo y santo
Del Albaicín quedaba despoblada;
No hay pluma que a explicar se atreva el llanto
Que en la transmigración desventurada
Aquella triste gente en sí mostraba,
Puesto que parte de él disimulaba.

Con guarda bien armada a todos lados
En larga procesión a paso lento
Al hospital real eran llevados
Para trazarse allí su apartamiento . . .)
(10.94–95.1–4)

(Yendo imitando pues desta manera
Un miserable ejemplo de vencidos,
Y tal, que a compasión mover pudiera
Los corazones más endurecidos . . .)
(10.96.1–4)

(Ya con armada gente y comisarios,
Religadas las manos a cordeles,
Eran llevados a lugares varios,
Padeciendo infortunios más crueles;
Trasplantados de allí nuestros contrarios,
Quedaron en Granada los fieles
Con menores recelos de alzamientos,
Mas sin comodidad de alojamientos.)
(10.102)

These octaves focus on the conditions of the deportation, itself: sadness, tears, ropes, defeat. But they are separated by thirty-six lines that are ostensibly about something else. Just as the pathos of the story swells to what feels like an intolerable level, the narrator abruptly shifts to an anecdote that bears no trace of the emotion he has kindled in the lines immediately previous and that, in fact, threatens to overturn the dynamics of the deportation narrative. In a move to repress his account of the evacuation, the authorial voice recounts an incident about a Morisco prisoner who attacked one of the soldiers overseeing the operation. Apparently overcome with emotion at the human misery he relates, Rufo marks the monumental disruption that the evacuation of the Albaicín provokes in his text by repressing the deportation story. The narrator turns his gaze from the slow procession of bound figures and refocuses it on a lone Morisco who dared to wound a soldier and was torn to pieces ("Fue hecho piezas mil el mahometo," 10.97.3). During four octaves, Rufo weighs the possible motives of the assailant, then concludes that the attack on the soldier was unprovoked and that the incident is

> . . . a prodigious example:
> for he who dared to die in this manner
> would undertake any treason for the right price.
>
> (. . . un ejemplo prodigioso;
> Que quien morir osó desta manera
> Cualquier traición al precio acometiera.)
> (10.100.6–8)

The anecdote serves, then, as a means of repressing the evacuation story and covering it over with a narrative designed to prove the rightness of the deportation, as well as the incorrigibility of the hard-hearted Moriscos.

The priority of Rufo's text is especially evident when one compares his account of the Albaicín evacuation to that of Hurtado de Mendoza. In the *War of Granada*, the deportation story comprises roughly forty-four lines of prose—one long paragraph—on the printed page. Of those lines, only eight refer to the incident of the attack on the solder:

> They displayed a kind of forced obedience, their heads hung low more out of sadness than repentance; of the latter, they showed not a trace; for one of them wounded the man closest to him: they say he meant to assail Don John, but the truth of it could not be ascertained because he was torn to bits: I, who found myself present, would say that it was an impulsive act of rage against the soldier, rather than a premeditated decision.

> (Mostraban una manera de obediencia forzada, los rostros en el suelo con mayor tristeza que arrepentimiento; ni de esto dejaron de dar alguna señal; que uno de ellos hirió al que halló cerca de sí: dícese que con acometimiento contra D. Juan, pero lo cierto no se pudo averiguar porque fue luego hecho pedazos: yo que me hallé presente diría, que fue movimiento de ira contra el soldado, y no resolución pensada.) (79)

Hurtado de Mendoza, who seems to exonerate the Morisco of pre-meditation, dedicates much more space to the conditions that made the deportation necessary, the procedures followed, and the misfortunes that befell the Moriscos on their way to exile.

> It was an exodus that caused great compassion in those who had previously seen them living in comfort and luxury in their homes: many died from the hardships of the journey, from fatigue, from grief, from starvation, from irons, robbed and sold into captivity by the very men who were supposed to guard them.
>
> (Fue salida de harta compasión para quien los vio acomodados y regalados en sus casas: muchos murieron por los caminos de trabajo, de cansancio, de pesar, de hambre, a hierro, por mano de los mismos que los habían de guardar, robados, vendidos por cautivos.) (80)

Rufo's text comes close to suppressing any mention of the atrocities committed against the Moriscos on their way out of Granada, but this almost complete silence ("suffering the most cruel misfortunes," 10.102.4) is what Barbara Johnson might call a "significant gap."[33] It is one of those eloquent silences that attempts to write misery out of a text that wishes to assert the fundamental justification of the expulsion "according to a just and holy proclamation."

Unpublished official documents of the period, however, fill in the gap of Rufo's epic in a way that leaves no room for doubt about the terrible suffering the Moriscos endured. Documents referring to the relocations of 1570 indicate that the voyage was made without proper provisions, and that men traveling with wives were slowed down so much that they simply could not make the trip.[34] What became of them, we do not know. Because the number of Moriscos being moved was so great and because they carried so much baggage, they could not be put up in churches.[35] There are signs that some of them starved to death during the voyage because the villages did not want to feed them and the authorities did not provide means to do so, with the result that "every day they die coming down those roads" (cada día se vienen muriendo por esos caminos).[36] Some villages refused to receive the Moriscos, asking that they be sent to a different place, where they could live "in all

---

33. For Barbara Johnson's articulation of the concept of the "significant gap," see her *A World of Difference*, 49–85.

34. Archivo General de Simancas, Cámara de Castilla, *legajo*, 2157, folio, 11 (hereafter abbreviated AGS, CC, with *legajo* and folio numbers following).

35. AGS, CC 2557/14.

36. AGS, CC 2157/18.

comfort" (*con toda comodidad*), though they could not indicate where that place might be.[37] On receipt of a shipment of Moriscos in a galley under the supervision of Don Sancho de Leyva, a letter from Seville states that the immediate task is to "see to it that all of them do not die of starvation, because they have arrived very sick, robbed, and so mistreated by the sea that it is the greatest compassion in the world to see them" (procurar que no mueran todos de hambre, porque vienen muy enfermos y robados y tan maltratados de la mar que es la mayor compasión del mundo verlos).[38]

The 1571 relocations provoked equally woeful comment. Documents written by the magistrates or mayors (*corregidores*) of towns in Castile list the number of Moriscos from Granada received by each one, in response to a royal decree (*real cédula*) that is summarized in these terms: "it is fitting that the Moriscos removed from the realm of Granada after the uprising should be distributed as sparsely as possible throughout the places of these realms" (conviene que los moriscos que se han sacado del Reino de Granada después del levantamiento se repartan lo más menudamente que sea posible por todos los lugares destos Reinos). The officials then allude to the crown's request for census information about the Morisco population. Some of the figures are difficult to make out, but in many cases the number of Moriscos received was at least 100 men, women, and children (*mozos y mozas*) per town, sometimes many more. These documents invariably indicate that the Moriscos arrived in miserable condition and with no clothing. Many of them were so sick that they could only be placed in hospitals. There is almost always an indication of the number of those who did not make it, as compared to that of survivors. Occasionally there is a reference to slavery; Murcia, for example, says it has received a number of Moriscos from Granada and that there are many slaves (*esclavos*). Of 950 Moriscos received by Segovia, 260 died.[39] Ávila received 1000 Moriscos and dispersed them to many nearby villages; the document says that many of the parents were so sick that their children had to serve in their place, and the children—who could only do "light work" (*trabajo liviano*), such as waiting and carrying water—worked so badly that the local people quickly tired of them.[40] A letter from Montanches documents receipt of a shipment of Moriscos from Córdoba who arrived in such a deplorable state—"since they are so sick and abused with hunger and common need" (según andan enfermos y maltratados con hambre y común necesidad")—that many of them died.[41]

37. AGS, CC 2157/30.
38. AGS, CC 2157/42.
39. AGS, CC 2162/27.
40. AGS, CC 2162/30.
41. AGS, CC 2162/33.

When placed side by side with this kind of archival evidence, the repressions in Rufo's text seem even larger and more telling. His account of the evacuation of the Albaicín, from which he, himself, seems to shy away, is a very significant moment of textual disruption. It is to Juan Rufo's epic what the carnage of Cañete is to *La Araucana*. Albarracín Sarmiento writes that when Ercilla laments Spain's loss of truth and condemns Spanish greed, his poem shows a contradictory revelation that "carries it toward self-destruction" (lo lleva a autodestruirse).[42] But Ercilla's poetic project comes much closer to self-destructing after Cañete, when the figure of the poet has seen enough blood and gore and removes himself—and his narrative—to the untarnished landscapes of southern Chile. If there is an equivalent threat of self-destruction in *La Austriada*, it is when Rufo writes the Morisco deportation from the Albaicín. The poet's own unease with the expulsion is shown by his decision to displace guilt onto the lone Morisco who attacks the Spanish soldier.

Still, there is sufficient sympathy for the Morisco plight in the octaves that surround the story of this incident to show that Rufo, like Ercilla, could not look on this magnitude of human affliction without feeling deeply torn. In the Spain of this period, the Moriscos did not arouse the same kind of ardent defense that the Amerindian occasionally did, even though they, like the Araucanians, were subjects of the Spanish crown.[43] This does not mean that Spaniards, generally, were not of two minds about the relocations, which produced new difficulties elsewhere while supposedly solving the problem in Granada. For one thing, relocated Moriscos were more difficult to spot and control than they had been in Granada, where the social markers were easy to recognize. The Morisco, however, was a more familiar "other" than the Amerindian. If the Moor of the past could still be romanticized, present-day Moriscos were usually detested. There was, in addition, an ancient perception of the Moor as treacherous and untrustworthy. Even Caro Baroja refers to the "enormous instability of character, a perfidy which not without cause has been associated with the 'punica fides' of which Sallust speaks."[44] The fact that this "perfidy" was confirmed by the historical facts of the War of Granada in the assassina-

---

42. Carlos Albarracín Sarmiento, "El poeta y su Rey en *La Araucana*," 111 n. 17.

43. On the ramifications of the legal status of vassals of the crown of Castile, see Anthony Pagden, *The Fall of Natural Man: The American Indian and the Origins of Comparative Ethnology*, 33.

44. Caro Baroja discusses the new problems caused by the relocations in *Moriscos del Reino de Granada*, 215–17; he alludes to the romanticization of the Moor, 131, and reaffirms the stereotype of Moorish treachery, 189.

tions of Abenhumeya and Abenabó by rivals within their own ethnic group only strengthened a well-established image of the Moriscos as duplicitous. If Ercilla invented Araucanian treachery, all Rufo had to do was narrate the events of the war as they had already unfolded.

Juan Rufo's ambivalence and compassion toward the Moriscos, whose communities were being dismantled all across Spain as he wrote, comes across most strikingly in scenes like the sack of Válor, with its condemnation of greed, and in the opening strophes of his narration of the emptying out of the Albaicín. In many other places, his epic reaffirms images of the Morisco (or the Moor) that were well established in his own culture and its traditions. What he has taken from Ercilla is the opportunity to problematize—if only slightly—those stereotypes of a close Islamic "other" whose military and religious linkage with the Ottoman Turks *La Austriada* articulates over and over again. The relocation of the Moriscos did not resolve any of the tensions Christian Spaniards felt toward them; in fact, those tensions seem to have escalated more rapidly once the Moriscos were scattered throughout the regions of Andalusia, Extremadura, and Castile. Unlike Ercilla's figures of faraway Araucanian braves, the image of the Morisco derived from a very old cultural complex of anti-Moorish beliefs that Spaniards from different regions believed they could confirm through daily experience.

It is thus all the more remarkable that Juan Rufo should summon so much sympathy for the suffering Moriscos in his verses, at the same time that he glorifies the military commander who defeated them. *La Austriada* revels in the triumph at Lepanto, which it promotes as the historical moment in which imperial power and true religion coincide. But no less does the epic of Juan Rufo criticize the routine capture and enslavement of Morisco women and children by the soldiers of Philip II during the War of Granada. The poet's internal stife crystallizes around the story of the evacuation of the Albaicín and forced resettlement of the Moriscos of Granada, which he does not seem to be able to narrate without discernible anguish. If all epic is intrinsically political and given to black-and-white representations of opposing sides, one might expect *La Austriada* to be even more so, since it was commissioned by one member of the royal family and written in praise of another. That its author was able to partially avoid stark, negative representations of the Moriscos, and show great compassion for the plight of the defeated, suggests that a highly ambiguous epic writing of the "other" was very thinkable in the 1580s. That this should happen so soon after the publication of part 2 of the *Araucana*, with Ercilla's equally ambivalent depiction of Araucanian warriors and widows, is surely not a coincidence.

3

Rape and Redemption
Virués's *El Monserrate* and Reading Golden Age Foundational Myths

Epic has been associated with foundations at least since the *Aeneid*, which set the key foundational myth of empire in the story of the Trojan survivors' flight to the new imperial city of Rome. Certainly not all epics are about foundations, yet they all function as foundational myths that reaffirm the origins and the preordained ascendancy of the political body. Alonso de Ercilla incorporated foundations and restorations of colonial towns and forts into his *Araucana,* and he showed the Spanish conquest of the south of Chile, which brought this virgin territory inside the Spanish polity. Juan Rufo does not write of foundations. By casting his hero, John of Austria, as a Christlike redeemer, however, he suggests an analogy between Christianized Granada and the new Jerusalem. In this chapter, I examine the story behind the foundation of a Catalan shrine, which the epic proclaims to be national: the Virgin's sanctuary at Montserrat. Unlike the authors of poems examined in previous chapters, Cristóbal de Virués reaches back into the Middle Ages for his material, but no less than the other epics studied here, his poem on the foundation at Montserrat is an encomium of Habsburg imperial monarchy. *El Monserrate* relies heavily on the category of gender for the construction of Spanish heroic identity. Although it differs from *La Austriada* (and, to some extent, from *La Araucana*) in this regard, it is by no means the only epic of the imperial age that bears witness to the role played by gender in narrating heroic national myths.

At the end of an essay on cultural violence in *Daphnis and Chloe,* John J. Winkler poses a methodological question that is particularly pertinent for those of us who study Renaissance literatures while living in a postmodern world: should the author's meaning be the goal of our reading? Winkler goes on to ask, "Should we concede that much authority to the writers we read? If our critical faculties are placed solely in the service of elucidating an author's meaning, then we have already committed ourselves to the premises and protocols of the past."[1] Winkler's dilemma is also ours, and it cannot be evaded. One might even argue that wrestling with this difficult matter is especially urgent in the case of older texts that offer a challenge to modern readers, both on the level of establishing authorial meaning, and on that of values or belief systems immanent in them, but no longer palatable to us. A reader who is guided by the criteria of twentieth-century feminism or recent critical theories such as deconstruction, for example, may be genuinely disturbed by Golden Age texts that attempt to set aside gender and other kinds of difference in order to affirm meaning.

Renaissance texts, moreover, may present another kind of problem if the author's meaning is obscured by echoes of meaning from the texts that have informed it, and whose voices still speak in it and through it. It might appear that only a philological approach could serve to disentangle so many story lines. In the case of *El Monserrate*, as in all of Golden Age epic, there exists an abundance of intricate intertextual relationships that problematizes the inference of meaning. In the Renaissance, as Colombí-Monguió has written, "*imitatio* generally produces—though not always—a functional relationship between the new text and its models, a refraction of the different voices which dwell in it together, thereby determining the mode of meaning of the text itself."[2] Under such circumstances, one grasps at the shape of the author's meaning by reconstructing the relationship of the text to its models, whether these be linguistically specific, literary subtexts, or easily recognizable story lines that might more generally be referred to as "sources." Especially in cases where several models play against one another in the new text, as in the case of *El Monserrate*, meaning can be subtly shaded, requiring more, not less, elucidation as the action of time erodes the relationship of models to text.

In these pages, I will attempt to weigh the mandates of two very different types of reading as they pertain to a Golden Age text that is problematic for the modern reader in various ways, and to scrutinize the advisability of approaching such a text from the vantage point of feminism or poststructuralist theories without enlisting the aid of formalist approaches. Specifically, I will focus on the problem of whether it is possible to achieve a thorough reading—one that takes into account inter-

---

1. John J. Winkler, "The Education Of Chloe: Erotic Protocols and Prior Violence," 30. Winkler's essay, as well as those of Coppélia Kahn and Patricia Klindienst Joplin cited in this chapter, appear in *Rape and Representation*, ed. Lynn A. Higgins and Brenda R. Silver.
2. Alicia de Colombí-Monguió, *Petrarquismo peruano: Diego Dávalos y Figueroa y la poesía de la Miscelánea Austral*, 140.

textual relationships, among other things—of a text in which Castilian male discourse erases, or writes over, regional and feminine identities, without entering into complicity with the author's meaning.

El Monserrate is a religious epic about the discovery of the Virgin's image and the subsequent founding of a monastery at Montserrat, just outside Barcelona. Its author is the Valencian Cristóbal de Virués, who earned the rank of captain during military service in Italy and who fought, according to Don Cayetano Rosell, "with great valor" (*con gran denuedo*) in the battle of Lepanto. There has always been some controversy over the publication date of the first edition, which Pierce gives as 1587. Rosell, editor of the most accessible edition of the poem, rejects the claim that there was a 1587 edition, while a recent editor of *El Monserrate*, Mary Fitts Finch, explains that the authorization to publish (*privilegio*) was issued in 1587, whereas the work actually emerged from the presses of Querino Gerardo (Madrid) in 1588. Fitts Finch, who bases her 1984 edition on *El Monserrate Segundo* (Milan, 1602), is correct about the date of the authorization, but not about that of the epic's publication. The Biblioteca Nacional, Madrid, holds both editions, and the publication date is clearly indicated in both cases. There seems to be no doubt, therefore, that the princeps dates from 1587.[3]

Cayetano Rosell bases his edition on that of Gabriel de Sancha (1805), even though he admits that it contains many alterations when compared to that of Milan, which he considers to be "the most exact and correct one" (*la más cabal y correcta*). Conceding that the variants of the Milan edition are so numerous that he could not attempt to include them, Rosell defends the Sancha edition on the grounds that, despite its own abundance of variants, the latter "do not distort the thoughts of Virués in any way" (en nada desvirtúan los pensamientos de Virués). He therefore reproduces them, "except in cases in which the meaning, the wholeness or the spirit of the original would suffer" (excepto en los casos en que padecían el sentido, la integridad o el espíritu del original).[4] All of this hints at a certain arbitrariness in Rosell's editorial decisions, especially considering that the Sancha edition is so late, and that it is the 1602 edition that modifies the first *El Monserrate* in the most substantive way. The emendations or enlargements of the 1602 edition redraw the religious and political lines of the epic and move those themes to the foreground, implying, perhaps, that the poet restates the theology of his text in starker terms that reflect the intensifica-

3. For the controversy surrounding the date of the princeps, see Frank Pierce, *La poesía épica del Siglo de Oro*, 336; Don Cayetano Rosell, introduction to *El Monserrate*, by Virués, 503 n. 1; and Mary Fitts Finch, introduction to *El Monserrate Segundo*, by Virués, 10.

4. Rosell, introduction to *El Monserrate*, by Virués, 503 n. 1.

tion of religiousness that was already transforming Counter-Reformation culture, generally.

Because epic tends to textualize matters belonging to the public arena, that is, political matters, in ways that are usually intended to be serious and free of irony, this genre, perhaps more than any other Golden Age literary kind, unabashedly mobilizes discourses of imperial monarchy and myths of providential predetermination, as well as ones that suggest the fullness and just nature of empire.[5] Messianic myths of this type are in evidence in *La Austriada* and in *La Araucana*, as we have seen. Like those epics, *El Monserrate* sets out to construct the fiction of a homogeneous, Castilian self, in the process of attempting to suppress difference. Within this framework, it is fitting that Virués's epic should represent the battle of Lepanto as the ultimate test of Christian, specifically Spanish, military might against the Ottoman Turks, just as Rufo and Ercilla had done before him. Indeed, a large midsection of the poem glorifies an analogous victory of Christian forces, led by Spanish heroes, over Muslim warriors in Africa.

For a foundational text that makes explicit reference to the glory of Habsburg empire, *El Monserrate* has a rather unseemly beginning. The event that calls the rest of the work into being is the rape and murder of the count of Barcelona's daughter by a hermit who lives on the wild summit of Montserrat. It is this hermit, Juan Garín, who, after undertaking a pilgrimage of atonement, witnesses the founding of the sanctuary for the Virgin's image on the same site where he had earlier buried his victim. Virués modeled his text on a medieval hagiographic legend, a fact that has previously gone unnoticed by students of *El Monserrate*, but that is beyond doubt after Charles Allyn Williams's extensive work on the legend of the hairy anchorite, and Roger Bartra's meticulous tracing of the figure of the "Wild Man" in the context of the mythic origins of European otherness. Both scholars link the story of Juan Garín to the thirteenth-century legend of St. John Chrysostom.[6]

---

5. For the difficulty modern readers encounter in Renaissance epics that promote imperialism without irony, see Thomas R. Hart, "The Author's Voice in *The Lusiads*," 45.

6. Charles Allyn Williams, "Oriental Affinities of the Legend of the Hairy Anchorite," 116, 122, and "The German Legends of the Hairy Anchorite," 31–33; Roger Bartra, *Wild Men in the Looking Glass: The Mythic Origins of European Otherness*, 74–78. The travel notes of Hieronymus Münzer, published as *Itinerarium Hispanicum Hieronymi Monetarii* by Ludwig Pfandl in 1920, include a fifteenth-century retelling of the Juan Garín legend, of which there are also German variants. On the figure of the "Wild Man" in early modern literature, see Richard Bernheimer, *Wild Men in the Middle Ages: A Study in Art, Sentiment, and Demonology*; Alan Deyermond, "El hombre salvaje en la novela sentimental"; John D. Williams, "The Savage in Sixteenth-Century Spanish Prose Fiction"; and the dissertation of Oleh Mazur, "The Wild Man in the Spanish Renaissance and the Golden Age: A Comparative Study."

Unlike the Catalan hermit, John Chrysostom was a priest who, according to legend (as opposed to Church teachings), forswore his oath and committed both rape and murder. There are numerous French, Italian, and German renditions of Chrysostom's story. The specific circumstances of the man's transgression vary from version to version of the legend. The German versions have John Chrysostom throw his victim over a cliff, for example, whereas Virués's hermit disposes of her body in a different way. The single characteristic of *El Monserrate* that sets it apart from other versions of the legend is the protagonist's arduous odyssey of repentance; there seems to be nothing like it in any other variants of the John Chrysostom tale. Since Martin Luther published the legend in 1537 as part of a polemic directed at Pope Paul III, and since the motive behind the pilgrimage of Virués's protagonist is to obtain papal forgiveness, it seems plausible that the Spanish epic is written, in part, as a rejoinder that reaffirms the pope's authority. In all the versions of the story, including that of Virués, John's penitence is the same: he lives like a hairy beast, walking on all fours, until God forgives him. Similarly, all interpretations of the legend show a miraculous happy ending.

Virués's text appears to presuppose a reader who is comfortable with the pro-Castilian view of state and empire it promotes. That regional alterity was "written out" of the text when Virués chose to compose his royal octaves in Castilian Spanish, rather than in Catalan—long the literary language of his native Valencia—would presumably not be problematic for such a reader, nor would the suppression of gender difference.[7] Both erasures, however, are likely to trouble a twentieth-century reader who, on the one hand, acknowledges linguistic and cultural diversity as a fact of sociopolitical life, and on the other, is no longer satisfied to adduce contemporary social mores in order to justify misogynous representations of women or acts of violence against female characters in an early modern text.

Let us consider the poet's choice of Castilian Spanish (*castellano*) as his literary language. Roughly speaking, the abandonment of nondominant vernacular tongues throughout Europe can be seen to coincide with a period of nation-state consolidation. Throughout the continent, due to

---

7. There is a difference of opinion among present-day *valencianos* as to whether the literary language of Valencia prior to 1540 was actually Catalan or a language closer to the language used in Valencia today. Specialists in this area inform me that there was virtually no distinction between Catalan and the language in which Valencian writers wrote prior to their adoption of Castilian Spanish. Without wishing to offend anyone, I have tried to remain as faithful as possible to the historical and linguistic facts.

reasons of cultural hegemony as well as political primacy, the languages of the dominant regions, which Benedict Anderson calls "print-languages," began to be used almost exclusively for the purposes of publication, but in most places this happened slightly later. In Spain, *castellano* had been the literary language of the court of Castile for hundreds of years, but by the sixteenth century its preeminence extended to the administrations of the semiperiphery, as mentioned in the Introduction. Braudel writes that language is an important sign of national identity, noting that "the Castilian language spread over the whole Iberian peninsula in the sixteenth century, and became the language of literary expression used by Aragonese writers from the time of Charles V."[8] Having been adopted by the upper classes throughout the country, Castilian was hegemonic and became a symbol and abbreviation of the nation-state as a whole, while other regional languages began to lose what public voice they possessed, as their own writers gradually began to produce manuscripts in the language of Castile. These developments cannot be divorced from the emphasis contemporary Spaniards placed on the vital role language would play in imperial expansion. The place given to language in the project of empire had been made quite explicit (by Antonio de Nebrija, Juan de Valdés, and numerous others) from the very beginning.

Against this general background, there are specific factors that contributed to the adoption of Castilian Spanish as Valencia's literary language in the sixteenth century. These factors include the increasing pressure brought on Valencian writers by local publishers to write exclusively in *castellano* for commercial reasons, the establishment of pro-Castilian viceroyalties in Valencia at Charles V's behest, particularly the court of Germana de Foix, and demographic changes that further strengthened the position of Castilian over Catalan. According to Berger, over the course of a decade (1540–1550), nearly all Valencian writers shifted to Castilian.[9]

Virués's text was published some thirty years after Castilian had achieved this dominant position in relation to the literary production of Valencia. The poem is manifestly deferential to *castellano*, though there are pertinent variants in the different editions. Describing the terrain of his native Montserrat, the Catalan hero remarks:

> It is as if the crags had been sawed off,
> or as if they had been split by hand,

8. See Benedict Anderson, *Imagined Communities: Reflections on the Origins and Spread of Nationalism*, 43–44; and Fernand Braudel, *The Mediterranean and the Mediterranean World in the Age of Philip II*, 1:163.
9. Philippe Berger, *Libro y lectura en la Valencia del Renacimiento*, 332–33. I owe this reference to José Luis Peset.

in some places less or more raised up,
according to whether they had grown less or more;
seeing them cut up in this way,
and the mountain divided up in so many parts,
people called it Mont Serrat in Catalan,
which is the same as calling it "sawed mountain."

But the universal language of Spain,
changed it from Mont Serrat to Monserrate,
and that is how this mountain will be called
by anyone who speaks about her in that tongue:
anything else would be a strange affectation,
and a way of stripping the language of its karats,
for this name is already proper in that tongue,
so it is right, lord, that I call her thus.

(Están las peñas como si aserradas,
O partidas a mano hubiesen sido,
Menos o más en partes levantadas,
Según menos o más hayan crecido;
Y de vellas la gente así cortadas,
Y el monte en tantas partes dividido,
Fue Mont Serrat en catalán llamado,
Que es lo mismo que decir monte aserrado.

Pero la universal lengua de España,
De Mont Serrat llamóle Monserrate,
Y así se ha de llamar esta montaña
Por cualquiera que en tal lengua della trate:
Fuera otra cosa afectación extraña,
Y quitar a la lengua su quilate,
Pues es en ella propio ya tal nombre,
Y así es razón, señor, que yo la nombre.)[10]

The second octave does not appear in any edition prior to Sancha's (1805), which Rossell takes to be completely reliable. Although Virués may have expressed a wish to include this strophe, it is at least possible that the new octave was composed by Sancha himself.[11] The nineteenth century, after all, had its own reasons for republishing the epic poems of

10. All quotations of *El Monserrate* are taken from the edition of Don Cayetano Rosell, Biblioteca de Autores Españoles 17 (Madrid: Rivadeneyra, 1851). Rosell does not number the octaves. I have made my own numbering of the stanzas, excluding from my count an octave that summarizes the plot, which appears above the text proper at the beginning of each book. Hereafter, in the text the canto number will be indicated first, followed by octave and, where appropriate, lines, in this case, 5.10–11.

11. Fitts Finch is cautious, but she is clearly aware of this possibility. See her introduction to *El Monserrate Segundo*, by Virués, 10.

the Golden Age, not the least of which was to construct a genealogy for the full-blown nineteenth-century nationalist conception of Spain. Virués's ninth-century character takes no offense at the Castilian modification of the mountain's name. On the contrary, he seems to take for granted that, in time and thanks to the fullness of empire, the Castilian name of "Monserrate" will achieve greater currency than its Catalan equivalent (*Mont Serrat*, or *Montserrat*).

It is also worth noting that Valencia is only mentioned once by name in the text of Virués, while the poet invokes the greatness of the Castilian throne many times. Toward the end of the poem, Pope Leo IV prophesies the glory of the Habsburg line, noting that the marriage of the future Philip III will take place in Valencia:[12]

> With the highest divine consolation
> and joy throughout all Spain, generally,
> in particular on Valencian soil,
> where the sumptuous wedding will take place;
> a land favored by heaven
> in gratitude for your Gothic lineage,
> and rightly so, since Valencia will have
> very great excellence when that day arrives.

> (Y con divino altísimo consuelo
> Y gozo en general de España toda,
> Y en especial del valenciano suelo,
> Donde será la suntüosa boda;
> Suelo favorecido por el cielo
> En grato ser a vuestra sangre goda,
> Y con razón, porque tendrá Valencia
> En aquel tiempo altísima excelencia.)
> (16.27)

The reference to Virués's birthplace is made in the most encomiastic terms, but the mention of that "land favored by heaven" is preceded by the "joy throughout all Spain, generally," a result of the matrimonial celebration of Philip II's heir. That the marriage occurs in Valencia only exemplifies the ability of a consolidated central power to reach into the semiperiphery it already controls. Virués, who, after all, had fought with

12. The marriage of Philip III and Margaret of Austria did indeed take place in Valencia in 1599. One wonders how Virués could know this when preparing his manuscript for publication in the late 1580s, unless, perhaps, the marriage had been prearranged. However, even this could not account for Virués's clairvoyance, because the wedding was supposed to take place in Barcelona and was switched to Valencia at the last minute. I owe this point to Elizabeth Wright.

distinction under Don John of Austria at Lepanto, paints a happy picture of a Valencia whose identity is uncomplicatedly subsumed under that of "España toda," metonymically rendered in the Castilian court of Philip II and his offspring. The poet represents Habsburg dominion in Valencia as a condition that will lead his native region to plenitude and fruition. The notion of "Spain as Castile" is further inscribed into the text through the Castilianization of Montserrat itself. The mountain and its monastery, transformed into an emblem of Catholic Spain, are revered by Isabella and Ferdinand as well as by Philip II, to whose Escorial the Catalan shrine is explicitly likened here.

El Monserrate, therefore, belongs to a category of texts that, according to Pérez Montaner, "comprise part . . . of Castilian literature, the culture of the colonizing capital."[13] In light of gains won by the Autonomous Communities of Spain in the latter part of the twentieth century, Virués's inclination to downplay local difference, linguistic and political, might seem to have a backward ring to it. At a time when the local languages of the País Valenciano and of the other regions that make up the Spanish state have been vigorously (though not unequivocally) reestablished, the centralist tendencies that the epic promotes might constitute an obstacle for those modern readers who find themselves at odds with the political program that informs Virués's thought. Those readers are then forced to carry out a "resisting reading" of El Monserrate.[14]

However, the neutralization of female otherness in Virués's text, specifically the violence against women that goes unchallenged here, may well be a more insurmountable obstacle for the twentieth-century reader. After the opening scenes of sexual violation and murder, the epic deftly turns the reader's attention to the terrible remorse and repentance of the hermit Garín. One supposes the inscribed reader of Virués would interpret the poem as a variation on the story of the Fall, a tale of penitence and rehabilitation. Since the epic culminates in the foundation of the monastery at Montserrat, the same reader would interpret it as an affirmation of the values of organized monastic life over the more independent vocation of hermitage. However, the initial episode of rape could also be seen as a problem that constitutes internal evidence for another kind of reader, one who is immediately offset by gender and

13. Jaume Pérez Montaner, "Nacionalismo y cultura en el País Valenciano," in Las nacionalidades del Estado español: Una problemática cultura (The nationalities of the Spanish state: a problematic culture), ed. Cristina Dupláa and Gwendolyn Barnes, 161–62.
14. The idea of a "resisting reading" is by no means new. Feminists have propounded such a reading of male-authored texts for some time. See Judith Fetterley, The Resisting Reader: A Feminist Approach to American Fiction.

who may well resist Virués's attempt to gloss over other kinds of difference in order to fashion a suppositious universal subject in his text.

The rape scene in *El Monserrate* serves as a pre-text for the main plot, but it does not authorize revenge in the text of Virués, as it does in other representations of rape, such as that in Shakespeare's *Lucrece*.[15] This is largely because in *El Monserrate*, the assailant is turned into the victim, tempted and deceived by demonic forces of evil. Joffré Velloso (Guifre, or Winifred I, Count of Barcelona, ?–897) brings his nameless virgin daughter to the hermit Garín so that he can exorcise the evil spirits that possess her. The count, duped by one of Satan's minions, leaves his daughter in Garín's cave for nine days, during which time the hermit experiences temptations of the flesh such as he has never known, since he has lived almost all his life in the solitude of Montserrat. The hermit finally resists no longer, but even at the moment of his transgression, Virués seems to go out of his way to blame the woman: "from a man, and such a good one, he turns into a wild beast, as if possessed by Medea or Circe" (de hombre, y tan bueno, se convierte en fiera / Cual si Medea o Circe le prendiera, 2.21). It is perhaps not a coincidence that this was one octave that Virués rewrote to accentuate the demonized representation of the woman, here likened to the witches Medea and Circe. The 1588 edition simply reads, "he turned into an irate beast" (se convirtió en una brava fiera). The Milan edition shows the emendation, which has appeared in all subsequent editions of the poem.

Garín's loss of control is thus carefully encoded in language that deliberately summons images of lethal female sexual power. There are many instances of this "lethal female" archetype in Golden Age epics. In his *Jerusalem conquered*, Lope de Vega draws on this type of dangerous female for the character of the Jewish woman Raquel, whom the married Castilian king finds irresistible, though she is a threat to his family and his throne. Virués's text frames the rape according to a masculinist perspective, and the young woman, who is not a true subject, but rather a negative foil to the hermit-hero, is nullified.[16] Indeed, even as she is being violated, the count's daughter remains speechless:

> The honest damsel turned her eyes,
> sad, disturbed, astonished and confused,
> as if to ask, "What new act is this,

15. See Coppélia Kahn, "Lucrece: The Sexual Politics of Subjectivity," 141.

16. An analogous situation occurs in Greek drama. For the role of woman as "radical other" to a self identified with the male, see Froma I. Zeitlin, "Playing the Other: Theater, Theatricality, and the Feminine in Greek Drama," in *Nothing to Do with Dionysus? Athenian Drama in Its Social Context*, ed. John J. Winkler and Froma I. Zeitlin.

oh father, which your hand executes?"
And he, though he understands, makes no response,
for he knows well that he has no excuse;
nor does he desist from the blind, clumsy act,
overcome by the sensual, furious fire.

(Volvía los ojos la doncella honesta,
Triste, turbada, atónita y confusa,
Como si preguntara, ¿qué obra es ésta
Tan nueva ¡oh padre! que tu mano usa?
Y aunque él la entiende, no le da respuesta;
Que bien conoce que no tiene excusa;
Ni desiste del acto torpe y ciego,
Rendido al sensual furioso fuego.)
(2.25)

Like Philomela, whose rape and silencing Virués will evoke through the poignant song of the nightingale later in the poem, the daughter of Joffré Velloso does not speak. Even if she were inclined to do so afterward, she cannot seek redress because Garín, following the advice of Satan who reappears to him in the form of another hermit, slits her throat (the verb later used to recall the act is *degollar*). Juan Garín then buries her body.

Some twentieth-century critics reaffirm the blame that Virués's text places on the victim. Meo Zilio, for example, writes that the episode "culminates when the two protagonists break the unstable tension between attraction and repulsion ('The weapons of conscience now torn asunder'), and they no longer resist the call of nature."[17] This interpretation manages to turn the rape into consensual sex between two frantically passionate adults, carried away by their lust for one another. The passage quoted above, however, makes it clear that the sexual act was unthinkable to the young woman, who was "sad, disturbed, astonished and confused," lacking all understanding of what was happening to her. Meo Zilio's interpretation collapses two separate problems into one: the representation of rape, on the one hand, and the negative stereotype of the "bewitching woman," on the other. *El Monserrate* reads very differently if one distinguishes between these two representational acts.

Immediately filled with remorse, the hermit Garín prays for forgiveness. His prayer for absolution, however, is an enumeration of abstractions containing not one specific reference to his own offense. Absent from his confession is any mention of the woman whose body he has violated, then

17. Giovanni Meo Zilio, *Estudio sobre Hernando Domínguez Camargo y su "San Ignacio de Loyola, Poema Heroico,"* 259.

mutilated. The specific (life, woman, rape) is buried first as referent, then as signifier, under an avalanche of generalizations about sin. The impression that the reader is meant to place the previous rape and murder scenes under erasure is borne out by repeated subsequent allusions to Garín's virtuous life. Fleeing Montserrat to escape the just wrath of the count of Barcelona, Juan Garín comes upon a ship preparing to set sail for Naples. Invited on board by the Italian general who leads the armada, Garín is offered dinner, which he refuses because, the text announces, he is a "man whose life is characterized by continence" (varón de continente vida, 3.45). His virtue thus restored in the framework of a masculine construction that is also related to the gendering of national identity, Garín embarks on a pilgrimage to Rome that is frequently textualized as a heroic fight for his life, in other words, the life of his soul. His objective is to make a full confession to the pope, who will establish proper penitence for his sin: Garín must crawl on all fours from Rome across the Alps and back to Montserrat, where he will remain in that position until a small child tells him that his repentance is ended. The nameless daughter of Joffré Velloso is practically forgotten in the telling of Garín's trials and tribulations, even though all the narrative action issues from the scene of her rape. Implicitly characterized as a tempting "Eva" to the Virgin's "Ave," and as a sacrificial lamb on whose broken body the monastery at Montserrat is founded, the female figure vanishes for the better part of the text. According to John J. Winkler and to Patricia Klindienst Joplin, the inscription and later elision of rape in narrative is, in fact, so common as to constitute an unsettling pattern. The rape is "written out" of the text but the erasure is imperfect, so the repressed "prior violence" lingers and threatens to return.[18]

However, if one reads back into the rape and murder all the sexuality and the violence that Virués seemingly has removed from his text, that is, if one treats rape not as a metaphor but as violence suffered in the female body, then it becomes difficult to read the story of Garín's spiritual regeneration with the same enthusiasm one imagines early readers of *El Monserrate* to have felt. This lack of affinity with what might be called Golden Age sensibilities is a problem that the reader who wishes to decenter misogyny or other ideologies that inform the text must confront, because for the contemporary reader as for Virués, the hermit's drama was presumably quite compelling. After all, one of the meanings of the text is a fundamental teaching of Christianity: that forgiveness is available to all, even to the author of a heinous compound crime like Juan Garín. Indeed,

18. See Winkler, "Education of Chloe," 18–20; and Patricia Klindienst Joplin, "The Voice of the Shuttle Is Ours."

one need not go back as far as the sixteenth century to find living exam-
ples of this kind of penitence; images of Holy Week processions from the
entire Spanish-speaking world readily come to mind. The religious belief
system that informs *El Monserrate* may strike us as remote, excessively
austere, or overstated. In this, it is not alone among the epics. Many twen-
tieth-century readers have little tolerance for the gory representation of the
crucifixion in *La Christiada*, for example. However, the central tenet of this
devout ideology—that penitence and forgiveness are effective and extend
even to the most despicable acts—was an organizing principle of spiritu-
ality for Cristóbal de Virués and others like him.

Accounting for ideological difference is an important step in reconsid-
ering Renaissance texts, but the kind of "rereading" executed in the first
part of this chapter smuggles an agenda into the scholarship, one that calls
for an indictment of ethnocentric, sexist, and other values promoted by the
Golden Age text that are noxious in that, to some extent, they have helped
shape Western culture and continue to hold it in their sway. The issue of
literary representations of rape is one that has real and vital consequences,
for, as Higgins and Silver point out, "literary and artistic representations
not only depict (or fail to depict) instances of rape after or as if they have
occurred; they also contribute to the social positioning of women and men
and shape the cognitive systems that make rape thinkable."[19] What is
objectionable about Virués's narrative is, finally, not the promise of
redemption for the rapist's soul, but the relentless masculine perspective
that turns the episode of the woman's rape into the reason for Juan Garín's
narrative, while depriving the female character of subjectivity. Expedient
to Virués for reasons of narrative strategy, and disturbingly dispensable in
human terms, the woman may not voice outrage over what has been done
to her. Still less does she seek revenge, even when at the end of the poem,
her father, having pardoned Garín "because God had pardoned him,"
finds her still miraculously alive. Instead of demanding satisfaction, the
daughter of Joffré Velloso, with the iridescent scar gleaming like an opa-
line choker around her neck, declares her resolution to remain forever
within the newly built monastery on Montserrat.

The above reading of *El Monserrate* is grounded in feminism. However,
by focusing intensely on a moment of disruption in the text (the rape), it
veers away from feminism in a deconstructionist move that is susceptible
to appropriation by New Historicism. According to this reading, one might
well conclude that it is the monastery, not the penitent, that becomes a

---

19. Lynn A. Higgins and Brenda R. Silver, "Introduction: Rereading Rape," *Rape
and Representation*, 3.

metaphor or an icon for the Spanish state. Habsburg Spain, like the apparently solid and unassailable shrine at Montserrat, was nevertheless constructed on a foundation of suppressed alterities. The author of *El Monserrate* fabricates a literary analogue to real, historical events; in the same spirit that the Spanish state systematically dismantled Jewish and Morisco communities throughout the country, and colonial administrations subdued the Amerindian peoples of Spain's recently conquered territories, Cristóbal de Virués sacrifices the count of Barcelona's daughter in order to ground his foundational text. But as the recent resurgence of nationalism in eastern Europe and other places suggests, otherness abated remains a potentially destabilizing force that the state must continually contain and neutralize in order to preserve itself. If this were not the case, if nationalist and masculinist values really were preordained and firm, Virués would probably not have had to assert them so resolutely in his text.

To summarize: a feminist theory that "rereads" rape can alert us to textual problems that more traditional methodologies avoid; it can help focus our attention on those elements that the text covers over or appears to forget. Feminism, likewise, can sometimes point to a surprisingly suggestive correlation between the female body and the body politic, for which it may stand.[20] It can also assist us in asking tough questions of the Golden Age text.

But it is no less true that any critical reading of a long text that rests primarily on the ramifications of a single episode (in this case, the rape scene) hazards excessive narrowness. It discards too many elements, even ones consistent with its own arguments. Some might argue that the feminist reading is anachronistic, thereby raising questions about sixteenth-century reception of the poem. In fact, there is evidence to suggest that contemporary readers may have been put off by Virués's use of demonic elements in his epic, not because of the link they established between the feminine and the diabolical, but because they threatened verisimilitude. The poet's friend Baltasar de Escobar wrote that Virués's use of the marvelous almost went too far when the poet attributed it equally to Satan and to God, but that in the end, "that which is realistic in this poem tempers the marvelous so that it does not become excessive, and when it seems that the marvelous will become excessive, being attributed now to God, now to the Devil, verisimilitude saves the situation . . ." (lo verosímil siempre en este poema

---

20. The body politic as political metaphor is much older than the more specific use alluded to here. See David George Hale, *The Body Politic: A Political Metaphor in Renaissance Literature*; for one of many examples of the use feminists have made of this metaphor, see Amy K. Kaminsky, *Reading the Body Politic: Feminist Criticism and Latin American Women Writers*.

va templando lo maravilloso para que no pase al exceso, y lo maravilloso cuando parece que va a exceder, atribuyéndose a Dios, o al Demonio, se salva con lo verosímil . . .). Escobar's letter, which appears for the first time in the 1609 edition of the poem, has not been reprinted in any modern edition. It stands as a reminder to proceed with caution when applying twentieth-century ideas to a sixteenth-century text. Still, the Golden Age did not condone rape any more than the twentieth century does.

Given the resonances of classical epic that still vibrate in the heroic poems of the Spanish Golden Age, it could be objected that a feminist or a poststructuralist reading centered outside the text does not take into account the ways in which the various subtexts inform and actually constitute meaning in the new text. While conceding that the argumentation of the feminist rereading is not defective, critics might contend that it lacks erudition. There is a grain of truth in this. Specialists in the field who regularly impart Golden Age texts to students who do not have a working knowledge of the main subtexts that echo through the literary texts of the time (classical mythology, ancient epic, the Bible) will acknowledge that this unfamiliarity makes it more difficult to achieve a reading that does not vitiate the text. In the second half of this study, we will consider to what degree the awareness of such intertextual relationships enhances the ability of competent readers to accomplish a thorough reading of the Golden Age text, regardless of how much affinity they may have for its ideological base. One ramification of this issue might be that a conscious formalist approach, because it looks for textual unity that creates meaning, precludes the possibility of carrying out feminist or poststructuralist readings of the text.

In the prologue to his *El Monserrate*, the poet reaffirms Horace's recommendation that poetry must of necessity demonstrate "sweetness and usefulness" (*dulzura y utilidad*) if it is to achieve excellence. This is especially true, according to Virués, in "that principal poetry called epic or heroic poetry" (aquella principal poesía llamada épica o heroica, 503). Virués, like Ercilla and others, looked to the ancients for many of the materials they used to fashion their own poems. Writers such as Homer and Virgil provided them with a recognizable repertoire of conventions, devices, and themes that smuggled the "sweet" (the pleasurable or entertaining) into the new text. By the late Spanish Renaissance, however, reading material increasingly needed to be religious or moralistic in order to qualify as edifying (*útil*). From this perspective, the *translatio studii* project underwent an adjustment as the Bible took a privileged place beside the writers of antiquity as the other great subtext for literary endeavors of the period. It would be inaccurate to create the impression that this was a new development, since religious epic had been written since the beginning of the Renaissance.

Important Italian models from this period were Sannazaro's *De partu virginis* (1526), the *Carmen Paschale* of Sedulius, Macario Muzio's *De triumpho Christi* (1499), and the *Cristias* of Marco Girolamo Vida (1535). In Spain itself, abundant examples of religious epics appeared from early in the sixteenth century to well into the seventeenth. The catalogue of Spanish epics included at the end of Frank Pierce's *La poesía épica del Siglo de Oro* demonstrates this quite clearly. What one begins to notice in the religious epic of these years, however, is an intensification of austere and somber themes such as that of repentance and graphic—even gory—representations of the religious hero's torment, a tendency that culminates in works such as Diego de Hojeda's *La Christiada* (1611). Nonetheless, if one stops to consider that Virués's poem was published only eighteen years after part one of *La Araucana*, a text that in important ways was the model for Spanish epic of the period, and that Virués himself was a captain at Lepanto, then the highlighting of religious elements in his poem appears to signal an important shift away from profane epic. That Virués should wish to redefine the sacred epic makes a good deal of sense because by 1588, the Tridentine mandate had grown strong enough to propel him in that direction.

Virués seems to have thought deeply about how to write an epic that would be equal to the occasion: one that would preserve enough characteristics of ancient epic to qualify it as belonging to that poetic kind, while satisfying the religious demands that the Counter-Reformation increasingly placed on writers. These constraints may have influenced his choice of subject, but the subject in turn intensified the need to cast the religious as heroic, to make the repentant pilgrim a figure who is larger than life. What was there in classical epic that could serve as a model for such a hero?

Because of his travels and the almost consecrated sense he had about leading the surviving Trojans to Italy and founding Rome, "pious Aeneas" might well have been the poet's chosen example. Indeed, Mary Fitts Finch's interpretation follows this line. Comparing Virués's poem to the *Aeneid* and Philip II to Augustus, Fitts Finch finds such examples of Virgil's influence as Garín's being torn between God and the Devil, his narration of the story of his life, his being warned by a groaning voice emerging from a cave that he has no place in paradise, a dream telling him to continue on his original plan, the Magdalen's appearance in Garín's dream warning him of imminent danger, and the fact that "the future is revealed to both Aeneas and Garín."[21] While these similarities between the *Aeneid* and *El Monserrate* are real enough, they are traceable in large part to conventions of epic, generally.

---

21. Fitts Finch, introduction to *El Monserrate Segundo,* by Virués, 29–32.

In truth, the case for influence is much stronger between the *Odyssey* and Virués's poem. The Valencian poet looked to the Homeric epic for much more than just poetic imagination, since he patterned entire episodes of the main body of *El Monserrate* on portions of the *Odyssey*, specifically on the section referring to the "Great Wanderings" of Odysseus (9–12).[22] Although the idea of mission or pilgrimage does not attach to the profile of the Homeric hero in a particularly sharp way, Odysseus is an archetype of the wanderer whose final homecoming is less significant than the delays and reversals of fortune that befall him on his journey, as modern poets such as Constantine Cavafy still remind us:

> When you start on your journey to Ithaca,
> then pray that the road is long,
> full of adventure, full of knowledge.
> Do not fear the Lestrygonians
> and the Cyclopes and the angry Poseidon.
> You will never meet such as these on your path,
> if your thoughts remain lofty, if a fine
> emotion touches your body and your spirit.
> You will never meet the Lestrygonians,
> the Cyclopes and the fierce Poseidon,
> if you do not carry them within your soul,
> if your soul does not raise them up before you.[23]

If Juan Garín could have known Cavafy's verses, he might have saved himself a lot of trouble.

From *Odyssey* 9 Virués takes the figure of Polyphemus, whom he transforms into an Italian cyclops named Formínolo, leader of the *lestrigones,* a monstrous people also of Homeric provenance (*Odyssey* 10). Homer's Laistrygones are giants, whose leader, Antiphates, devours human flesh. Odysseus and his men barely escape from them by ship. In the text of Virués, Juan Garín and his Italian travel companians are taken prisoner by the equally anthropophagous *lestrigones,* whose caves are kept well supplied with potential "meals" (13.55–61). Shortly thereafter, Formínolo, whom Virués identifies as a direct descendant of Homer's Antiphates ("de Antifates y Lamio derivado," 13.55.3), chooses ten young men to be cooked for his dinner, then selects others of the Italians to be thrown to beasts that the *lestrigones* keep as pets:

22. Richmond Lattimore, introduction to *The Odyssey of Homer,* trans. Richmond Lattimore, 1. All quotations of *The Odyssey* are taken from the translation of Robert Fitzgerald, and appear hereafter in the text by book and line.
23. Constantine Cavafy, "Ithaca," in *The Complete Poems,* trans. Rae Dalven, 36.

Serpents and panthers in confusion,
dragons and griffins, tigers and lions,
manticores, corocottas and other wild animals,
each different in strength, weapons and nation,
within that enclosure are prisoners
of the Laistrygones, who are more ferocious than they,
raised there only for the pleasure
of sustaining them with human flesh.

(Confusamente sierpes y panteras,
Dragos y grifos, tigres y leones,
Mantícoras, crocutas y otras fieras,
Varias en fuerzas y armas y naciones,
Son en aquel cercado prisioneras
De los más fieros que ellas lestrigones,
Solamente por gusto allí criadas
De ser de humana carne sustentadas.)
(14.8)

Formínolo picks Garín as one of the victims to be placed in the lions' den, and only a last-minute rescue by the Castilian hero, Diego Florel, saves the praying hermit from being devoured.

Virués also takes from the *Odyssey* two enchanting but deadly female figures, Circe and the Siren. In fine Homeric form, these figures tempt Juan Garín to abandon his pilgrimage of repentance. Homer's Circe is a sorceress with a beguiling song and the power to turn men into swine (*Odyssey* 10). This is the fate of Odysseus's crew. When the hero foils her attempts to enchant him, as well, she marvels at his lucidity, restores his men to their original state, and entices them to remain with her for a year, which they do, as if in a trance. As witnessed in the first part of this chapter, the Circe figure of *El Monserrate* is none other than the daughter of the count of Barcelona, who, at the moment of her rape, is compared to both the Homeric sorceress and Medea (2.21). This pejorative characterization of the woman encourages us to view the hermit not as a perpetrator, but as a victim who has fallen prey to an irresistible female force that transforms him from man to beast, as Homer's Circe had done with Odysseus's men. This is the misogynist underpinning of a female representation that actually reaches beyond misogyny, since in this case, it explains away rape and murder as the inevitable result of temptation by dark powers that give their host superhuman strength. Virués embodies this evil force in a young woman, thereby associating her sex with diabolical power. The Homeric episode, which already presents a negative representation of Circe but no corresponding atrocity, is in fact much milder than *El Monserrate* in this regard. In Homer, Circe finally sends

Odysseus and his men on their way with proscriptions designed to vouchsafe their return home.

Homer's "Seirenes" are quite another matter. Scylla and Charybdis have the power to "sing a man's mind away" (12.44), then whisk him overboard and eat him (12.246). Something of this deadly might attaches to the siren that appears in *El Monserrate*, though a thoroughly Christian cosmology and demonology have overturned the pagan ones so wondrously present in Homer's text. Virués's narrator apostrophizes Satan who, disguised as another hermit, planted the seed of temptation in Garín's heart in the first place, calling the Devil a wild beast, a cruel monster that with a siren's voice and face enchants the wisest and most valiant of men (2.9). The reader thus stands forewarned when Garín comes upon the figure of a *sirena* as he makes his way to Rome, seeking absolution from the pope. Coming upon an earthly paradise with a palace set on crystal foundations in the middle of a lagoon, the hermit hears the siren's song, then follows it through a labyrinth until he sets eyes on her. Her beauty is equal to that of any of the women in so many Petrarchan sonnets (her attributes include a crimson dress, golden hair, "hands that in their whiteness surpass untouched snow," a soft breast, etc.), and her song reproaches Garín for fleeing from sweet human love (12.52–54). An angel warns the exiled protagonist against sleeping in so soft a bed as can be found in such a place, whereupon the hermit awakens to find a damsel (*doncella*) beside him. Garín recognizes her as the daughter of the count of Barcelona, who claims to be waiting for his love and tries to ensnare him with her tongue and hands, finally resorting to tears and threats. This is a far cry from the mysterious song of Homer's Sirens and their rapid dispatch of six of Odysseus's men. For here, the terrible attributes of the siren are displaced onto Juan Garín's dead victim, now demonized in a manner that seems disquieting even when viewed in the very different terms of the sixteenth century. Since Garín's crime was prompted by a temptation from the Devil, Virués's text suggests, in the same vein as an old Spanish proverb, that woman is literally and metaphorically "the skin of the devil" (*la piel del diablo*). *El Monserrate* insists, perhaps a bit too tenaciously, that Satan is a wolf in sheep's clothing, and that he can dupe us because he can take on any form. One wonders why this text is so quick to absolve Juan Garín from responsibility for his deeds, and why it seems to have so little to say about free will.

This question is a bit perplexing, especially in a text as religious as *El Monserrate*, which is filled with biblical allusions and figures. Far and away the most prominent of these is Mary Magdalen. In this epic, the Magdalenic figure stands for both eroticism and the power of penance.[24]

---

24. For a feminist "re-visioning" of the Magdalenic figure, see Elizabeth B. Davis, "'Woman, Why Weepest Thou?' Re-Visioning the Golden Age Magdalen"; Marjorie

Virués establishes links between the New Testament figure and the hermit Garín on several different levels, beginning with the story of Garín's birth, which resembles that of Venus in all respects: both are sea creatures, washed ashore on large scallop shells. The repentant Mary of Magdala has, of course, been widely interpreted as a belated reincarnation of the figure of Venus. The Magdalen's hard ascetic practices now cloak the splendid beauty of the ancient goddess in sackcloth. In this explanation of Garín's origins, there is already a foreshadowing of the kind of complications and the eventual dénouement in his own narrative.

But aside from this hint of identity between Garín and the Magdalen, the epic makes the connection between the two quite explicit in other places. For example, there is an episode in which Garín's ship puts to port at Marseille, and the hermit disembarks to visit Mary Magdalen's temple and the nearby cave where she lived out her last years of penitence and ascesis. On the walls of a monk's cell at Magdalen's temple, Garín sees iconographic representations of the Eucharist, the Immaculate Conception, the Assumption, Mary Magdalen's conversion, and the stories of St. Agueda and Judith and Holofernes. An explanation in verse accompanies each scene. The narrator seizes this occasion to make the point that poetry can prove the truth of pictorial art by joining together "heroic nobility and heartfelt sweetness" (heroica alteza y cordïal dulzura, 6.13). He continues:

> Those who imitate heroic gravity
> found their poems on two things,
> with sweet voices singing supreme achievements
> of grave examples which move people to virtue;
> these same poets, to obtain noble garlands
> of eternal laurel, fit themselves out with everything;
> for if the sweet is accompanied by the useful,
> everything will be held to its necessary point.

> (Dos cosas en que fundan sus poemas
> Los que la heroica gravedad imitan,
> Con dulce voz cantando obras supremas
> De ejemplos graves que a virtud incitan;
> Y estos, para alcanzar nobles diademas
> De eterno lauro, en todo se habilitan;
> Pues si a lo dulce lo útil fuere junto,
> En todo se tendrá el debido punto.)
> (6.14)

M. Malvern's *Venus in Sackcloth: The Magdalen's Origins and Metamorphoses* continues to be the most important book on the subject.

This is as close as Virués comes to an art of poetry, and it elaborates on the idea of blending the sweet with the useful, already expressed in kernel form in the prologue. The most recurrent elements are those of sweetness in the manner of expression ("with sweet voices"), and gravity and exemplarity in the subject matter ("supreme achievements of grave examples which move people to virtue"). That this formula is expressed in the context of religious ekphrasis suggests that Virués automatically accords "grave" or heroic status to the sacred subject. Apart from the fact that the poet could have wished to hold at bay critics who might challenge the gravity of his own work, this passage constitutes a reaffirmation of the idea that the religious subject be deemed appropriate for epic. As noted above, the 1580s renewed the engagement of writers with religious epic, and there followed a veritable flowering of sacred epics in countries where Spanish was the literary language. Of this more will be seen in the next chapter.

Garín's final confession upon arriving in Rome binds him even tighter to the image of Mary Magdalen. Humbling himself by kneeling at the pope's feet as Magdalen had done at the feet of Christ, the hero weeps: "he pours out his tears with internal pain" (el llanto vierte con dolor interno, 16.4.4). The pope listens to "the crying of the contrite penitent" (el lloro del contrito penitente, 16.4.8), then hears his confession, and orders him to return the next day to receive penance and absolution. Since the conversion scene is the pivotal moment in Mary Magdalen's narrative, Virués similarly induces his readers to privilege the tearful confession of Juan Garín. In the same way that Magdalen's tears were said to be the most perfect confession because they were wordless, Garín's tears mark a kind of closure on his wretched past, though his tale is far from over.

The stories of the many biblical figures who inhabit the ostensibly epic world of *El Monserrate* inform the epic's meaning in various ways. A case in point is the passage in which three such figures converge: the scene in which Garín is lowered into the lions' den of the *lestrigones*. At this point, the narrator compares Juan Garín to Job for his patience, while Garín compares himself to Paul, saved from a tempest at sea, and to Daniel, who suffered the same kind of torment he now faces. These are only brief allusions, and the text does not attempt to set up elaborate analogies between Garín and the three biblical characters mentioned. But the mention of the names is enough to signal such analogies in a deeply religious culture. The hermit points to the example of Paul because God has already delivered Garín from a maritime storm. The comparison he makes between his present ordeal and Daniel's understandably turns into a prayer for salvation.

The suggested comparison between Garín and Job is more intriguing, but also more problematic in some ways. As in Garín's case, it was

Satan who instigated Job's trials. In both cases, the Devil's motive was to devastate the life of a virtuous man and, by destroying him, to affront God. But in Job's case, the Adversary had God's permission to tempt the man. The *Monserrate* does not show corresponding terms. The most salient difference between the epic and the biblical story, however, is that when tempted and tormented, Job never cursed God. In the case of Juan Garín, as noted earlier, there was hardly any resistance to sexual temptation, and the hermit compounded his own crime by taking his victim's life. The poet wants us to focus on Job's patience as a way of endorsing his own hero's suffering, thereby suggesting his virtue. By the time Virués writes, the virtue most commonly associated with the Job figure is his patience, yet, as Moshe Greenberg writes, the Book of Job and the character for whom it is named are far more complex than the "late passing reference to Job's patience" would have it.[25] In fact, one can only find proof of the hermit's gravity and exemplarity (his "heroic gravity" and "grave examples") by searching out, in his conduct, the sole attribute of Job's that fits: his patience. Because Juan Garín is not, in a strict sense, a righteous man, as was Job. He is a criminal and sinner in search of forgiveness, which he ultimately finds on his return to Montserrat.

By dint of the intricate interweaving of biblical and classical narratives in *El Monserrate*, Spanish heroism itself seems to have suffered radical redefinition at the hands of Cristóbal de Virués. For here, in the story of the hermit Garín, the poet focuses on an epic battle that has cosmic proportions yet is intensely private and internal. By fashioning his hero after Mary Magdalen and Job as much as after Odysseus, Virués stretches and recombines the codes of epic to include disciplinary trial and repentance of the virtuous.

Having taken into account the strongest classical and biblical subtexts that *El Monserrate* revises to its own ends, let us now return to our point of departure: is it possible to trace these stories of trial and repentance, as Virués has deliberately intertwined them with his own hero's narrative, without entering into complicity with the poet's meaning? The answer, it appears, is no, but surely this does not entail an automatic commitment to "the premises and protocols of the past," to use Winkler's words. Nor does it have to constitute a call for a return to formalism. The dismissal of regional and feminine identities in the discourse Virués mobilizes in his epic are profoundly disturbing, but there is much more to *El Monserrate* than the problem of rape and its erasure, enormous as that problem is. To

25. Moshe Greenberg, "Job," 283, in *The Literary Guide to the Bible*, ed. Robert Alter and Frank Kermode.

say this, however, is not to put an end to the discussion. For one thing, the author's meaning itself is not simple. For another, it is perfectly possible to explicate authorial meaning without subscribing to it.

There is always the danger that an excessively archeological approach to a text precludes the possibility of opening it up to more productive readings. However, there is a great deal in the philological study of this text that a strong feminist analysis can use profitably. Homer, after all, is the *Urtext* for all the stories of lethal sorceresses. The *Odyssey*, therefore, can shed light on some problems of negative female representation in *El Monserrate*, and it can do more.

Virués's refashioning of these Homeric episodes focuses attention on three categories that appear to be intrinsically connected in *El Monserrate:* the feminine, the bestial (or wild), and the monstrous. This configuration of categories is neither random nor inconsequential, nor is it unique to this epic. Quint's analysis of the ideology of epic shows that the "other" opposing the Western "self" is usually depicted as Eastern, female, chaotic, monstrous, and plural.[26] The categories that Virués sets in motion all through his text— the feminine, the bestial, the monstrous—are very suggestive of the degree to which Quint's observation is applicable to the Spanish-language epics of this period. What is more, these categories stand in direct relation to, and are repeatedly associated with, the deep semantic structures of *El Monserrate*. They also reactivate a fourth category that was established early in the text, that of the diabolical. The epic of Virués mobilizes these categories at many points so that their connotations seem to accumulate and repeat. In other words, they are deliberately redundant. This reiteration and interplay of meaning suggests that the major semantic level of connotations in the Homeric episodes of *El Monserrate*, and in many other epics of imperial Spain, is the threat of chaos: that which is inhuman, irrational, uncivilized. By grasping the pattern of this constant semantic repetition, one can explore some of its ramifications for this text, as well as for the epic of the Spanish empire, generally.

From the beginning, the poem affirms the bestial nature of Satan and his followers. In canto 1, when he decides to make war on Garín, Satan tells his helpers to fly to Montserrat, addressing them as his lions (*mis leones*). Shortly thereafter, when the count of Barcelona brings his ailing daughter to Garín for help, the reader learns that the "wild dragon of hell" (*fiero drago, infernal dragón*) has devastated her body. Since the satanic force dwells inside her body (she is possessed), the diabolical and the feminine can only be apprehended as the inside and the outside aspects of the same

26. David Quint, "Epic and Empire," 3–4.

entity. Thus Satan, referred to in this textual site as a wolf, a tiger, and a drone, is always covered by a facade that appears harmless (first the young woman, then the false hermit) but is, in fact, quite deadly. And so the text links the violated woman to mythical females eternally associated with the power to transform men into beasts, or kill them outright.

The diabolical, the feminine, and the bestial thus appear inextricably linked even from the first pages of the epic. After the rape, the narrator moralizes about the force of lust in a way that appears to generalize it away from the scene just witnessed. But since the flesh is associated with the strength of lions (it has "poderosas fuerzas de leones"), a beast already associated with Satan and his band, and since the text now makes Garín into a pitiful creature capable of moving lions and serpents to compassion ("quedó tal, que mover pudiera / a compasión leones y serpientes," 2.36.3–4), Virués does not remove the onus of sexual provocation he has already placed on the woman. In fact, he reinforces it by placing Garín's pathetic state in the foreground.

But in abandoning restraint, the hermit has also sunk to the level of bestiality. Garín, always a "Wild Man" figure since he grew to manhood in the wilderness of Montserrat, has "othered" himself by giving in to the "power of lions" (first Satan, then the female). Having been disabused of his error, he now undertakes an odyssey of repentance. On the walls of the Italian ship the hermit surveys decorative carvings along the stern that insert the Habsburg imperial program (specifically, the victory at Lepanto) into Virués's religious narrative. At the same time, however, the ekphrasis that describes the sculpted panels reaffirms the bestial, the feminine, and the monstrous together in one thematic nucleus, since one panel contains the story of the abduction of Europa, and another, the head of Medusa framed by her serpentine locks. Garín at once takes in apparently unrelated messages—the triumphalist ethos of imperial victory and the constant threat of feminine destruction—which appear contradictory in content, but which complement one another as myths that promote Western triumphalism.

When the Italians are shipwrecked in Portofarin (Africa), a land of "barbarous infidels," the text deftly displaces Garín's guilt onto the external, Muslim "other." Among the great African warriors is one Tulipante, who was "born and raised among lions" and has "the heart of a ferocious tiger" (8.18). Virués easily reattaches the same animal metaphors previously used to characterize Satan's strength to the "untamed" Africans, also referred to as dogs (*gente perra*) and insolent, bloody barbarians (*insolente bárbaro sangriento*). In this section of the poem, all the undomesticated tendencies until now associated with Garín are respatialized and reassigned to an enemy, the barbarian, whose wildness differs from that of the archetypal Wild Man in one crucial respect. The West has always perceived the barbarian threat not as individual, but as a collective threat against civilization. Since antiquity, barbarians have been considered a worthy foe, whose tribes possess legal and social organization but are always imagined to be somewhere distant. "The home of the barbarian," according to Hayden White, "is conventionally conceived to lie far away in space, and the time of his coming onto the confines of civilization is conceived to be fraught with apocalyptical possibilities for the whole of civilized humanity." For White, guilt and shame are two strains that converge in the image of the barbarian "at times of cultural stress and decline;" in the same vein, the image of the Wild Man incarnates both desire and anxiety in the early modern period.[27] The confrontation with the Muslim "barbarian" that occurs in this section of *El Monserrate* serves to disconnect Garín's own "otherness" (the ad hominem threat of the Wild Man), then reattach it to a remote, external "other" whose belief system differs in fundamental ways from that of the Christian Spaniard of the sixteenth century. The text reduces geopolitical and religious difference to one and the same. As if to underscore that fact, in a metadiegetic narrative, Virués turns Pope Leo IV into a "Christian soldier" who dons armor to fight Muslim intruders threatening to occupy Rome (canto 9). The notion of the militant Christian seems to inform Virués's text in the same way it does the *Jerusalem conquered* of Lope de Vega. Garín, however, is not a warrior and he does not take up arms. Briefly captured by the enemy during the African battle scene, the hermit goes about the business of nursing the wounded and baptizing dying Muslims. But though he does not take up a sword against the infidels, this section of the poem represents a significant step toward the removal of Garín's guilt by transferring it to a more terrible enemy whom Virués has unexpectedly brought into the thick of the unfolding events.

Having successfully displaced much of his own shame onto the Muslims, Garín resumes his penitential journey. When he arrives on Italy's shore, he encounters the siren, with whom the text unequivocally identifies the count of Barcelona's deceased daughter. The categories of the bestial, the feminine, and the monstrous are all implicit in this identification, which makes manifest the misogyny in the text. The narrator's ensuing denunciation of "human love" (by which he can only mean carnal love, or plain lust) does nothing to rehabilitate the woman's denigrated image. This passion of "human love," he soberly asserts, has the power to "soften the Nemean lion, the African tiger" (ablanda al nemeo león, al tigre africano,

27. Hayden White, "The Forms of Wildness: Archaeology of an Idea," in *The Wild Man Within: An Image in Western Thought from the Renaissance to Romanticism*, ed. Edward Dudley and Maximillian E. Novak, 20, 10.

12.54.5). It is perhaps one of the ironies of the epic that the "hero" appears effeminate from the beginning, in consonance with his Venuslike origins and his affinity with Mary Magdalen. Garín may have a beast inside, but he did not put up much of a fight and so he did not need any "softening." As noted in chapter 1, in the codes of the epic, softness and effeminacy are constant dangers to virile warriors who must be on guard against decadent, "Eastern" mores.[28] Garín, however, is none of these things. His "savageness" is so repressed that it can only emerge as a distorted and horrible image of himself, as it did in the rape scene. Here, just after the military confrontation in Africa, the epic reaffirms the threat of the Wild Man in a passage that makes luxury ("human love") seem more feared than the Muslim, and graver than the powers of Satan, the first "lion" in the text.

In the final analysis, though, Garín is not the target of the narrator's moralizing discourse on lust. The siren scene explicitly assigns that passion to a different kind of "beast:" woman. The representation of the count of Barcelona's daughter as a poison-tongued serpent who tries to hold onto her prey through typically "feminine wiles"—she grabs at Garín with her arms and cries "lethal" tears—shifts the blame for the rape onto the victim, depicted as deceitful and cunning, thanks to the allusion to Circe. When the female figure pulls at her hair, she stirs our memory of the earlier appearance of the Medusa head, with its deadly connotations. In an important turn of events (peripeteia), this time Garín triumphs over the "beast within himself." His bestiality is thereby repositioned onto the female figure, who then slouches away howling, like a mother tiger whose cub has been stolen. It is perhaps consistent with the misogyny of the entire episode that it almost snatches the satisfaction of Garín's victory from him. By focusing attention exclusively on the truly horrifying image of the siren/woman, one almost fails to notice Garín's recovery of his self-restraint. Still, it is clear that Virués intended this scene as a second instance of guilt displacement in a text carefully structured to purify the sinner, at least symbolically, even before he reaches Rome.

The episode of Polyphemus-like Formínolo and his Laistrygones, on the other hand, brings the protagonist face-to-face with what might have been his worst possible destiny. The cannibalistic *lestrigones* stand in the text as a warning and as proof of what happens to human beings who surrender to the beastly nature and antisocial ways of the cyclops, a figure that Bartra writes "represents an implosion, a primeval void," but which "in its autarchy, becomes symbolic of the human need to communicate with the Other."[29] *El Monserrate*, in terms more explicit than those

28. David Quint, *Epic and Empire*, 24.
29. Bartra, *Wild Men*, 31.

used by Homer, establishes the *lestrigón* identity as monstrous and bes-
tial; Virués's creatures are "half bull," and they are fleet-footed monsters,
sons of tigers (14.23). The Laistrygones feed on humans and serve them
up to their pets, but they are human enough ("more beast than men") for
Garín to be able to recognize in them the lower side of his own nature, as
well as his urgent need to distinguish himself from them. He must
reaffirm his identity as thoroughly human. When the *lestrigones* throw
him into the beasts' den, it is really the beast inside himself that Garín
confronts.

In each of these three encounters (the Muslim infidel, the siren, the
lestrigones), Garín achieves a measure of inner peace by displacing his
culpability and by facing, then vanquishing, that which is wild in him-
self. By the time he reaches Rome, then, he has already done much of the
spiritual work necessary for his own redemption. The pope, who
receives Garín together with the Castilian hero Diego Florel, hears the
fallen hermit's confession, then prophesies the future of imperial Spain.
Specifically, he foretells how Charles V will tame (*domar*) monsters who
adore Bacchus and remain deaf as asps to virtuous Catholic hymns:

> Taming wild monsters, for to tame them
> amazes both heaven and hell:
> dreadful monsters, which will try to
> take the world by storm, worhipping Bacchus.
>
> Monsters motivated by the furies
> and rage of that ungainly idol,
> their bodies and souls will be
> submerged in an abyss of lies;
> monsters deaf as asps to the lyres
> which delight Catholic ears,
> their faces entirely turned away from virtue,
> and they, entirely unbridled to do vice.
>
> (Monstruos fieros domando, que domarlos
> Al cielo y al infierno maravilla:
> Monstruos horrendos, que querrán a saco
> Poner el mundo, idolatrando en Baco.
>
> Monstruos que de las furias y las iras
> De aquel ídolo torpe conmovidos,
> Tendrán en un abismo de mentiras
> Sus almas y sus cuerpos sumergidos;
> Monstruos sordos, cual áspid, a las liras
> que regalan católicos oídos,
> A la virtud del todo el rostro vuelto,
> Del todo el freno para el vicio suelto.)
> (16.20–21)

In this important prophecy, the political program of Hapsburg empire is stated according to the terms of a discursive formation that has associated the bestial and the monstrous with internal and external enemies of both the polity and the individual, all throughout *El Monserrate*. In this way the destiny of the Spanish state, iconically symbolized by the monastery at Montserrat in this foundational narrative, blends with and reinforces, on many different semantic levels, the rehabilitation of John Chrysostom as it is remodeled and recontextualized by Cristóbal de Virués.

When Leo IV finally dictates the terms of Garín's penitence, the hermit can assume the posture and other visible characteristics of the beast he might have been, but now does not have to be. In other words, when Juan Garín assumes his position on all fours, he projects onto a physical but purely external plane the "wild animalness" that he demonstrated when he raped and murdered the young woman. He becomes on the outside the beast that he might have been on the inside for all time. This is the most important part of the John Chrysostom legend, according to Bartra, for "by becoming part of the world of beasts, immersed in nature, leading a savage existence, and feeling the laws of the Cosmos in the flesh, one is able to attain wisdom or saintliness."[30] Similarly, by externalizing the beast and communing with nature, Virués's Juan Garín gains the prophetic powers he will use to reveal the future of the Virgin's monastery on Montserrat at the end of the poem. Literally made into a beast, Garín is led to the count of Barcelona's palace in chains that are reminiscent of the metaphorical shackles that bound him in lust at the moment of the rape. Here his penitence comes to an end, he makes a less than candid confession to the victim's father, and he is forgiven. Once the slain woman is discovered to be miraculously alive, Garín delivers his prophecy of the future of the monastery. This speech projects the categories of the monstrous and the bestial onto a political and military plane that alludes one last time to the triumph of Habsburg empire. Speaking this time of Philip II, Garín foretells how the Castilian monarch will wage just war against ferocious enemies, subjugating thousands upon thousands of hydras and monsters:

> Philip will wage just war
> against the wild men of the opposing camp,
> subjugating a thousand hydras and a thousand monsters.

> (Militará Felipe en justa guerra
> contra los fieros del contrario bando,
> mil hidras y mil monstruos sujetando.)
> (20.40.6–8).

---

30. Ibid., 77.

Virués manages to reattach the bestial and monstrous, those same categories that he first associated with Satan and with the rape victim, not only to Islam, but also to the impious and debauched, and ultimately to all who belong to the enemy camp ("los fieros del contrario bando"). These elements cover a wide scope. At one end of that range, the beastly "other" is a personal lack of virtue and a broken relationship with God. But at the other end, the "others" are groups of real people that hold different beliefs: groups that can be expelled and ones that cannot, groups that—in the American conquest, for example—run the risk of enslavement and death. All of these "othered" entities are interconnected and viewed as equally pernicious within the belief systems of *El Monserrate*.

This epic is thus a fable about the taming of the beast, the wild "other." But the "other" that Virués's text urgently wishes to domesticate is both internal and external. Internal not just in reference to groups marked as different within sixteenth-century Spain, but also in personal terms as the lower self that threatens to estrange humanity from itself; external not only in reference to the African Muslim but to all ethnic and racial groups that contravene the drive to establish homogeneity and oneness in the body politic. Only after Juan Garín "becomes" what he already was at his worst moments, a beast, does the Virgin's image appear to the shepherds on Montserrat. Only after they have discovered the image does Garín obtain pardon from the count of Barcelona. And only after he has pardoned the hermit does the count make plans to build the monastery, the future of which (with that of imperial Spain) Garín then prophesies. In the end, the epic asserts control and triumphs over the chaotic impulses represented by these various "others" made manifest in its pages through the feminine, the bestial, and the monstrous.

Thus, even though formalism probably cannot avoid entering into complicity with authorial meaning, it can nevertheless uncover many layers of meaning in the text itself that sometimes encode subversion. The overly negative representation of the rape victim in the "siren" episode is a suggestive example. The strong negativity of the representation undercuts Virués's ability to make the moral point he wants to make about Juan Garín's redemption. The solution to the problem posed by Winkler, and incorporated into the fabric of this chapter, is, perhaps, not so much to move away from formalism altogether as to reincorporate a formalist approach within a more sophisticated framework, while still allowing the impulses of feminism or poststructuralist theory to pulsate in our critical analysis. If there is a danger in applying exclusively poststructuralist approaches to early modern texts, it surely lies in neglecting the important study of sources and subtexts that affect and create meaning in the new text, even as one attempts to carry out analysis that has its theoretical base outside the text.

By bringing to feminism or poststructuralist analysis the benefits of a conscious formalism, good work will be strengthened, not diluted. Thus, a feminist analysis of *El Monserrate* could take advantage of more traditional scholarship to discuss such aspects as the feminization of the hero through his association to Venus and through constant and sustained identification between Garín and the figure of Mary Magdalen. Likewise, starting from a position of familiarity with *Aeneid* book 4, such an analysis would have cause to point out that Garín is not a virile, Aeneas-like hero, who seduces a Carthaginian queen and abandons her, indirectly provoking her death, but a character who does suffer and pay for his crime.

The literary critic who is determined to read old texts in a new way does not have to remain hopelessly at odds with a work like *El Monserrate*. On the contrary, it is possible for twentieth-century readers to confront a text such as this one "in acceptance of difference," to use Elizabeth Rhodes's phrase, not with the idea of endorsing, but in seeking to understand the religious discourses that govern it. In her study of another neglected text of the period, Luis de Granada's *Libro de la oración y meditación*, Rhodes calls for an approach that entails "a willingness to consider the old book as a subject, not an object, as a self-determining entity of semiotic independence whose original boundaries should be respected and whose original significance can and should be at least partially recovered, and appreciated instead of altered or ignored."[31] The lesson of this chapter has been that once the "original significance" of the old book has been recovered, once the author's meaning has been recaptured, merely the first part of the critical task is completed. Only when these things are accomplished is the reader at liberty to adopt an attitude toward authorial meaning and respond to those questions that previous generations of scholars did not ask of the text.

31. Elizabeth Rhodes, "Spain's Misfired Canon: The Case of Luis de Granada's *Libro de la oración y meditación*," 45.

4

The Old World in the Poet's Gaze
Christian Heroism and Alterity
in Diego de Hojeda's *La Christiada*

By the beginning of the seventeenth century the subject matter of many epics had shifted away from the stories of war that typified ancient epos and toward conflicts of a more symbolic nature. The reasons for this shift are no doubt complex, especially since the horrors of war and conquest had not disappeared from the landscape of seventeenth-century Europe, and certainly not from the recently acquired American territories. Murrin argues that epic finally surrendered to a "slow but complete revolution, mostly but by no means solely through the development of firearms," and that when poets such as Spenser and Milton began to write "peaceful epic," they called into question the viability of the genre itself. The Christianization of classical epic and the allegorization of ancient myth throughout humanism and into the post-Tridentine period also had an impact on the genre. Even epics with a profane subject could not escape this pervasive religious ethos; as Greene writes, "virtually all epic poems through the seventeenth century show at least a tincture of Christianity."[1]

Some literary critics describe religious epic as largely unsatisfactory, reasoning that sacred epic is founded on an intrinsic flaw that could lead to insoluble contradictions, not the least of which is that the formal requirements of the ancient genre would damage or detract from a story that Christians cherished above all others. Curtius, for example, calls biblical epic a "hybrid with an inner lack of truth," while Greene writes of Sannazaro's *De Partu Virginis* (1527), "The wonder is that the Gospel story is not crushed by the elevated tone and the extrinsic pagan apparatus." Another potential problem of biblical epic was the temptation on the part of devout poets to amplify religious content at the expense of the objective action that had characterized the genre since antiquity. Especially in the seventeenth century, when there was an abundance of devotional lyric types

---

1. Michael Murrin, *History and Warfare in Renaissance Epic*, 8, 17; and Thomas M. Greene, *The Descent from Heaven: A Study in Epic Continuity*, 170.

that had achieved great popularity, the religious poet might be tempted to either lyricize biblical epic or turn it into a sermon. "The problem," writes Kurth, "lay not so much in his use of Biblical figures in place of the pagan gods and heroes as it did in the fact that the Biblical materials immediately introduced religious associations which were not always in harmony with the epic action."[2]

It is clear, however, that seventeenth-century religious poets did not gauge the range of viable possibilities so narrowly. In England, for example, there was no serious debate about whether or not it was fitting to adapt biblical materials to the form of pagan epic until the second half of the century. In Spain, sacred epic of this period makes no particular claim to adhere to the precepts of the genre's foundational texts, though it does attempt to assimilate their best-known conventions. Whether there was a need for religious literature to compete with profane works or simply a burning desire to write epic with a sacred theme because of the genre's lofty position within the hierarchy of poetic types, the fact is that in the sixteenth and seventeenth centuries, religious epics abounded in the Spanish-speaking world. Meo Zilio lists more than eighty-five poems of this type published between the years 1552 and 1694. From the point of view of cultural history, biblical epic's success or failure in its attempt to appropriate for itself the machinery of ancient epic is perhaps less important than the writers' computable determination to arrive at a form that expressed, more or less adequately, their own vision of the Christian heroic. Kurth is right to view the religious epic of this period as "not merely the result of an artificial crossbreeding of Scripture and pagan epic, but rather the working out of a distinct form of the heroic genre which could best express Christian themes and concepts."[3]

Thus, much of seventeenth-century epic moves away from physical battle and onto a spiritual ground, where the prestigious ancient genre struggles to retain its legitimacy by adapting to the specific needs of Christian theology. This is the context in which we must examine Diego de Hojeda's *La Christiada*, an epic on the subject of Christ's Passion composed in viceregal Lima and published in Seville in 1611. As Greene has noted, Hojeda blends some trappings of classical epic into a story line that is directly traceable to the Gospels. Sister Mary Edgar Meyer, for her part, has identified a wide range of other sources from Josephus Flavius to

---

2. Ernst Robert Curtius, *European Literature and the Latin Middle Ages,* 462; Greene, *Descent,* 155; Burton O. Kurth, *Milton and Christian Heroism: Biblical Epic Themes and Forms in Seventeenth-Century England,* 18.

3. Kurth, *Milton and Christian Heroism,* 12, 107; Giovanni Meo Zilio, *Estudio sobre Hernando Domínguez Camargo y su "San Ignacio de Loyola, Poema Heroico,"* 264–68. See also Lily B. Campbell's classic study, "The Christian Muse."

fourth-century patristic writings against heresy that the poet, a member of the Order of Preachers, used to compose his poem. This admixture of components issuing from diverse kinds of material creates an epic text that can be called "impure," to use Pierce's term, but that may be considered one creative solution to the dilemma of how to write epic that is ostensibly not about war, but about the foundations of Christian faith.[4]

My examination of La Christiada has two main foci. The first pertains to the remarkable architecture of Hojeda's epic. The Dominican set out to compose an epic poem about the death of the man Christ. As the narrator declares in the epic's *propositio,* the purpose of La Christiada is to "sing of God's Son, human and dead" (Canto al Hijo de Dios, humano, y muerto).[5] But as these pages will show, Hojeda found it difficult to fulfill his epic program without digressing to include matters extraneous to his plot yet fundamental to his Christian view of universal history. In the first section of this chapter, there will be a need for some close readings to show the complexity of Hojeda's treatment of the Incarnation theme and his depiction of the "suffering Messiah." The second section examines Hojeda's use of hagiography to recontextualize and validate the story of the Passion. The ultimate goal will be to arrive at a more holistic view of the poem's structure.

The second focal point of the chapter has to do with how theology and ancient prejudice condition the writing of cultural identity in La Christiada. Hojeda's epic representation of Christ as "suffering Messiah" grows out of a much earlier Dominican evangelizing project that influences the writing of Christian heroism at the same time that it scripts otherness along anti-Semitic lines. Finally, consideration will be given to the ramifications of Hojeda's decision to turn his gaze away from Andean indigenous all around him in order to belatedly enunciate this older alterity.

The Suffering Messiah:
Incarnation, Atonement, and Christian "Truth"

The idea of writing an epic on the Incarnation and the Passion of Christ was not a new one, by any means. Marco Girolamo Vida's Cristias (1535),

4. Greene, *Descent,* 232; Sister Mary Edgar Meyer, *The Sources of Hojeda's "La Christiada"*; Frank Pierce, *La poesía épica del Siglo de Oro,* 264.

5. All quotations of La Christiada are taken from the critical edition of Sister Mary Helen Patricia Corcoran (1935), which is based on a manuscript located in the Bibliothèque de l'Arsenal (Paris), the only one that predates the princeps. Corcoran does not number her stanzas, using the folio markings instead. I have made my own numbering of the octaves, excluding from my count an octave that summarizes the plot, which appears above the text proper at the beginning of each book. Hereafter references in the text indicate first book number, followed by octave and lines, in this case, 1.1.1.

an important model for Hojeda's poem, had already adapted the gospel narrative to classical epic form with limited success. In early modern Spain, besides some twenty epicoreligious poems on the life of Christ, there was a considerable corpus of devotional writing on the Sacred Humanity. Loyola's *Spiritual Exercises* routinely appealed to scenes from the life of Christ to bring about the desired spiritual state in the practitioner. Hojeda's epic, though a much more sophisticated literary endeavor, draws on an extensive tradition of prose commentaries and poetic renditions of the Passion story.[6]

The Dominican's plan to focus on the suffering and death of the man, Jesus of Nazareth, appears to define the priority of the poem, above all because of what it obligates the poet to de-emphasize. Similarly, the choice to acclaim Christ's humanity curtails the repertoire of New Testament episodes Hojeda can use to construct the plot line of his epic. To a point, it does so. The narrative focuses principally on the crucifixion and the episodes immediately prior to it, all of which is in keeping with a decision to emphasize not Christ's divinity, but rather that aspect of his nature that is most susceptible to epic treatment: the side that suffers pain and tribulation, as do human beings. Greene, who considers the enigma of the Incarnation to be the "binding theme" of *La Christiada*, writes that "It is typical of Hojeda that he intensify rather than mitigate the anguish of this crisis. For if incarnation is to be apprehended at all, one cannot minimize its fearful paradoxicality; one must dwell both on God's ineffable grandeur and on the lowliness of His indignities."[7]

The hagiographic visions Hojeda includes in the epic show that the poet was familiar not only with the long defense of the mystery of the Incarnation by church doctors and other religious, but that he perceived a need for constant vigilance against heretical views on this doctrinal matter that he esteemed central to Christian faith. There is more at stake, however, in Hojeda's decision to represent the Savior incarnate as vulnerable to affliction. If Christians themselves could not always agree on the fine points of the doctrine of incarnation, non-Christians found it very difficult to accept that the Christian divinity could send a son into the world to agonize. For

---

6. For evaluations of Vida's *Cristias*, see Kurth, *Milton and Christian Heroism*, 87; and Greene, *Descent*, 171. On Spanish-language poems on the life of Christ, see Meo Zilio, *Estudio sobre Hernando Domínguez Camargo*, 264; and Frank Pierce, "Diego de Hojeda, Religious Poet," 588–89. This essay by Pierce, cited several times in this chapter, appears in *Homenaje a William L. Fichter*, ed. David Kossoff and José Amor y Vázquez. For the influence of Ignatius of Loyola's *Spiritual Exercises* on metaphysical poetry of this period, see Louis L. Martz, *The Poetry of Meditation*.

7. Greene, *Descent*, 232.

Judaism, in particular, the notion of a "suffering Messiah" seemed to be a contradiction in terms.[8] This fundamental incompatibility resulted in centuries of Christian theological discussion of Christ's torment and Crucifixion, which served the dual purpose of reaffirming atonement for Christians and explaining salvation to Jews, who supposedly misunderstood its spiritual, not carnal, nature. To write about the suffering Messiah was to attempt to demonstrate that the Messiah had come, that his victory was not a military conquest, and that he had brought a new law to supersede the Law of Moses. Viewed from this perspective and as a continuation of this tradition, Hojeda's epic is not just a baroque contemplation of the Sacred Humanity, but a militant evangelizing text designed to affirm Christian truth over the claims of Judaism and other faiths.

In keeping with the wishes of its founder, the Dominican Order of late-medieval Spain fostered the study of Arabic and Hebrew for the purpose of converting Spanish Muslims and Jews through debate with their own sacred texts. The records of some of these debates are preserved, along with many Dominican treatises and sermons from the thirteenth through fifteenth centuries that expound the evidence of Jesus' Messiahship. Since the Dominicans always accompanied their arguments with a repudiation of Jews who continued to reject the Christ, these writings were intended, at least in part, as proselytizing tools.[9] During the nine years of intense study that led Hojeda to become a bachelor of sacred theology (*presentado*) in his order, the author of *La Christiada* would have to have examined the writings of Spanish Dominicans from this period. Two of these, Raymund of Peñafort and Vincent Ferrer, appear in the hagiographic prophecies contained in *La Christiada*, so there is no question about Hojeda's admiration for them and their message. Paulus Christiani and Raymund Martini were two other Dominicans who profited from instruction in Semitic languages. At the Disputation at Barcelona in 1263, Paulus Christiani debated Rabbi Moses ben Nachman (Nachmanides)—unsuccessfully, it seems—on whether the Messiah had come and "whether the laws and ceremonies have ceased, and ought to have ceased, after the coming of the Christ." Hojeda incorporates a similar disputation into book 3 of *La Christiada*, where the Jewish council debates whether or not the Messiah must be a military leader, or whether his wars might be "metaphorical" (*metafóricas*, 3.45.7), as Hojeda's character Gamaliel puts it. Raymund Martini, for his part, wrote the *Pugio Fidei* (*Dagger of faith*, 1278), a work meant to "divide the bread of the Divine word to Jews, or to slay their impious falsehoods." Williams writes that a main

8. A. Lukyn Williams, *Adversus Judaeos: A Bird's-Eye View of Christian 'Apologiae' until the Renaissance*, 253.
9. Ibid., 244–46.

part of Martini's thesis was that the Jews mistook the spiritual meaning of salvation because they rejected the notion of a suffering Messiah.[10] This formulation of Christ's vulnerability is intrinsic to the particular strain of heroism *La Christiada* promotes. It is highly probable that the Dominicans in Peru held works such as the *Dagger of faith* in their libraries, but whether or not Hojeda knew this specific treatise, he certainly had access to the ideas and the conversion strategies of his predecessors in the Order of Preachers, and their writings undoubtedly informed his thought.

Because it gave precedence to Jesus' degradation, rather than just prefiguring his glory, *La Christiada* served both as a reminder to Christians of the founding stories of their faith and as a tool for converting unbelievers. On the one hand, by placing the sacrificial figure of the Redeemer, as opposed to the conquering Christ of the Harrowing of Hell or the exemplary figure of the teacher and teller of parables, in the foreground, Hojeda could write of Christ's death in human terms recognizable to those already familiar with the New Testament. This was appropriate, since those readers were supposed to be able to reconcile themselves to God through Jesus' expiation. In this vein, Pierce has remarked on Hojeda's tendency to dwell on the brutality of the Crucifixion "with apparent fascination." Likewise, Greene notes that although the poet attempts to justify Christ's Passion in three or four passages, "the weight of the poem falls not upon the achievement but the agony."[11] At the same time, by textually privileging Christ's indignities, Hojeda could carry on the tradition of Dominican evangelists who argued that the Messiah's death was necessary for the correct understanding of Christian salvation. To the extent that *La Christiada* accomplishes this, it gains ground as an evangelizing text.

The degree of Hojeda's success in resisting the temptation to highlight the Resurrection story is one indicator of whether he fulfilled the goal he set for himself in the epic's *propositio*. His theological training and his worldview inevitably induced him to foreshadow Christ's victory over death. However, in order both to corroborate the suffering nature of the Messiah and to adhere to his original epic program, the poet needed to stress the hardships that befell Jesus of Nazareth in his life on earth, especially during the events leading up to the Crucifixion. Furthermore, there was a genealogical advantage to imposing human constraints on the representation of Christ. If Hojeda could emphasize the hero's afflictions and stress his steadfastness at the expense of other attributes, the outlines of *La Christiada*

10. Ibid., 251–53.

11. On the various roles of Christ, see Kurth, *Milton and Christian Heroism*, 82. On the emphasis of Hojeda's poem, see Pierce, "Hojeda, Religious Poet," 594; Greene, *Descent*, 237–38.

could be made to coincide with those of earlier attempts at biblical epic that
had established a concept of Christian heroism as virtuous forbearance in
the face of adversity, poems that focused on long-suffering heroes such as
Job, whose uprightness in the face of difficult moral choices proved unwa-
vering. Kurth describes these biblical narratives as texts that concentrate
upon "temptation, trial, and suffering as the most significant experiences
for the Christian hero and the chief measures of his faith, virtue, and forti-
tude."[12] *El Monserrate* is just one example of the religious epics written in
Spain or her colonies during this period that combine these elements.

The materials from the Passion narrative that best conform to this
model of Christian heroism come from the agony in the Garden of
Gethsemane and from crucial moments of Christ's torment and death,
such as his silence during Herod's interrogation, or his anguished cry of
abandonment from the cross. The happenings at Gethsemane, based on
the synoptic Gospels, are significant not only, or even primarily, because
this is the place of the arrest, but because everyone forsakes Jesus here.
Hojeda's treatment of this narrative nucleus reinforces the depiction of
Christ as human by establishing him as the model for heroism defined as
faithful endurance of suffering. But even here, as we will see, the poet can-
not refrain from suggesting Jesus' divinity in various ways. The writer of
La Christiada affirms Christ's identity as "suffering Messiah," while com-
plicating the plan stated in the poem's proposition.

Hojeda's extensive treatment of the events at the Garden of
Gethsemane (books 1–3 of 12) suggests their significance for the narrative
line as a whole. Furthermore, the poet carefully structures the Gethsemane
episode to foreshadow events to come, in the Passion story and beyond. In
this sense, the agony in the garden acts as a window opening onto a much
broader text. The lengthy episode breaks down into three segments, each of
which includes Jesus' solitary prayer and his interaction with the sleeping
apostles. Each of Christ's meditations is more portentous than the previous
one, so that there is a steady increase in dramatic tension, culminating in the
hero's arrest.

Hojeda borrows from all four Gospels to weave together the threads
of his plot. At first, he follows the synoptics closely. As soon as the last
supper and the institution of the Eucharist have concluded, Jesus leaves
for the garden in the company of Peter, James, and John. Telling the three
that he is ready to offer himself "in sacrifice and perfect holocaust to the
Father" (en sacrificio / de holocausto perfecto al sumo Padre, 1.86.1–2),

12. Kurth, *Milton and Christian Heroism*, 30. For the strategies Hojeda used to fore-
shadow Christian triumph, see Elizabeth B. Davis, "The Politics of Effacement: Diego
de Hojeda's Humble Poetics," 347.

Christ goes off to pray alone, asking his disciples to watch with him. They quickly fall asleep. In his prayer, Jesus declares that his spirit has never faltered, "even if the flesh is always followed by weakness" (Si bien sigue a la carne su flaqueza, 1.87.2). Hojeda takes his cue from Mark 14:38, where Christ admonishes the sleeping Simon Peter: "Watch and pray so that you will not fall into temptation. The spirit is willing, but the body is weak." To highlight his hero's vulnerability, the poet of *La Christiada* redirects these words and applies them to Jesus' own human frailty and internal conflict.

In consonance with this representation of Christ as weak and wavering, Hojeda draws attention to his forlornness. The ungrateful apostles sleep, while he remains awake like a father who watches over his sleeping daughter and worries about finding her a suitable bridegroom (1.93–94). Thus, the disciples symbolically desert Jesus early in the events that culminate in the Crucifixion, as they will do toward the end of book 3 in a more conscious and radical way. René Girard's work on culture's scapegoat mechanisms makes it clear that the Passion is a founding murder of the type that occurs when people take out their personal conflicts or "scandals" on a public substitute or "collective target." For the scapegoating to be successful in the gospel story, according to Girard, the frenzied crowd had to absorb even those closest to Jesus.[13] By glossing the theme of the disciples' ingratitude and their inability to watch and pray, Hojeda alerts his reader to the men's contamination by the will of the crowd and their imminent abandonment of Christ, while highlighting Jesus' sense of desolation.

Christ's first meditation at Gethsemane centers on the description of an elaborate cloak woven from threads of the seven sins of man. This passage, as suggested by the recent examination of ekphrasis as political device in the work of Krieger and Bergmann, is significant both theologically and from the viewpoint of early constructions of national identity. In it, Hojeda puts the great sinners "in their place" in separate infernal dungeons, but as it happens, the enemies of Catholicism are also those of Spain. Luther appears under the sin of Pride, while Mohammed, the legendary Count Don Julian, "drawn among Moors" (entre moros dibujado, 1.122.4) because he precipitated the Moorish invasion of Spain (A.D. 711), and Elizabeth of England are in the domain of Anger. Henry VIII's character defects are so numerous that he appears in five separate categories: Gluttony, Laziness, Luxury, Greed, and Anger. Reading Hojeda's epic in the 1930s from a religious perspective, Corcoran rejected a nationalist interpretation of the poem

13. René Girard, "The Question of Anti-Semitism in the Gospels," in *The Girard Reader,* ed. James G. Williams, 216.

on the grounds that, in contrast to epics such as *Paradise Lost* or the *Messias* of Klopstock, "*La Christiada* is a poetic interpretation of the Bible, as well as an invitation to read the Sacred Scripture." Pierce, on the other hand, who would later argue that Tridentine Spain was "semi-theocratic" and that the epic muse of the period was "shaped as the organ of the Church Militant and its ally, Imperial Spain," does not hesitate to interpret the passage on Elizabeth of England as proof of Hojeda's "bitter sectarianism."[14] Today it would be difficult to deny the confluence of religious and early national ideologies in the ekphrastic passage about the cloak of sins, which contains Christ's meditation on human iniquity. It is, after all, the Lutherans and the British, enemies of Golden Age Spain and her official faith, whom Hojeda explicitly condemns in the verbal picture of sin.

As intriguing as this meditation on sin may be from the point of view of emergent Renaissance nationalisms, it is a departure from epic action that disrupts the poem's unity. In general, threats to Hojeda's narrative unity come not from vying plots, as in Ariosto's *Orlando Furioso,* but from the poet's expansive commentary on doctrinal matters. On the other hand, this type of commentary can establish important thematic links between different sections of the epic. For example, the description of the cloak of sins attenuates plot development because of its length (46 octaves), but it ultimately constitutes an apology for the Passion. Furthermore, by associating the themes of sin and redemption, this ekphrasis attaches the agony in the garden to later episodes in which first the Jewish leaders, then Lucifer and his demons, and finally Pontius Pilate dispute Christ's Messiahship (books 2, 4, 5), much as Paulus Christiani and Nachmanides had done in 1263. Although Hojeda's plot unfolds slowly, the connections between the various segments of his epic are adroitly executed.

In offering a justification for the Crucifixion, the vision of human sin frames Jesus' death in theological terms that reach far beyond his personal fate to imply the benefits his death will accrue to the human race as a whole. After all, the scene in which Christ takes human sin upon himself does not make much sense if Jesus of Nazareth is a man who dies like any other. Already in book 1, therefore, Hojeda begins to move away from his original plan and toward a larger purpose.[15] The poet, however, is not able to invoke

14. Corcoran, introduction to *La Christiada*, by Hojeda, lii–liii; Frank Pierce, "The Spanish 'Religious Epic' of the Counter-Reformation: A Survey," 178–79; Frank Pierce, "Hojeda's *La Christiada*: A Poem of the Literary Baroque," 209–10. For the political implications of ekphrasis, see Emilie Bergmann, *Art Inscribed: Essays on Ekphrasis in Spanish Golden Age Poetry;* and Murray Krieger, *Ekphrasis: The Illusion of the Natural Sign.*

15. For another example of the "unfulfillment" of a program stated or implied at the beginning of an epic poem, see Ramona Lagos, "El incumplimiento de la programación épica en *La Araucana.*"

a grander, more providential perspective without mitigating his hero's suffering, which he cannot do without contradicting the priority of his text. To counterbalance this discrepancy, he immediately reaffirms Christ's humanity by calling attention to his fear. When Jesus sways to the ground under the burden of the accumulated sins, Hojeda, following Scripture, makes him ask God to remove their weight: "Father, Father, if it is possible, let this terrible burden pass from me" (Padre, Padre, si es posible, / Pase de mí esta carga terrible, 1.146.7–8). These words, which demonstrate Christ's anxiety about his impending ordeal, reveal a deep ambiguity in the text. Hojeda asserts Jesus' human reaction of dread and his desire for exemption from an awful death, but in appealing to a greater good, the poet details the reasons why the Crucifixion must take place. In this one textual locus, therefore, Christ's humanity and his divinity stand in unavoidable contradiction. In response to Jesus' anguished plea, God the Father, who does not recognize his own Son attired in the despicable cloak (human iniquity has "othered" him), takes flight: "He does not shun Christ; he shuns the sin which He sees represented on Christ" (Mas no huye de Cristo, del pecado / Huye que en Cristo ve representado," 1.148.7–8). Once the Redeemer has "put on" the sins of humankind, even God abandons him. These lines serve as an eerie premonition of Jesus' lamentation from the cross: "'Eloi, Eloi, lama sabachthani?'—which means, 'My God, my God, why have you forsaken me?'" (Matt. 27:46, Mark 15:34). By ending the ekphrastic passage this way, the author makes Christ's fear and solitude at Gethsemane perceptible long before the arrest occurs. What is more, Hojeda uses these lines to build a bridge between book 1 and Jesus' forlorn cry near the end of the Crucifixion, a cry that calls attention to the Redeemer's human vulnerability and his elusive relationship to God.

Hojeda's Christ figure then rises to look for his disciples and finds them sleeping. This time he scolds them lovingly, then returns to prayer and sees a ghastly vision of his own death:

> Out of mockery, she appears to him
> dressed in radiant purple
> and carrying a reed she had been given
> for a scepter, which they use to hurt her face:
> this is death, who vanquished life on the cross,
> and for this reason, the cross shines in her;
> she comes already crucified: o fierce death!
> God sees you, God fears you, and God awaits you.

> (De rutilante púrpura vestida,
> Y por mofa vestida se le ofrece,
> Y una caña por cetro recibida,
> Con que el rostro le hieren, aparece:

> Es muerte que en la cruz venció a la vida,
> Y así la cruz en ella resplandece;
> Crucificada viene: ¡o muerte fiera!
> Dios te ve, Dios te teme y Dios te espera.)
> (1.153)

Jesus' terror comes not from his divine essence, but from his mortal existence. On seeing the graphic image of his own approaching death, Christ "fell to the ground, bathed in sweat and trembling, for even God fears death and sin" (Sudó, cayó en tierra asombrado; / Que aun Dios teme a la muerte y al pecado, 1.157.7–8).

Reacting to the horror of this image, the Son complains to the Father in a state of panic. These verses suggest that Christ's awareness of his role in God's redemptive plan cannot console him now:

> God is humiliated, but still terrible death,
> that ferocious female Samson, does not leave him:
> he repeats his second complaint to the Father,
> and grief gives weight to his demand:
> his human will seeks advice
> from his great fear, while the Divine person
> holds sway over human reason;
> for God is a man, and as a man he resolves his inner differences.

> (Humillado está Dios, y no le deja
> La muerte horrenda, la feroz Sansona:
> Repite al Padre la segunda queja,
> Y su aflicción y su demanda abona:
> La voluntad humana se aconseja
> Con su grande pavor, y la persona
> Divina rige a la razón humana;
> Que es hombre Dios, y como tal se allana.)
> (1.159)

Contrary to what the text says, Jesus does not repeat his previous objection to the planned Crucifixion. For in these lines, Hojeda exposes the painful paradox of Incarnation. As a man, Jesus' will is controlled by overwhelming fear. His human ability to reason, however, is still governed by the divine aspect of his being. The phrase "for God is a man" is full of ambiguity that is both linguistic and conceptual. The deliberately polysemous words encode Christ's humanity, but they also express the mystery of hypostatic union: he is a "Man-God." For theological reasons, the poet decides to affirm Christ's superhuman comprehension of the unfolding events, even if by doing so, he contravenes the simple statement of the epic's *propositio*. At every step, however, the text reaffirms Jesus' identity as

a suffering Messiah, which is an indirect way of invoking Christian supe-
riority over other religions. Hojeda finds himself in a kind of double bind
that he can only resolve by broaching the subject of Jesus' dual nature quite
directly. Gone, perhaps forever, is the notion that he can sing only of
"God's Son, human and dead."

Christ's new rejection of his imminent execution is twofold. Describing
his beautiful human features—"this mouth of immense beauty, . . . this
noble throat and pleasing neck, . . . this chest of God, this chosen chest"
(esta boca de inmensa hermosura, esta noble garganta y cuello amable,
este pecho de Dios, pecho florido)—Jesus accuses the Father of allowing
their mutilation. Christ's second allegation is that humans are ungrateful
and that they will neither appreciate his sacrifice, nor put it to good use:

> "The men for whom I suffer all this
> are bound to be ungrateful for this service!
> On their account I offer myself up to a base death,
> and will they make poor use of this great gain?
> Good Father! In dying, I deserve
> for virtue to live and vice to die
> in men: if it is possible, let the reward
> pass to them, to me the horrible death."

> ("Y ¡que los hombres por quien tal padezco,
> No me han de agradecer este servicio!
> Por ellos a tan vil muerte me ofrezco,
> Y ¿usarán mal de tanto beneficio?
> ¡Ah mi buen Padre! Yo en morir merezco
> Que viva la virtud y muera el vicio
> En los hombres: a ellos, si es posible,
> Pase el premio, y a mí la muerte horrible.")
> (1.167)

This octave, like the one cited above, is full of ambiguity. The first four
lines expound a good reason why the Father should spare Jesus: he should
not have to die for a host of ingrates who do not comprehend or value his
death. It feels as though the hero is leading up to a repetition of the previ-
ous request ("let this terrible burden pass from me"), but in an unexpected
about-face, the Christ character accepts his destiny, wishing only to negoti-
ate the results of his expiation ("let the reward pass to them"). The phrase
"pase a mí" stands in direct opposition to the "pase de mí" of octave 146.
The image of his own death is fiercer than the allegorical vision of sin, but
here, too, the text shows an explicit link between the Gethsemane episode
and later events in the epic, such as the scourging (book 9) and the grue-
some details of the Crucifixion itself (book 12). This connection is further

proof of Hojeda's deftness in joining together material that in the Gospels is disconnected. In this passage, Hojeda's Christ does not contradict himself as much as he changes his mind, after considering how his death will benefit humanity. Thus, "pase de mí" becomes "pase a mí."

Hojeda immediately develops a juridical simile designed to illustrate the predicament of Father and Son together. He likens God to a magistrate who must take bail from a friend who has not committed any crime. Reason obliges the judge to accept the bail, but friendship reminds him that it is for an infraction committed by someone else, a crime that is "alien" (*ajeno*). For now, the Father suspends Jesus' sentence by postponing it. Christ, so filled with despair that his "soul does not fit in his chest" (en el pecho el alma no le cabe, 1.171.4), gets up to look at his sleeping disciples but does not wake them.

Once again the Savior returns to prayer, this time seeing a vision of God's providential plan that encompasses past, present, and future, in a manner consistent with the scope of classical epic. He sees, as well, the Trinity and the allegorical personification of Charity, in whose name he will later carry his cross. The dominant theme of this prayer is that human sin offends God. But though Jesus understands this, and though he contradicts himself, he implores God to let the stipulation of death (the chalice) pass from him. Hojeda switches the prepositions ("a" reverts to "de"), a substitution that seems to cancel out the previous prayer.

> Seeing that his Father was offended,
> the beloved Son was suspended in mortal sorrow;
> but with intense pain, he broke
> the knot of silence tied to his throat:
> "Oh Father, affronted by men,"
> (he said, contemplating their great shamelessness),
> "if possible, may they no longer offend thy glory;
> let this terrible cup pass from me."

> (Vio a su Padre ofendido el Hijo amado,
> Y estaba con mortal pena suspenso;
> Mas rompió del silencio el nudo atado
> A la garganta con dolor intenso:
> "¡O Padre, de los hombres afrentado
> (Dijo mirando aquel valor inmenso)!
> No agravien más tu gloria, si es posible;
> Pase de mí este cáliz tan horrible.")
> (1.184)

Jesus denounces the sin of humans, while simultaneously asking the Father to spare him.

Book 1 ends on this unresigned and unresolved note. The allegorical figure Prayer (*Oración*) collects Christ's reasoned arguments and delivers them to the Father in his heavenly palace, where Hojeda brings together the angels in "celestial courts" (*cortes celestiales*) structured in opposition to the demonic councils of ancient epic. Interceding on the Son's behalf, *Oración* probes the Father's intentions, summarizing the theologically meaningful events of Jesus' life prior to the epic's action. This account of Christ's life reinforces the concept of Christian heroism as patient suffering that informs the entire epic at the same time that it substantiates a thoroughly Christian conceptualization of the Messiah through intimations of his mortality and foreshadowings of his terrible death.

Pleas cannot sway the Father, who had predestined the Redeemer to die on the cross from the beginning; he hands down the terrible sentence, "Let him die" (*Muera*). The words of Hojeda's text stir the resonance of Abraham's readiness to sacrifice his son, Isaac (Genesis 22), which stands in typological relationship to the Passion narrative. Yet, even for the reader who knows both stories well, the harshness of the sentence signals a disruption that mimics, on a textual level, the historical significance of the Crucifixion for a writer like Hojeda, who understood it as a rupture that resulted in the birth of a new law and a "true Israel." For the Dominican from Seville, the hated cross is transformed into a loved object through Christ's death. The Father says, "I will give eternal life to whomever loves the abhorred cross" ([daré] eterna vida / Al que amare la cruz aborrecida, 2.123.6–8). From this moment on, crucifixion, symbolic or real, becomes the most perfect way for humans to follow Christ's example. Hojeda thus lays the groundwork for the hagiographic sections of the poem and thematically binds those sections to the Passion story.

The seventeenth-century Dominican, writing from his mission in Peru, intended to write an epic about the death of the man Jesus, but as these pages suggest, he could not carry out his original plan without seriously complicating it through numerous digressions and detours to events and to a kind of understanding that surpass human limitations. Hojeda's problem was aesthetic, theological, and ultimately unavoidable, because, though he wanted to let his reader know that Christ suffered the agony and fear of the Crucifixion just the way any other human being would do, he also wanted to argue, as his Dominican forerunners had done, that Jesus was the Messiah. The writer could not accomplish that without alluding to Christ's divinity in various ways, and this resulted in the kind of tension witnessed throughout the Gethsemane section of the epic. "Christ," as Kurth writes, "was the ultimate Hero, or measure of heroism, yet as a subject for heroic poetry the figure of Christ was too complex, too paradoxical, to be encompassed in a single or restricted vision, whether it be cosmic or human."[16] In response to just such a problem, and determined to perpetuate an earlier Dominican preoccupation with the "suffering Messiah" as a marker of Christian ascendancy, the poet strives to hold his gaze on the tortured carpenter from Nazareth while filling out his destiny by giving him superhuman consciousness, marvelous emissaries who wing their way between heaven and earth, and triumphalist prophecies to console him in his agony. The delicate connections Hojeda makes between Christ's prayers at Gethsemane and events that take place much later in the Passion narrative are based on theology, on evangelism, and on a dazzling intuition about the possibilities of epic structure.

La Christiada and Hagiography

When Hojeda moved away from the focus on Christ's humanity stated in the proposition of La Christiada, he showed his purpose to be the narration of something infinitely more comprehensive. But let us not rush to the conclusion that in broadening the scope of his epic to encompass the glory of Christian ascendancy, the poet gave up a tenable epic program. What he gave up was a deliberately oversimplified early statement of epic action. The propositio of any epic is important in that it is the first sign the poet gives the reader about what the poem's principal subject matter will be. Due to its succinctness, however, it cannot suggest the range of themes the text itself holds. When Hojeda swerves from the original proposition, therefore, he does so to include elements indispensable to the completion of his Christian epic vision.

Hojeda buttresses the Passion story of La Christiada with a series of prophetic visions, most of which are hagiographic in nature. Because they tell stories of sainthood and martyrdom, these passages textualize the themes of abuse of power and suffering for righteousness' sake in a context that is intrinsically religious and political. Stemming from Roman martyrology (passiones) and from saints' lives (vitae), they are Old World legends of persecution of the just. From colonial Lima, Hojeda's gaze remains fixed on these narratives of early Christian heroes to flesh out his own account of the Crucifixion. Pierce has written that these sections of the poem are not of much interest to the modern reader and may even constitute a defect in the poem, but in fact, they are indispensable to the culmination of Hojeda's project, partly because they reinforce and reaffirm the same kind of Christian heroism that operates in the Passion

---

16. Kurth, Milton and Christian Heroism, 85.

narrative proper. Prophecy is an important component of ancient epic machinery because of its ability to construct a political genealogy for the narrated present and then link that present to a triumphant future. *El Monserrate* boasts examples of this device and, as the next chapter will show, it plays a pivotal role in Lope de Vega's structuring of Spanish identity in *Jerusalem conquered*. The vatic quality of Hojeda's hagiographic segments lends them transcendental importance. Furthermore, recent scholarship has shown that the stories of saints' lives, which were enormously popular in the Middle Ages and the Renaissance, make up a fertile area of study in their own right. Alison Goddard Elliott, for example, has found important narrative patterns in both the *passiones* and the *vitae*, which she studies specifically as literature.[17] That said, the modern reader of *La Christiada* indeed faces a dilemma in the hagiographic sections of the poem, though not precisely the one Pierce had in mind. Because they imitate Christ crucified, the virtuous figures that make up the prophetic visions of Hojeda's epic are crucial to our full reception of the poet's message, yet most modern readers are not generally possessed of the ability to recognize any but the most celebrated among them.

There are some ten prophecies in the epic of Hojeda, including those spoken by the descending angels Gabriel and Michael. Meyer has traced the sources of two of these, the vision of heresies that will threaten the Church's unity (book 7) and that of the destruction of Jerusalem (book 10), while Pierce has studied the vision of Hell (book 4), not as prophecy but in its relation to literary tradition.[18] These visions illustrate through negative example the importance of right thinking on doctrinal matters and the necessity for perseverance in virtue. The same issues appear in the other prophetic visions of *La Christiada,* which express the struggle against heresy and for the defense of monastic life in affirmative terms that echo the concept of heroism as steadfast suffering elsewhere in evidence in Hojeda's poem. These prophecies constitute the very sections about which

17. Pierce, *Poesía épica*, 274; Alison Goddard Elliott, *Roads to Paradise: Reading the Lives of the Early Saints*. I owe the latter reference to Maureen Ahern. See also Kenneth L. Woodward, *Making Saints: How the Catholic Church Determines Who Becomes a Saint, Who Doesn't, and Why*.

18. The angel Gabriel descends to Christ in Gethsemane (book 1), to announce the Resurrection to the Virgin (book 6), and to foretell the Ascension (book 10). In book 8, the angel Michael enunciates the prophecy of the early martyrs, which, unlike Gabriel's visions, is truly hagiographic. The reach of the hagiographic prophecies is much greater than that of Gabriel's visions, which are closely connected to the events of the Passion. See Davis, "Politics of Effacement"; and Frank Pierce, "The Poetic Hell in Hojeda's *La Christiada*: Imitation and Originality."

Pierce expressed reservations: the panorama of religious persecuted for Christ's sake (book 4), the vision of the church doctors (book 5), the rejection of the just (book 6), the prophecy of Christian martyrs (book 8) and that of what Hojeda calls the "Gentile Church" (book 11).

The visions of Christian exemplars stand more neglected than their infernal counterparts, perhaps because vice is more inherently interesting than virtue, but surely, too, because of the hagiographic material they contain. Whether it is a question of indifference or unfamiliarity, the result is the same: these revelations, the ones that can tell the reader the most about Hojeda's visionary conceptualization of the Church's future, remain ignored. The twentieth-century reader may come to these prophecies unsuitably schooled, but they probably offer the best access we have to the worldview of Hojeda and his contemporaries. As mentioned earlier, Hojeda's talent for interconnecting remote parts of his poem and for using early events to foreshadow later ones is quite remarkable, even when he is compared to the ancients. The effect of the linking strategy in *La Christiada* is so powerful that by the end of book 12, the reader has the impression of having read the same story in different versions multiple times. This is not a fortuitous perception, but a natural response to the deliberate redundancy achieved through the inclusion of innately repetitive hagiographic material that echoes key aspects of the Passion story. The five visions are not only intrinsically significant; they illustrate the importance of hagiography for the writing of a heroism that is not bellicose. These considerations shed new light on the structure and substance of Hojeda's epic.

"Despised for Christ's Sake:" *Pro vita apostolica*

Previous critics have not accurately stated the subject of the first prophecy in *La Christiada*. Meyer identifies some sources for this section, especially the *Golden Legend* of Jacobo de Voragine—like Hojeda, a Dominican—Ribadeneira's *Flos sanctorum* (*Glory of saints,*) and Marieta's *Historia eclesiástica de todos los santos de España* (*Ecclesiastic history of all the saints of Spain*). Pierce says that it is a view of "martyrs who followed Christ," yet none of the saints appearing in the vision was martyred.[19] They are, more precisely, exemplary religious who epitomize the perfection of monastic life, the *vita apostolica* that had become the next best thing to martyrdom in an era when the high-pitched fervor of the early perse-

---

19. Meyer, *Sources*, 87; Frank Pierce, introduction to *La Cristiada*, by Hojeda, 14. This is a late, much abbreviated edition of the poem done by Pierce; in it, the spelling of the title has been modernized.

cutions of Christians had waned.

The early Christians considered martyrdom the greatest blessing they could receive from God, and this belief persisted even in Golden Age Spain. Teresa de Jesús, for example, tried as a child to run away with her brother Rodrigo to Moorish lands so they could be beheaded and quickly enjoy the gifts of heaven that she had read about in stories of saints' lives (*Libro de la vida* 1.5). The frustration she experienced at finding practical obstacles in her path—in this case, the greatest problem was having parents—had been felt by the zealous ever since Christianity had become acceptable and even fashionable. With the Peace of Constantine (A.D. 313), the secular world entered the Church en masse, and many of the most fervent promptly left, withdrawing to the desert and to monasteries. (This, of course, was ultimately Teresa de Jesús's solution, as well.) There they took vows that, if strictly followed, had the desired effect of turning their austere daily lives into a kind of permanent martyrdom. Thus, they fulfilled their hearts' desire, to suffer in imitation of Christ.[20] In a roundabout way, therefore, Pierce was correct when he referred to these examples of religious life as "martyrs"; they intended their lives to be simulacra of martyrdom.

The backdrop of the first prophecy is the physical abuse of Jesus during the night before Caiaphas interrogates him. Deprived of sleep, slapped and spat upon, kicked in the forehead and taunted, Christ meditates on the "great fruits of his great patience" (los grandes frutos de su gran paciencia), a gallery of "men scorned for Christ's sake" (hombres . . . por Cristo despreciados, 4.73). This is a glimpse into a life led in submission to God's will, prophetic from the perspective of Christ's time, historical from Hojeda's vantage point. In it appear the founders of eremitical monasticism, Antony and Pachomius, and some founders of cenobitical monasticism, such as Dominic and Francis of Assisi. Also present are figures like John Damascene, whom Hojeda remembers for speaking out against heresy and for his persecution by coreligionists, Saints Teodora (Hojeda calls her "Teodoro" because she entered a monastery attired as a man), and Alexis, who fled marriage in the defense of chastity.

What these model Christians have in common is a lifestyle of mortification, humility, fortitude in refusing temptation, and rejection of worldly society which exemplifies the codes of Christian heroism in evidence in *La*

---

20. Joseph F. Chorpenning argues the point in "The Monastery, Paradise, and the Castle: Literary Images and Spiritual Development in St. Teresa of Avila." On the values of monastic life and its relation to martyrdom, see Christopher Brooke, *The Monastic World, 1000–1300: The Rise and Development of the Monastic Tradition;* Henry Chadwick, *The Early Church;* and M.-D.Chenu, *Nature, Man, and Society in the Twelfth Century: Essays on New Theological Perspectives in the Latin West.*

Christiada. Behind each of the figures is a story familiar to most seventeenth-century readers. As Elliott has demonstrated, it was not necessary to know the particulars of a saint's story because in significant ways, all the saints' lives followed a similar pattern, "in which was encoded much of the meaning of the story." By dint of this repetitious pattern, Hojeda can present the hagiographic material in almost telegraphic form, sometimes through a mere allusion meant to tip off the reader "in the know." Such a reader would bring to Hojeda's visionary words traditional ideas, many of them thoroughly medieval, about the monastic life and about asceticism, such as the belief that the desert was the way to Paradise, that the preservation of virginity was an equivalent of martyrdom, and that marriage was a chain that bound the religious to more onerous material and social concerns, which was why it had to be avoided.[21]

The saints' lives grew out of the Crucifixion narrative, which was their foundational text and also Hojeda's. In the Dominican's poeticization of his Passion, Christ, the ultimate model for all religious, looks into the future and sees the reward for his torment: men and women who apply their will to imitating him in suffering and patience. In this prophecy, it is as if Christ were looking through a glass to see himself reinterpreted by those who scorn the world and whom the world scorns. Hojeda refers to Antony and Pachomius, for example, as "Wise in the ways of heaven, crazy according to those of the earth" (Del cielo sabios, locos de la tierra, 4.74.2). Their activity, judged by secular standards, is irrational; it only makes sense seen in the context of Christ's example and thus of his agony. By the same token, however, the Redeemer's suffering acquires meaning only if future generations prove him right by following in his footsteps. In this sense, the hagiographic segments of *La Christiada* are not extraneous to the plot; they are, rather, essential to its fullness. For Hojeda, the monastic life was, in some respects, the finest legacy of the Incarnation.

"A Heaven Filled with Stars:" The Doctors of the Church

The second prophecy, that of the church doctors, occurs during Pilate's interrogation of Christ. Hojeda seizes this opportunity to open up the issue of Jesus' identity as Messiah. As indicated above, the debate about Christ's Messiahship is a recurrent theme throughout the epic and one that Spanish theologians debated as late as the fifteenth century in their effort to convert Jews and other unbelievers. The way Hojeda frames it, therefore, the utterance belongs to an evangelizing discursive formation. Book 5 opens with nature's plea for darkness to hide Jesus' degradation, a request that seems ironic in the context of a section that

21. Elliott, *Roads to Paradise*, 2, 137, 43, and 96.

consistently opposes Christ's "light" to the "dark" obstinacy of the incredulous. The antithesis of light and darkness that is the dominant semantic field of this prophecy has its roots in the New Testament (John 3:19, 2 Cor. 6:14), but it has been used to symbolize Christians and Jews, respectively, throughout the history of Christianity.[22] Jesus either does not respond to Pilate or he answers enigmatically, whereupon the poetic speaker chides the "learned of the law" present in the crowd who, with all their knowledge of Mosaic Law, have no lights to see that the man standing before them is God incarnate. In analogous fashion, Christ's light blinds Herod: "But with his immense light, he becomes confused and blind" (Mas con su inmensa luz se ofusca y ciega, 5.125.4). When the king of Judaea regains his equanimity, Hojeda makes him ridicule Jesus by dressing him as a ridiculous impostor king: "He perceived him as a king, but as a buffoon king" (Viéndole como rey, pero rey loco, 5.134.8). These words are strangely reminiscent of the epithet Hojeda gave to the desert fathers (*locos de la tierra*), and they serve to underscore Christ's role as the model for monastic detachment from worldly power and glory.

In keeping with the imagery of light and darkness, Hojeda presents the church doctors as heavenly stars: "an extended and shining heaven, drawn with infinite lights" (un estendido y refulgente cielo, / Con infinitas luzes dibujado, 5.146.5–6). The text opposes these "lights" of the Church to the scholars of the old law and claims that the former are infinitely superior. The church doctors shine brighter; they have greater sight and vision. Their wisdom, the text affirms, compensates for Herod's derision of Christ (5.147). Hojeda begins with the four Gospel writers whom he calls stars that reflect (because they record) the light of Christ, the eternal sun: "wise chroniclers of the sun who take part in its very light" (del sol eterno sabios coronistas, / Y dél mismo la luz participando, 5.150.3–4). In the first part of the vision, the poet mentions some of the church fathers, such as Dionysius the Areopagite, Gregory Nazianzen, John Chrysostom, and Saints Augustine, Jerome, and Ambrose. Continuing to develop the stellar imagery with which he started (he calls Augustine a "great fire"), Hojeda honors these church scholars for defending the doctrine of the Incarnation—a *conditio sine qua non* of Hojeda's brand of Christianity—for struggling against heresies within the Church, and for enduring defamation and exile, forms of mistreatment to which Hojeda himself was especially sensitive.

22. Williams, *Adversus Judaeos*, 263–64. On the opposition between light and darkness in anti-Semitic discourses, see Moshe Lazar, "The Lamb and the Scapegoat: The Dehumanization of the Jews in Medieval Propaganda Imagery," 40, 75 n. 21. The essay of Lazar and that of Nicholas de Lange, both cited in this chapter, appear in *Anti-Semitism in Times of Crisis*, ed. Sander L. Gilman and Steven T. Katz.

The rest of the vision classifies the church doctors according to religious order. Hojeda's attitude toward imperial power is uneasy, at best, but since this prophecy connects a theological elite to the Christian foundational story, its effect is to validate an ecclesiastical status quo that in the seventeenth century is not separate from the state. It is, therefore, eminently political. Pride of place goes to the Dominican theologians, among whom Hojeda names Dominic and Thomas Aquinas—"of the true theology, a mighty river of waters and shafts of light" (de la teología verdadera / Río de aguas y rayos caudaloso, 5:161.2–3)— Peter Martyr, the Valencian Vincent Ferrer, Raymund of Peñafort, founder of canon law, and several others. The only woman Hojeda includes is Catherine of Siena, a member of the Dominican lay sisterhood known for her mystical experiences. Among the Franciscans, he designates Francis of Assisi, Bonaventure, and John Duns Scotus. Meyer identifies the Augustinians and Mercedarians in the vision, which draws to a close with an octave dedicated to the Jesuits, though none is named, and a polite nod to "Carthusians, Bernardines, and Benedictines" (cartuxos y bernardos y benitos).[23]

This prophecy, lengthy compared to the others (it spans twenty-four octaves), shows Hojeda's tendency to represent matters of faith as uncompromising struggle between two antagonistic positions. His praise for the learned who put their talents at the service of the Church is as vehement as his rejection of those who remain locked in the "darkness" of ignorance or error. Even within the Church, Hojeda articulates doctrinal struggles in the terms of battle for the correct view. That is why he emphasizes the importance of patristic writings against heresy, though he also admires the fathers' translations of ancient texts, exegetical works on Scripture, and commentaries on Aristotle. He values preaching, as well. Some of the figures named here also appeared in the first vision and will reappear in the third. Changing only his angle, Hojeda repeats their names in order to achieve overlapping and redundancy, which hagiographic tradition valued positively, although the twentieth century generally does not.[24] In contrast to the first vision, what interests Hojeda here is Christian erudition. Through the specific connection he makes with the Passion story, the poet opposes Church "luminaries" to rabbinical tradition, which he depicts as punctilious about the letter of the old law and blind to the spirit of the new.

"Righteous yet Scorned:" The Rejection of the Just

In the middle of book 6, the narrator interrupts Gabriel's prophecy of the Resurrection to return to the Passion narrative just at the moment when

---

23. For Hojeda's attitude toward empire, see Davis, "Politics of Effacement." For the identifications of Augustinians and Mercedarians, see Meyer, *Sources,* 20-21.

24. Elliott, *Roads to Paradise,* 8.

Pilate offers the Jews the option of liberating Jesus or Barabbas. When the crowd demands Christ's Crucifixion, the poetic speaker ponders the injustice of their choice, affirming Jesus as the model and consolation for all who will suffer oppression in the Church. The prophecy of the persecuted just, which bears a thematic relationship to the vision of the early monastics, revisits figures appearing among the church doctors: Gregory Nazianzen, removed from the see at Constantinople; John Chrysostom, exiled at the hand of the Empress Eudoxia; and Jerome, who patiently endured the popularity of the heretics John, follower of Origen, and Rufinus. Hojeda also includes the apostle Peter, who tolerated Simon Magus (Acts 8:9–24).

This prophecy weighs the righteousness of the persecuted against ecclesiastical abuse of power, such as removal from one's post by opposition within the Church and banishment of religious—ironically, the very thing that would happen to Hojeda just five years after he completed his poem. Because the pious protagonists of this vision have fallen from favor, they are, as Hojeda says, "just men scorned" (*justos despreciados*) who endure affliction with the dignity that is their inheritance through Christ.

"A Lineage Vast and Marvelous:" An Army of Martyrs

In the 1960s, Thomas Greene observed that what is found in Hojeda is "the lonely and passive heroism of the afflicted saint, Milton's 'better fortitude of patience and heroic martyrdom unsung.'" Frank J. Warnke has also written that "martyrdom and sacrifice are glorified as acts of the highest heroism throughout the literature of the Baroque age, narrative as well as dramatic, in the works of both Catholic and Protestant authors." Indeed, seventeenth-century epic privileges spiritual struggle over acts of war, but there is nothing new about heroic narratives of martyrdom and sacrifice, which are as old as the Roman *acta* of the Christian martyrs. Neither may the baroque hero be easily qualified as "passive," because sacrifice, as it is defined in hagiography, necessitates agency. As Elliott argues, there is a deliberate choice involved in the decision to give one's life for the founding of the faith. Christ's avowal that "whoever loses his life will preserve it" (Luke 17:33) is one of Christianity's fundamental beliefs and paradoxes. For seventeenth-century epic poets, the battles of the *milites christiani* were in every way as dangerous as the hand-to-hand combat of Homeric heroes, and their consequences equally far-reaching. Already in the medieval epic, as Bernard Huppé has argued, the fundamental conception of the hero is always grounded in the *imitatio Christi*: "there can be but one Christian hero, and that is Christ. Whatever is heroic is in imitation of him."[25]

25. Greene, *Descent*, 238; Frank J. Warnke, *Versions of Baroque*, 191; Elliott, *Roads to Paradise*, 36; Bernard Huppé, "The Concept of the Hero in the Early Middle Ages," in

Although the Passion narrative is the basis for all Christian martyrology, the structure of the *passiones* is different from that of the Crucifixion story, primarily because Jesus was the protomartyr and he suffered alone. Elliott argues that the *passiones*, in contrast, are social texts written in celebration of a religious community and in affirmation of its ideals. The most dramatic moment of these stories of martyrdom is not the death itself, but the trial scene, which always occurs in an acutely polarized atmosphere. The Roman *acta* invariably entail a sharp confrontation between the Christian and a pagan tyrant. The latter coerces the former to recant, whereupon the Christian delivers an impassioned refusal. In Christ's own trial (the interrogations by Annas and Caiaphas, then Pilate and Herod), there is none of this bravado; according to the Gospels, Jesus says almost nothing in his own defense. The *passiones* also move more rapidly toward resolution than does the Crucifixion story. Elliott refers to them as "centripetal narratives" in which "All roads lead to a known destination—to Rome, whether literally or figuratively, and thence to the Heavenly Jerusalem."[26] However, though they diverge from it in important ways, the *passiones* are written in imitation of the founding murder, without which they would not be. What the Crucifixion narrative and the early Christian *passiones* have in common is a radical confrontation of the new religion and the old, followed by torture and death.

Martyrdom, therefore, is an organizing principle of monasticism. In their determination to imitate precisely the most difficult aspects of Christ's life, all religious strive to attain suffering and symbolic death. Therefore, when Hojeda links the vision of martyrs to the bloody scourging of Christ, which he details in harshly realistic terms (book 8), he inscribes the essence of monastic life into his poem. And though he briefly encapsulates the martyrs' stories, sometimes giving no more than the name and one or two remarkable details for each, he could count on his readers to supply the missing information.

When the flogging ends, the angel Michael appears to comfort Jesus by prophesying the legion of martyrs who will follow his lead:

> If your affliction is great and also your sorrow,
> great is the good and many the reasons
> for you to be happy, seeing the heroic deeds
> of those you engender today in your heart.
>
> (Si es grande tu aflicción, tu pena mucha,
> El bien es grande, y muchas las razones

Concepts of the Hero in the Middle Ages and the Renaissance, ed. Norman T. Burns and Christopher J. Reagan, 23.

26. Elliott, *Roads to Paradise,* 18, 38, 24.

Por qué alegrarte, viendo las hazañas
De los que engendras hoy en tus entrañas.)
8.109.5–8)

Divided into two sections according to gender, the list of martyrs contains both familiar and unfamiliar names. Among the men are Steven, Peter, Paul, and Sebastian; Hojeda depicts the manner of death of each according to tradition. The poet also includes a group of Spanish martyrs: Lawrence, Vincent of Zaragoza, and Hermenegildo, who converted to Christianity against his father's will. Hojeda writes in imitation of Prudentius, who claimed that St. Lawrence, while burning on a grill, had jokingly asked his executioner to turn him over so that his flesh could cook more evenly. The Dominican also includes Ignatius of Antioch, of whom it is said that he joyfully gave himself up to be eaten by lions in Rome, and others. Finally, there is an array of little-known Dominican martyrs.[27]

Among the women, the poet identifies Saints Catherine, sentenced to death on a spiked wheel but beheaded when it broke down, and Cecilia, submerged in a boiling bath, then sloppily decapitated. Hojeda honors Saints Agatha, Agnes, Lucy, and Margaret for their chastity, then turns to the Spanish martyrs: Eulalia of Mérida and Eulalia of Barcelona (thought to be one and the same); then Justa and Rufina, two sisters from Seville martyred for refusing to sacrifice to pagan gods.[28] Hojeda, a Sevillian himself, refers to his native city with evident satisfaction in Justa and Rufina's octave.

And both were from the marvelous city,
queen of splendid cities, whose feet are kissed
by Betis, the river that embraces her walls,
groaning under the rich weight of pure gold.

(Y ambas de la ciudad maravillosa,
Y reina de ciudades admirables,
Que Betis besa el pie y abraza el muro,
Gimiendo al rico peso de oro puro.)
(8.136)

Several characteristics recur in this vision of martyrs. In keeping with the propagandistic tendency to promote his country of origin and religious

27. For the ludic aspect of St. Lawrence's martyrdom, see Elizabeth B. Davis, "Hagiographic Jest in Quevedo: Tradition and Departure," 316–17; for the identity of the Dominican martyrs, see Meyer, *Sources*, 89–90.

28. For the identities of the Spanish female saints, see John J. Delaney and James Edward Tobin, *Dictionary of Catholic Biography*, 389, 639. For the importance of Saints Justa and Rufina as local models for gender ideals in early modern Spain, see Mary Elizabeth Perry, *Gender and Disorder in Early Modern Seville*, 33–37.

order, Hojeda grants a favored status to Spanish and Dominican martyrs. More important, however, he makes all the martyrs share a determination to die joyfully, which is a guiding principle in Christian hagiography. Another tenet is that greater suffering leads to greater glory. It is not uncommon to find stories of horrible executions in which the martyr jubilantly rushes toward death. Similarly, hagiographic paintings of the period show saints undergoing ghastly ordeals with a placid countenance. In places, Hojeda's epic reflects the festive tone that characterizes Christian hagiography, generally. His treatment of women martyrs is not as imaginative as one would have liked. The decision to safeguard their virginity almost always leads to their death, whereas the men's stories show a wider variety of situations and motives (though chastity was a keystone of monastic life for men, as well). In part, the redundant theme of female chastity can be traced to the repetitive nature of the poet's sources. In Hojeda, as in tradition, the tyrant invariably requires the woman to surrender her body or worship his gods; she always prefers death. Frequently, mutilation is a part of her ordeal.

Appropriately, the angel Michael is the first to admit that Christ has no need of this prophecy:

> "Innocent beauty, o martyrdoms of red,
> purple-colored roses among white lilies!
>
> But it would be impossible to relate them all,
> good Lord! You can see them,
> and in your divine eye revisit them,
> since it is you who will grant them such favors:
> I only wished to reveal them in outline form;
> You, who surpass us in learned conceits,
> will bring the appropriate shadows
> and brightness to their praise."
>
> ("¡O cándida beldad, rojos martirios,
> Purpúreas rosas entre blancos lirios!
>
> Pero será imposible referirlas
> Todas, ¡o buen Señor! Tú verlas puedes,
> Y en tu divina mente repetirlas,
> Pues tú les has de hacer tales mercedes:
> Sólo en bosquejo quise descubrirlas;
> Tú, que en sabios conceptos nos excedes,
> Acabarás de dar a sus loores
> Propias sombras y vivos resplandores.")
> (8.137–138)

All of this simply underscores the irony of "revealing" anything to God's Son, yet this is probably the most important of the prophetic visions of *La Christiada*. It was easy enough for Christians of later ages to idealize the first centuries of Christianity. Hojeda was not different from Teresa de Jesús and others who thought of early church times as the period of ultimate Christian experience. They imagined every day to have been dangerous and exhilarating. The Dominican's text transmits a certain nostalgia for times when ideas had to be defined and struggled for on a daily basis, times when defending one's beliefs could bring death. The organization, and later the reform, of monasticism was an attempt on the part of the most zealous Christians to recapture or rekindle some of that spirit. Teresa de Jesús's move to return her order to its primitive rule is a fitting example.

Needless to say, all of this enthusiasm about the idea of martyrdom stems from the imitation of Christ. Precisely because of its mimetic nature, its literally consuming desire to follow the Savior, martyrdom was viewed by monastics as the surrender of body and will to Christ and as an end to life on earth, a life they thought of as transitory and imperfect. Teresa de Jesús, for example, often complained that earthly life was an exile (*destierro*) from God. Martyrdom was thus a way to "go home," which is why the monastics longed for it and did their best to simulate it through constant self-sacrifice and mortification. In this sense, the prophecy of martyrs bridges the gap between the vision of monastic life and the main plot of Hojeda's poem as nothing else could have done.

"A Pious People Who Believe Him:" The Gentile Church

The last prophetic vision of *La Christiada* occurs in book 11, as Christ, burdened by the cross, makes his way toward Calvary. Hojeda's poem moves slowly here, focusing on each detail of the *via crucis* and meditating on the various stations of the cross. Seeing Jesus falter, the soldiers constrain Simon of Cyrene to carry the cross for him. The narrator, contemplating the person of Simon, celebrates in him the future of the Church, which, he says, will be the "Gentile Church," now that the Jews have rejected Christ. Pierce says that this is a vision of founders, and that is partially true.[29] In this passage, Jesus stares at Simon and sees in him a prefiguration, a "figure" (*figura*), of all the Gentiles who will take up the cross of Christ. Among these will be martyrs, confessors, virgins, penitents, servants, and noblemen, "all shining as they carry their crosses" (Y todos con su cruz resplandecientes, 11.75.4). Hojeda specifies the desert fathers, with whom he groups the apostle Mark, claiming that he found-

29. Pierce, introduction to *La Cristiada*, by Hojeda, 14.

ed the Essenes, an ascetic desert sect.[30] The poet then pays homage to
Saints Benedict, "blessed in name" (bendito en nombre, 11.81.5), Bernard
of Clairvaux, Dominic, Francis, Augustine, Jerome, Peter Nolasco,
Raymund of Peñafort, and Ignatius of Loyola. The Carmelite reformers
come into view, but only John of the Cross is named at first. Here, as in
the vision of martyrs, Hojeda reaffirms a traditional construct of monas-
ticism that is intrinsically gendered. Subsequently, the poet acknowl-
edges that there are women founders, but he names only Teresa de Jesús,
whose name appears at the end of the Gentile Church prophecy. Hojeda,
who probably had no way of knowing about St. Teresa's Jewish ancestry,
shows boundless admiration for her boldness in reforming the Spanish
Carmelites: "to Carmel, which was reduced to flat ground, you gave new
peaks, tall but also gentle/gentile" (Que al gran Carmelo, hecho humilde
llano, / Cumbres diste elevadas y gentiles, 11.94.5–6). There is a delicious
irony in the Dominican's pun about the gentility and "Gentileness" of
Teresa de Jesús, whose grandfather had done public penitence for
Judaizing in Toledo.

Whereas the interchange of light and darkness characterized the
poetic language of the vision of church doctors, it is the cross that gov-
erns the semantic field in this prophecy. The two visions manifest the
same anti-Jewish ethos, however. Taken together, they imply that the
Jews choose to remain in the "darkness" of Mosaic law, while the
Gentiles are open-minded and insightful. The latter "take up the cross"
that the Jews refuse to carry. Hojeda's iconic representation of the cross
in this vision is consistent with a primary narrative that has already
endorsed it as an adored object and established crucifixion, real or sym-
bolic, as the best imitation of Christ. In an obvious reference to Matthew
16:24 ("If anyone wants to come after me let him deny himself and bear
his cross and follow me"), Hojeda suggests that the Gentile founders,
among whom he counts Teresa de Jesús, bear their cross with élan. This
notion is compatible with the conception of monastic life as martyrdom
that reverberates all through *La Christiada*. St. Teresa is not necessarily
complaining when she writes that God wants her to have nothing but
"cross and more cross" (cruz y más cruz) in her life.[31]

In Gabriel's prophetic revelations to the Virgin (book 10), he explains
the meaning of his prophecy in these terms: the church before Pentecost

30. There is no basis for the attribution of the Essenes to Mark. The Essenes were a
pre-Christian group of Jews, brought into prominence in the 1940s by the discovery of
the Dead Sea Scrolls.
31. Teresa de Jesús, letter to Father Domingo Báñez, *Obras completas de Santa Teresa*,
918.

has eyes but cannot see, a tongue but cannot speak, feet but cannot walk, hands that cannot work (10.101); after the coming of the Spirit, the church will have all her faculties and use them fully. She will have "prelates and prophets and doctors, strong martyrs, simple confessors" (prelados y profetas y doctores, / Mártires fuertes, simples confesores, 10.108.7–8). As we have seen, all of these appear in the prophetic visions Hojeda includes in his epic. Taken together, and in relation to the main plot, these visions tell us how Hojeda chose to conceive of the church's future. By assembling the prophecies into one panoramic vista of church destiny, which the poet invokes as "the incomparable ordering of the Church" (El orden de la Iglesia incomparable, 11.154.6), we can view the overall design of the poem. Much more than an epic on the humanity of Christ, *La Christiada* is a compendium of the whole of church history. It is only by dint of ekphrasis, prophecy, and careful interlinking of parts that the writer could carry out such a monumental task. The extraordinary structure of the epic is a result of this elaborate articulation (enunciation, but also joining together) of bits of church history. Pierce credits Menéndez y Pelayo with the recognition that *La Christiada* "has the best plan of all epics in the language."[32] More than just a good plan, however, the interconnected parts of the epic facilitate a global understanding that far surpasses the Passion story. If the central theme of *La Christiada* is the Incarnation, then these prophecies reveal its legacy, which is the Christian view of universal history as Hojeda understood it. That is the source of their visionary power.

According to the belief system that informs this epic, monastic life as a simulacrum of martyrdom is the guarantor of the Church's future. The intentionality of the text is quite clear: it does not matter that the world despises or persecutes religious since the monastic state is fundamentally separate from the world, anyway. In a "recollection forward," Hojeda's Christ looks toward his imitators for fulfillment, just as they look back at him for authorization. The text is not eloquent on the subject of powerful earthly adversaries, such as the dubious characters of Caiaphas and Herod, because what it promotes is the renunciation of worldly power. Hojeda is not concerned with empire, unless it be the "empire of virtue," in the words of the angel Gabriel:

> And this is the holy kingdom of David,
> this, the true monarchy
> which I promised to you as an official emissary,
> saying that his Father would give it to him:
> This, the always longed-for empire

32. Pierce, "Hojeda, Religious Poet," 587.

and the pious house of the new Jacob:
kingdom of souls, empire of virtues,
house of tender peace, may you never change.

(Y éste es el reyno de David sagrado
Esta la verdadera monarquía
Que yo te prometí siendo legado,
Y dije que su Padre le daría:
Este el imperio siempre deseado,
Y del nuevo Jacob la casa pía:
Reyno de almas, imperio de virtudes,
Casa de tierna paz, nunca te mudes.)
(10.112)

For Hojeda, the only monarchy that matters is the "kingdom of souls," and the only way to live one's life is to sacrifice it, to withdraw from worldly concerns and attend to the Church's business. He and religious like him seem to welcome abuse of secular power as an opportunity to suffer as Christ had suffered. But there is also, in these visions of saints and martyrs, a patient indignation at the misapplication of power, particularly if it occurs within the Church. And it is perhaps telling that when Hojeda witnessed such an injustice in his own order, he did not passively resign himself to it. When Father Alonso de Armería, ecclesiastical visitor to Peru, removed the recently elected Brother Nicolás de Agüero from his post as Provincial, Hojeda joined in a protest. Quirós writes that after Armería's arrival in Lima (1612), Hojeda and Fray Juan de Lorenzana "in private conversations had disapproved of the conduct of the very reverend father Visitor and General Vicar . . . and they had been of the opinion that a meeting of the Chapter should be called" (habían desaprobado en conversaciones particulares el proceder del reverendísimo padre Visitador y Vicario General . . . y habían sido de opinión de reunir Capítulo).[33] Shortly thereafter, Armería divested Hojeda and Lorenzana of their honors and rights. The ecclesiastical visitor then relocated Hojeda to Cuzco, and a few months later, to Huánuco, a village that was then nothing more than a remote frontier outpost. Eventually the poet's privileges were restored, but he died at Huánuco (1615) before he could ever enjoy his rehabilitated state. Thus, in a poignant way, the stories of the exiled just in the hagiographic sections of *La Christiada* unknowingly prophesied the poet's own end: unjust persecution within the Church he loved.

Nor was Hojeda's case unique. Contemporary documents show that in colonial Peru, such ecclesiastical abuses of power were not infrequent.

---

33. Quoted in Corcoran, introduction to *La Christiada*, by Hojeda, xxxiii.

in correspondence to Philip III, the archbishop of Lima himself takes up the cause of religious relocated to remote villages.

> Great are the affronts which the brothers receive from their Superiors, whenever the latter see fit, and since the remedy is so far away that only with difficulty can those who have been offended come to seek it, the Superiors fear nothing, and with shamelessness they proceed like this every day. In this way, if, during the election of a Provincial or a Prior, a religious got on the wrong side of the one who was elected, the latter will vex and harrass him at various times, and send them [sic] to convents that are 300 leagues from this city, or more. And this on the worst roads in the world, and without providing them with money for their expenses, forcing them—unless they have parents or relatives who can provide for them—to beg for alms. Even though these brothers, out of desperation and worry because they do not have the wherewithal to get by, nor anyone to give it to them, run away and become apostates. It would be fitting for your Majesty to ask his Holiness to provide in these realms someone with Apostolic authority to whom the Religious could turn with their complaints and ask for justice. I beg your Majesty to have this looked into and considered; and provide whatever would be most appropriate to the service of God, so that these violent acts and oppressions which they endure can cease.

> (Grandes son los agravios, que los frailes reciben de sus Superiores, cuando a ellos les parece, y como el remedio está tan lejos, y con dificultad los agraviados pueden acudir a pedirle, no temen, y con más rotura proceden en esto cada día, de manera, que si un Religioso faltó en la elección de Provincial o Prior a quien salió con el oficio, el tal le ha de vejar y molestar por momentos, y enviarles a conventos que distan de esta ciudad trescientas leguas, y más, y de los Peores caminos del mundo, y esto sin proveerles del gasto que han de hacer, obligándoles a que si no tienen padres, o deudos, que lo provean, lo pidan de limosna, y aunque de desesperados y apurados de no tener con que aviarse, ni quien se lo dé, se huyan y anden hechos Apóstatas; Convendría que V. M. se sirviese de pedir a su S. proveyese que en estos Reynos hubiese persona con autoridad Apostólica a quien acudiesen los Religiosos a quejarse y pedir su justicia; suplico a V. M. lo mande Ver y considerar; y proveer lo que más convenga al servicio de Dios, y para que cesen las violencias y opresiones que padecen.)[34]

---

34. Archivo General de Indias, Seville, Audiencia de Lima, 301 (hereafter abbreviated AGI, Lima, with *legajo* following), Bartolomé Lobo Guerrero (Archbishop of Lima) to Philip III, April 18, 1613. The *Catálogo de Pasajeros Abordo* at the AGI contains no record of [H]Ojeda's embarcation at Seville or of his exit from Spain.

In another letter written two years later, the archbishop specifically complains about Father Alonso de Armería, the man who caused Hojeda's misfortunes:

> Father Alonso's intent was to deceive both of us, as he did with his feigned hypocrisy, because later on so much shamelessness was uncovered in the matter of greed, selling Doctrines, in other things both tremendous and ugly, because his friars recount so many things—the same friars who vouched for him at the time—, that they offend the ears, and these things are deserving of exemplary punishment, if they are true.

> (. . . su intento de dicho Fr. Alonso fue engañarnos a ambos, como lo hizo con su simulada hipocresía, pues después descubrió tanta desventura en materia de codicia vendiendo las Doctrinas, en otras cosas enormes y feas, que son tantas las que dicen sus frailes que lo abonaron entonces, que ofenden los oídos, dignos de castigo ejemplar si son verdad.)[35]

The letter is specific enough to beg the question of whether or not reports about the ecclesiastical visitor's mistreatment of Agüero, Hojeda, and Lorenzana reached the archbishop's ears.

Such evidence sheds new light on the case of Hojeda's removal to Cuzco and then to Huánuco. It also substantiates multiple cases of religious who suffered abuse in the American viceroyalties but were too far from Spain to have ready access to appeal. If such events were as frequent as the archbishop's letters to Philip III suggest, Hojeda's case can be generalized to include numerous priests in the region who had to put up with similar indignities. This fact helps to account for the poet's special sensitivity to issues of religious persecution within the Church, an attitude in evidence throughout *La Christiada*.

The "Other" Scapegoat: Jew-Hatred in *La Christiada*

The last section of this chapter will explore an issue that previous scholars of *La Christiada* have not raised: Hojeda's rearticulation of a very old discursive formation, that of anti-Semitism, from his position as a Dominican missionary in colonial Peru, a place with a small Jewish population and an increasingly influential "New Christian" or *converso* community. At a time when writers of Spanish-language epic such as Alonso de Ercilla had already immortalized Amerindian deeds of resistance and

---

35. AGI, Lima, 301, Bartolomé Lobo Guerrero (Archbishop of Lima) to Philip III, April 25, 1615.

treachery, Hojeda appears unwilling to engage the nearby indigenous in a literary way, exploiting instead a well-established scripting of alterity to vilify the Jews in his poem. Although his subject matter places obvious constraints on his ability to incorporate New World themes into his poem, we have seen that the poet is capable of including a wide range of materials that depart from the epic's first narrative through ekphrasis and prophecy. He took the indigenous deities seriously enough to treat one of them, the Araucanian god Eponamón, as a devil.[36] Yet in *La Christiada* as a whole, Hojeda's gaze is fixed not on the Andean peoples around him, but on a Jewish "other" that he represents in deprecatory terms conditioned by theology and by tradition.

The appearance of the earliest accounts of Christian martyrdom in the fourth and fifth centuries, as mentioned above, coincided roughly with Christianity's new hegemonic status after the Peace of Constantine. These hagiographic narratives were one cultural means by which Christianity rewrote its identity at the very moment when the official persecution of Christians was drawing to a close. Another was through the creation of a new enemy, no longer pagan Rome, against which to array itself. So it is that in the same period when the martyrs' stories were recorded, Christianity constructed a new adversary—rather, it revived and embellished an ancient one—through the complex discourse of Jew-hatred that, in Christian Europe, eventually became the ultimate discourse of otherness.[37] It is probably not fortuitous, therefore, that both of these discursive types, hagiography and anti-Semitism, appear inextricably bound together in *La Christiada*.

First, a word about terminology. The terms *anti-Semitism* and *Jew-hatred* are used interchangeably in the following pages, though the latter is older and less pseudoscientific than the former. The particular brand of anti-Semitism that appears in *La Christiada* is fundamentally Christian, and it is largely traceable to patristic sources. But as Yehuda Bauer has shown, many claims that modern anti-Semitism makes about Jewish "racial" difference, the notion of a Jewish "conspiracy," and so on, have precedents in traditional Christian Jew-hatred. Although historians tend to analyze Judeophobia as a historically specific phenomenon, it is a belief system that has endured for centuries, partly by recycling and expanding its essential

---

36. Francisco Javier Cevallos, "Don Alonso de Ercilla and the American Indian: History and Myth," 18 n. 11.

37. Sander L. Gilman and Steven T. Katz argue that the "image of the Jew . . . not his/her reality" is necessary for Western self-definition, "an identity reflected in the structure of the Western fantasy about Europe's ultimate other, the Jew." See the introduction to their edition, *Anti-Semitism in Times of Crisis*, 1.

elements. As Lazar states, "In spite of the differences between the traditional articulations of antisemitic propaganda and modern ones which include racial overtones, the commonality of ideas and imagery as well as their dehumanizing purpose and effect are a clear testimony of continuity rather than of rupture."[38] Both because of this diachronic persistence and because none of these terms is completely free of semantic conflict, the terms *Jew-hatred* and *anti-Semitism* can be used more or less interchangeably.

It could be argued that Hojeda's attitude toward the Jews is derogatory because epic, in general, necessitates an odious "other" against whom the hero may prove himself superior. So, for example, Kurth adduces the need for a strong Satan to oppose Christ in Milton's *Paradise Lost*.[39] In primary epic, however, the genre still shows ample room for sympathetic representation of an enemy one fully expects to defeat. Homer's depiction of a disadvantaged adversary, for example, tends to be generally flattering. He calls Hektor glorious and handsome, a loving husband and father, a dutiful son. Hektor and Andromache's farewell at the Skaian gates is one of the most poignant moments in the *Iliad*, and the dragging of the Trojan warrior's corpse through the streets (22.395–405) tarnishes, rather than enhances, Achilleus's victory. That the Homeric representations of winners and losers should be so complex suggests a rejection of overly simplistic dualism in the characterizations of opposing sides since the very beginning of Western epic tradition. According to this logic, Hojeda could have gotten away with a less opprobrious depiction of the enemy, yet the only Jews he represents in a favorable light are the few (Gamaliel, Nicodemus, and Joseph of Arimathea) who rejected their faith because they "saw the light" of Christianity's eventual triumph.

Another way of looking at this issue is to say that Hojeda writes anti-Jewishness into *La Christiada* because it already appears in one of his sources, the Gospels. There is a grain of truth in this idea. Historians such as James Parkes, Marcel Simon, and Jules Isaac have long sought the roots of anti-Semitism in the early church.[40] Rosemary Ruether traces the "anti-Judaic myth" to central documents of Christianity, and Gilman and Katz trace the negative stereotype of the Jew directly to the Gospels,

38. Yehuda Bauer, "In Search of a Definition of Antisemitism," 10–11. Bauer's essay, as well as that of Jennifer Golub cited in this chapter, appear in *Approaches to Antisemitism: Context and Curriculum*, ed. Michael Brown. See also Lazar, "The Lamb and the Scapegoat," 78 n. 46.

39. Kurth, *Milton and Christian Heroism*, 118.

40. See James Parkes, *The Conflict of the Church and the Synagogue: A Study in the Origins of Antisemitism*; Marcel Simon, *Verus Israël: Étude sur les relations entre Chrétiens et Juifs dan l'empire romain*; and Jules Isaac, *Genèse de l'antisémitisme*.

where there is a gradual movement away from Jewishness as a positive marker of difference, culminating in the reduction of Jewish history to a "preamble" to the coming of Christ.[41] *La Christiada*, like so many religious texts of this period, establishes direct typological relationships between Hebrew Scripture and the Christian Lectionary. In this sense, Hojeda's poem takes for granted the notion that Jewish history is an important pre-text for Christian truth, nothing more.

But, while it is undeniable that the Gospels assign a negative role to the Jews in the Passion story, it was later exegesis of the New Testament that predisposed Christians, and certainly ones like Hojeda, to actively read anti-Jewish ideology into the gospel story. Ironically, Christianity's very similarities with Judaism strained the relationship between the two faiths almost from the beginning. In this context, Christians wrote against Judaism at least in part to establish their own separate cultural identity. In this spirit, Bauer observes that Christianity "emerged from Judaism and in opposition to it." Although it may no longer seem self-evident that Christianity and Judaism had to oppose one another, the need to distinguish the Christian faith from Judaism was undoubtedly quite strong in the early church. Lazar argues that "In its enterprise of demonizing non-Christian reality, adopting the structure and language of ancient Near Eastern, platonic, and gnostic dualisms (spirit/matter, sons of light/sons of darkness, *agnostos theos/demiurgos*), emerging Christianity engages in a relentless anti-Jewish campaign as part of its differentiation process from ancient Israel and its Torah."[42] Lazar, of course, is talking about a young faith striving to define itself negatively: Christianity is whatever Judaism is not. The remarkable thing is that so much of this militant spirit survives in the early seventeenth-century text of Diego de Hojeda, in the vision of church doctors, and in many other places.

Not all of Hojeda's sources were Christian. Meyer, interestingly, has traced some passages about Jews to Josephus Flavius's *The Jewish War*, which was the subtext for Hojeda's prophetic vision of the siege and destruction of Jerusalem by Titus (A.D. 70).[43] Josephus was not a pagan writer, but a Jewish military commander who surrendered to the Romans and wrote, under Roman supervision, what is considered to be the only eyewitness account of the siege of Jerusalem. Meyer documents

---

41. For some implications of Ruether's *Faith and Fratricide*, see Nicholas de Lange, "The Origins of Anti-Semitism: Ancient Evidence and Modern Interpretations," 27. On anti-Semitism in the Gospels, see Gilman and Katz, introduction to *Anti-Semitism in Times of Crisis*, 17.

42. Bauer, "In Search of a Definition," 15; Lazar, "The Lamb and the Scapegoat," 40

43. Meyer, *Sources*, 61–65.

Hojeda's borrowings from Josephus: the deleterious effect of Jewish fac-
tions on the defense of the city (*Christiada* 10.20–22, *Jewish War* 4.7.1 *pas-
sim*); the story according to which Mary, Eleazar's daughter, ate her child
so that the Romans could not enslave him (*Christiada* 10.28–29, *Jewish War*
6.3.4); unheeded warnings God sent to Jerusalem before its destruction
(*Christiada* 10.44–45, *Jewish War* 6.5.3); Arabian dissection of Jewish
deserters who had swallowed pieces of gold to smuggle their wealth out
of the city (*Christiada* 10.31, *Jewish War* 5.13.4); and numbers of Jews who
perished by fire in the Temple (*Christiada* 10.35, *Jewish War* 6.5.2).

What Meyer does not discuss is the strong anti-Jewish ideology that
permeates the particular episodes Hojeda takes from Josephus. The accu-
sation of factionalism is a means of characterizing the Jews as contentious
and treacherous. Ercilla levels this same charge at the Araucanian Indians
in order to make Spain's conquest of Chile appear inevitable, but Western
representation of Jews as "treacherous, disloyal, and the cause of discord
and dissension" antedates disparaging depictions of Amerindians by cen-
turies. Similarly, the imputation of cannibalism—in the specific way it
appears in both Josephus and Hojeda—is eerily similar to the patristic
accusation of Jewish sacrifice of Christian children in imitation of the
Crucifixion, a phenomenon Lazar refers to generally as "the ritual murder
libel." Goldberg points out that Jewish and female identities blend in the
story of Eleazar's daughter, who appears as "an unnatural, less-than-
human creature."[44] The story of the mother who eats her child had been
recycled in peninsular literature much earlier (it appears in the *Primera
Crónica General* 1.135), but its dehumanizing and demonizing functions
remain equally effective when Hojeda employs it at the beginning of the
seventeenth century. The criticism that Jerusalem ignored God's warning
is Hojeda's reworking of a traditional Christian appropriation of Old
Testament language of prophetic wrath. In the hands of Christian theolo-
gians, this language came to signify Israel's unwillingness to recognize
Christ as the Messiah and God's ensuing rejection of Israel. Finally, the
Arabian murder of Jews who transported pieces of gold out of Jerusalem
by swallowing them joins together two characteristics commonly associat-
ed with the negative stereotype of the Jew: avarice and astuteness used to
deceive others. Both texts, *La Christiada* and *The Jewish War*, indict the
Arabian soldiers, not the Jews, for greed. However, since the Jews had
used deception to slip the gold out of the city, both texts imply Jewish lust

44. Harriet Goldberg, "Two Parallel Medieval Commonplaces: Antifeminism and
Antisemitism in the Hispanic Literary Tradition," 95, 107. Goldberg's essay, which I cite
several times in this chapter, appears in *Aspects of Jewish Culture in the Middle Ages*, ed.
Paul. E. Szarmach. See also Lazar, "The Lamb and the Scapegoat," 57.

for wealth, as well as Jewish treachery. When the Arabians cut open the deserting Jews to take their gold, this perhaps represents an extreme, monstrously brutal form of the "out-Jewing of the Jew," a traditional folktale motif that appears in *El Cantar de Mío Cid* and other places.[45] In Hojeda, a presumably superior Western narrator can look on while the Orientalized Arabians commit atrocities against equally despicable Jews. In summary, Hojeda's recycling of Josephus already brings important components of an anti-Semitic discursive formation into view: the charge of Jewish factionalism and treachery, the ritual murder libel, prophetic anti-Judaism, and the image of the Jew as a wily swindler.

It was the church fathers, however, who developed a complex anti-Jewish ideology that has had a lasting effect on the writing of alterity in the West, the consequences of which are especially manifest in Hojeda's epic. As noted above, the elaboration of patristic anti-Semitism is particularly intense between the second and fourth centuries, a period that coincides with Christianity's ascendancy and with the recording of early stories of Christian martyrdom. If patristic Jew-hatred is the dominant way of writing the "other," the stories of martyrdom and persecution serve as a means to write a heroic identity for the Western "self." These two constructs are interdependent and they both serve Western cultural needs. However, Christian determination to forge an identity for itself by appealing to the foundational texts of the faith is not an ideological battle that takes place in isolation from political reality. With the Peace of Constantine, Christianity achieves enough civil power for theology to influence Roman law, thereby translating myth into legal codes that directly impact Jewry throughout the empire. Anti-Semitism now becomes "part of the public policy of the state."[46]

In the fourth century, as Lazar notes, "Anti-Judaism becomes more forcefully a doctrinal necessity, a guide for the 'teaching of contempt.'" In christological exegesis, there is in evidence a "symbolization process of both good and evil" that places the Jew in the realm of the diabolic along with Satan in his many disguises: Lucifer, Antichrist, Dragon, Dog, and Woman. During the Middle Ages, this same symbolization process was expanded to include the typological use of bestiaries, negatively applied to the Jew to produce an association between Jewishness and all sorts of poisonous or lowly animals: manticores, serpents, vipers, aspics, basiliscs,

45. On Israel's supposed apostasy and God's rejection of her, and also for the notion of "prophetic anti-Judaism," see Lazar, "The Lamb and the Scapegoat," 43. On the Jew's "wiliness" and the "out-Jewing of the Jew," see Goldberg, "Two Parallel Medieval Commonplaces," 100–101.

46. De Lange, "The Origins of Anti-Semitism," 35.

goats, pigs, ravens, vultures, bats, scorpions, vermin, cormorants, hyenas, and jackals.[47] For Chrysostom, Prudentius, and many others, the realm of the diabolic is also that of darkness and obstinacy, fundamentally opposed to the Christian "light" that Jews have rejected.[48] The works of these two men and those of Origen and Augustine, Hippolyte, Gregory of Nyssa, and Jerome repeatedly identify the Jew with the Devil, "a mythical image from which all the other negative attributes were to be genealogically derived: liar, deceiver, agent of corruption and debauchery, treacherous, poisoner and killer, horned beast, etc." Chrysostom's homilies against the Jews (*Adversus Judaeos*) probably contain more anti-Semitic vituperations than any other treatise from this period. Chrysostom, who was especially vexed with Judaizing Christians, blamed the Jews for slaying the Christ and explicitly called the diaspora God's punishment for the Crucifixion. These are convictions that permeate *La Christiada*. Chrysostom character-izes the Jews as dogs, stiff-necked and gluttonous, and as drunkards. He calls their synagogues "a brothel and a theater . . . a den of robbers and a lodging for wild beasts."[49] At the same time that this complex process of symbolization develops, the church fathers' pronouncements about the Jews grow less metaphoric and more aggressively propagandistic, creating the impression among the general populace that the culprits are not New Testament characters, but the "Jews living in their midst." The diaboliza-tion and dehumanization of the real Jew was thus accomplished. Christianized Europe now had what Lazar names "a memorable land-scape of fear" against which to imagine its own identity.[50]

Hojeda's anti-Semitism stems from his own Dominican predecessors and from this tradition of Jew-hatred that the church fathers enunciated so clearly and forcefully. In keeping with patristic Judeophobia, a filter through which he views (and rewrites) the gospel narrative, Hojeda identifies Judas Iscariot as the ultimate traitor, a disciple turned into a common thief motivated only by greed ("Ratero ladroncillo mal usado," 7.30.6). Attaching the typological epithet "modern Cain" (*Caín moderno*) to the Judas figure (7.63.7), the narrator links the accusations of envy and

47. The phrase *teaching of contempt* is Jules Isaac's; Lazar quotes it in "The Lamb and the Scapegoat," 40; he discusses the association of the Jew with diabolical forces and animals on 39, 56.

48. For the Christian association of Jews with darkness, see Williams, *Adversus Judaeos*, 133, 212.

49. For the identification of the Jew with the Devil, and for Chrysostom's charac-terization of Jewish synagogues, see Lazar, "The Lamb and the Scapegoat," 45, 48. See also Williams, *Adversus Judaeos*, 134.

50. On the fear of the real, not the metaphorical, Jew, see Lazar, "The Lamb and the Scapegoat," 44, 40.

fratricide with Iscariot, who stands in synecdochic relationship to the Jews, in general. In the same vein, Hojeda elsewhere refers to the tribes of Israel as "vile lineage of Adam" (linaje vil de Adán), and "lineage justifiably damned" (linaje con razón maldito).

By the same logic, the poet connects the vision of future heresies to Judas (7.64–117), whose contentious spirit reinforces the negative stereotype of Jewish factionalism and internal strife that appeared in kernel form in Josephus Flavius and arises throughout *La Christiada*. Hojeda expands the accusation of Jewish dissension to include some of the "enriched dehumanizing lexicon" that typified fourth-century patristic anti-Jewish propaganda.[51] For example, not content with describing the Jewish sects at the high priests' council as "dissenting" (*discrepantes*) among themselves, albeit "of one accord, when it comes to vices" (todos conformes en los vicios, 5.11), the narrator says that envy of Christ has blinded Caiaphas, who is "more ignorant than beasts" (más que las bestias bruto, 5.7.1). He then makes a sustained comparison between the Jews and "poisonous animals" (*animales ponzoñosos*), "new monsters" (*nuevos monstruos*) who snuff out a candle in the dark of night, not because they are enamored of it but because they are envious of its light (5.15–16). The face of Jesus, in contrast, mysteriously subdues savages: "With a humble face and a restrained look, he tames wild beasts and conquers asps" (Con rostro humilde y mesurada vista, / Que amansa fieras y áspides conquista," 5.20.7–8). It is not mere coincidence that Virués applies this same language to Philip II in *El Monserrate*.

Later, when Christ first contemplates the cross, Hojeda inserts an extended allegory on the figure of Charity. For her sake alone, Jesus allows the Pharisees and the Saducees, here likened to wild serpents and wretched dogs, respectively (*fieras serpientes, viles perros*, 11.39.1–4), to abuse him. Because it reinforces the symbolizing process that connects the Jew to the diabolic, Hojeda's sustained use of the analogy between the Jews and venomous creatures belongs to a separate category from the derogatory epithets he customarily uses to refer to the Jewish high priests—"savage people," "obstinate Hebrew council," "homicidal patriarchs" (*gente fiera, concilio pertinaz hebreo, patriarcas homicidas*)—or to the Jewish people, as a whole—"savage mob," "hateful people," "rough people," "vile Hebrew riffraff" (*turba fiera, odiosa gente, pueblo rudo, vil canalla hebrea*, etc.). When Hojeda composed *La Christiada*, these epithets were little more than topoi, and we may read them as generic ways of referring to Jews in early modern Spain and her colonies. By dint of repetition, however, they were still very effective for underscoring the bloodthirstiness and depravity that patristic writing had ascribed to the Jews much earlier.

51. Lazar, "The Lamb and the Scapegoat," 50.

During the long section that recounts Pilate's interrogation of Christ, Hojeda deploys a thoroughly traditional opposition between church and synagogue. The book of Revelation had already confused the Jewish temple with the "synagogue of Satan" (3:9), but it was the church fathers who articulated the opposition between church and synagogue as an intractable difference that they expressed in the terms of confrontation. The best example is the fifth-century pseudo-Augustinian *De Altercatione Ecclesiae et Synagogae* (*Dispute between the Church and the Synagogue*), but Chrysostom and others develop the opposition between synagogue and church as a confrontation between the Old (veiled) and the New (unveiled) Testaments that persists as allegory in medieval plays and other art forms. Lazar documents that in these allegories, *Ecclesia* usually appears as a young woman dressed in gold and carrying a chalice, which symbolizes the New Testament, as well as a cross. *Synagoga*, in contrast, appears as an old woman dressed in a dark, tattered tunic. A black veil covers her face. She carries a broken spear and two inverted tablets signifying the Mosaic Law and the Hebrew Scriptures. In medieval plays based on the confrontation, *Synagoga* usually drops the tablets and escapes from the church in tears.[52]

Hojeda's text, here as in so many other places, assumes the reader's familiarity with the conventions of the traditional confrontation:

> And if the inexorable synagogue,
> previously his mother and now his stepmother,
> does not adore the venerable Kir g she awaited
> for so long, seeing him dressed this way,
> the Church, beloved spouse and loving daughter
> of God, lady of a thousand earthly princes,
> receives, embraces and worships him
> with constant faith and sincere charity.

> (Y si la sinagoga inexorable,
> Antes su madre y su madrastra ahora,
> Al que tanto aguardó Rei venerable,
> Por verlo en este trage no le adora;
> La Iglesia, cara esposa e hija amable
> De Dios, y de mil príncipes señora,
> Le recibe y le abraza y le venera
> Con fe constante y caridad sincera.)
> (9.100)

La Christiada telescopes the whole altercation into one octave that calls *sinagoga* Christ's first mother, now turned "stepmother" because she does

52. On the *Dispute between the Church and the Synagogue*, see Williams, *Adversus Judaeos*, 326–38. On medieval theatrical representations of the dispute, see Lazar, "The Lamb and the Scapegoat," 52–53.

not recognize him in this pitiful guise. Badly beaten and wearing a crown of thorns, he does not look like the kind of Messiah she awaited, Hojeda implies. On the other hand, *Iglesia* appears as Jesus' wife and daughter who adore him. Hojeda's succinct version of the confrontation is obviously designed to assert Church's flawlessness and superiority over Synagogue and her law.

These examples suffice to suggest that Hojeda's brand of anti-Semitism conforms ideologically to a long tradition of patristic writings against the Jews. Although it feels virulent to the twentieth-century reader, the Judeophobia that surfaces in *La Christiada* is not exceptional or even particularly remarkable compared to that of the church fathers, themselves, or to other texts of the same period.

There are, however, one or two elements in Hojeda's anti-Jewish utterances that do not seem traditional. One is the accusation of Jewish uncleanliness, which Hojeda insinuates by making reference to a peculiar smell that the Jews carry with them into captivity. When Christ sees a prophetic vision of the destruction of Jerusalem and the Jewish diaspora, the narrator remarks that the Jews who go into exile are "loathsome, heads bowed, deep in thought, with an offensive smell and ugly tremors" (Infames, cabizbaxos, pensativos, / Con mal olor y con temblores feos, 10.41.5–6). This peculiar odor, which Hojeda apparently associates with the mark God put on Cain for killing his brother, Abel (Genesis 4:15), is an example of a dehumanizing strategy that generally accompanies the construction of a racial or ethnic stereotype. In this vein, Gilman and Katz remark that

> This fantasy of difference was played out within the social reality of the Middle Ages, with the creation of distinctive clothing required for Jews and, indeed, in the institution of the "ghetto" as a locus that labeled its inhabitants as Jews. If the "Jew's hat" was grotesque, if the "ghetto" stank of garbage and effluvia, that was because the Jews looked and smelled different. Thus the boundary between the self and the Other was drawn. The Jew was made to look different.[53]

Hojeda ties the notion of squalor to the thoroughly traditional image of the "wandering Jew."

The connection Hojeda makes between Jewishness and effeminacy does not have obvious origins in the writings of the church fathers. In *La Christiada* this idea finds subtle expression at the textual site of Simon Peter's denial of Christ after the arrest (based on Matthew 26:69–75) and his repentance, an episode that in Hojeda spans thirty octaves. The disciple

---

53. Gilman and Katz, introduction to *Anti-Semitism in Times of Crisis*, 6.

warms himself beside a fire outside Caiaphas's palace, and the flames seem to soften his resolve: "The fire with its burning flatters him, and little by little, melts him like wax softened by a light" (El fuego con su ardor le lisongea, / Y poco a poco ardiendo, le consume, / Como a la cera que la luz derrite, 4.91.5–7). Peter is already like soft wax when a servant girl, described as "naughty" (revoltosa) and "hungry to learn the latest news" (De saber novedades codiciosa, 4.92.1–3), asks him if he is not one of Christ's followers. There is a specific link between the female figure and the whole symbolizing process of evil mentioned above in regard to the Jew: the woman is a doorkeeper (portera) with a venomous tongue and a "poisonous look" (vista ponzoñosa, 4.92.7–8). Hojeda explicity likens her to the poisonous serpent who tempted "our mother," Eve. Nevertheless, Peter is exhorted not to let her intimidate him, since she is no more than a lone woman: "She is a woman, Peter, and she's alone; don't be taken aback" (Mujer es, Pedro, y sola; no te assombre, 4.93.20). Hojeda's version of the apostle's denial thus participates in a poetic tradition that pokes fun at Peter's cowardice by exploiting the sexual innuendo inherent in the situation.[54] La Christiada, however, takes the traditional derision of Peter a step further by linking his lack of bravery to the Hebrew name Simon, thereby suggesting that cowardice turns the rock (Peter) back into a "soft" Jew:

> . . . . he turns back
> from good to evil, and from his own name,
> a name of bravery, he reverts to detested weakness;
> therefore, let Peter be called Simon from now on.
>
> (. . . . . da la buelta
> Del bien al mal, y de su propio nombre,
> Qu'es de valor, a la flaqueza infame;
> Por tanto Pedro ya Simón se llame.)
> (4.93.5–8)

Penitence, however, eventually redeems the disciple, restoring his "hardness" along with his Christian name: "In this way he cried, resolved in tears, the good Simon turned into Peter" (Assí llorava, en lágrimas resuelto, / El buen Simón en Pedro convertido, 4.117.1–2).

The association of Jewishness with effeminacy, though not especially traditional, has an ideological connection with the Orientalizing tendencies of epic representations of otherness, as we have seen elsewhere. It may have been a particularly Spanish phenomenon. As Mariscal shows, in early mod-

---

54. Quevedo has an ovillejo on St. Peter's repentance that is filled with such sexual innuendo; see Obra Poética 1:335. On the relationship of this "disrespectful" poem to the lyric tradition of the tears of repentance, see Davis, "Hagiographic Jest," 327.

ern Spain, Jews and other groups considered "defective" were routinely assimilated into the woman's side of a construct according to which the female body was understood to be "naturally subservient" to that of the male. Furthermore, menstruation was commonly attributed to Jewish males.[55] Indeed, in Hojeda's version of the denial and repentance, it is a serpentlike woman who lures the favored disciple dangerously close to the soft Jewishness out of which Jesus had presumably called him. What the Dominican textualizes in this brief allusion to Peter's Jewish name is the supposed demonic force of woman and Jew together, set against a Christian, male self that must remain vigilant lest he backslide into a perilous "otherness" marked by both gender and ethnicity.

These are only some of the most striking elements in Diego de Hojeda's elaborate anti-Semitic discursive practice. In conclusion, let us ponder the purpose and the effect of the poet's decision to look away from nearby Amerindians in order to reenunciate the older, more established alterity of anti-Semitism from a place where the Jewish population was not demographically significant, but where there was a community of "New Christians," or converts from Judaism (*conversos*) that was beginning to play an important economic role in the city of Lima. The first consideration is that a large target group does not have to be present for racializing discourses to be mobilized. De Lange cites *The Merchant of Venice*, "written three hundred years after the Jews were banished from England," as an example of how anti-Jewish prejudice can continue to spread in the absence of Jews. In the same vein, Golub documents widespread negative perceptions of Jews in modern Japan, a country with a very small Jewish population.[56] One ramification of this is that the "truths" of Hojeda's text have as much to do with the imposition of Western belief systems as they do with the teaching of doctrine.

The second and more important consideration, however, is that the persecution of Judaizers was on the rise in Peru during the period in which Hojeda wrote *La Christiada*. During these years and immediately following, most of those denounced to the Inquisition on the pretext of Judaizing were identified as Portuguese, and they were generally considered to be converts to Christianity. Some of them, but not all, seem to have been recent arrivals from Buenos Aires, Brazil, Mexico, and a few other places. They were

55. George Mariscal, *Contradictory Subjects: Quevedo, Cervantes, and Seventeenth-Century Spanish Culture*, 42–43.

56. On the efficacy of invoking anti-Semitic discourses in places without Jews, see de Lange, "The Origins of Anti-Semitism," 34; and Jennifer Golub, "Antisemitism without Jews," 119. Judith Laikin Elkin grapples with this same issue in "Imagining Idolatry: Missionaries, Indians, and Jews."

almost all successful merchants in Lima, where they sold everything from "brocade to coarse woolen cloth, from diamonds to cumin." There is a clear indication that the Portuguese *conversos* were also involved in the lucrative slave trade: according to a letter from the period, they sold everything "from the most contemptible Negro of Guinea to the most precious pearl" (desde el más vil negro de Guinea hasta la perla más preciosa).[57] Their economic status alone would have made them tempting targets for the Inquisition, which could confiscate their wealth once they were arrested. Toward the end of the sixteenth century, a few of these *portugueses* were put to death, but the suppression of crypto-Judaism began in earnest in the early 1600s. This period of heightened anxiety about Judaizing led to the 1635 "great conspiracy" (*la complicidad grande*), in which the Inquisition rounded up some seventy Portuguese *judaizantes*. The whole affair culminated in the huge *auto de fe* of Lima in January 1639. These last tragic events occurred, of course, after the composition of *La Christiada*. But from the end of the sixteenth century on, the interest in persecuting the *portugueses* would certainly have brought a more intense focus to anti-Semitic discursive practices among the learned groups (*letrados*) of colonial Lima. This fact may help to explain the Jew-hatred that Hojeda's text promotes, as well as the poet's relative lack of literary interest in the indigenous to whom we may suppose he preached on a daily basis.

La Christiada, then, affirms Christianity's presumed superiority over Judaism and other religions by showing the spiritual nature of Christian salvation, but the value of this epic as a proselytizing tool extends beyond matters of faith into larger cultural issues, in part because of the anti-Semitic ideology it contains. When Diego de Hojeda wrote his epic poem in the early seventeenth century, the negative stereotypes of Jews present in the Crucifixion story had long served as what Gilman and Katz call "the central referent for all definitions of difference in the West."[58] Perhaps because they inscribed "otherness" according to codes then eminently transferable to other ethnic groups, those stereotypical representations were invaluable to Spanish missionaries like Hojeda. In fact, there is evidence to suggest that indigenous peoples assimilated Spanish religious and racial beliefs fairly

57. On the commercial success and the persecution of the Portuguese "Judaizers," see José Toribio Medina, *Historia del Tribunal de la Inquisición de Lima (1569–1820)*, 1:303–4; 2:45–46; 2:46 n. 1. I owe this reference to Susan Herman. For the identity of the Portuguese Jews, see Günter Böhm, *Nuevos antecedentes para una historia de los judíos en Chile colonial*, 33–38. On *converso* families in Mexico who were involved in the slave trade, see Gonzalo Aguirre Beltrán, *La población negra de México: Estudio etnohistórico*, chapter 2. I owe the latter reference to James R. Nicolopulos.
58. Gilman and Katz, introduction to *Anti-Semitism in Times of Crisis*, 18.

quickly. When Guamán Poma de Ayala calls for a "general Visitor of the holy mother Church" (Visitador general de la santa madre iglesia), he is careful to add that the ecclesiastic visitor should be neither a Jew nor a Moor.[59]

La Christiada may be understood as an instrument for the advancement of Christian faith and Western civilization. At the time of its composition, however, some forty years had passed since the publication of part one of Ercilla's prestigious *La Araucana*, with its occasionally magnificent representations of American Indians. At first blush, it certainly makes sense to ask why, in the context of Spanish overstepping of state and ecclesiastic power in colonial Peru, Diego de Hojeda wrote an epic poem about ancient power and its abuse in the ancient Middle East. From the cultural isolation of the "little Spain" that he and his associates in the Academia Antártica were attempting to create, Hojeda revived very old discourses that juxtaposed Christian martyrs and hated Jews. Meanwhile, according to the detailed sketches of Guamán Poma de Ayala's *Nueva corónica y buen gobierno*, Andean indigenous all around the Dominican were undergoing their own "martyrdom" of sorts, but Hojeda, whose cultural world was inhabited by Christian martyrs and Jews, did not register their distress. At approximately the same time as the poet from Seville penned his verses, a man from his own religious order, Domingo de Santo Tomás, was compiling the first Quechua grammar and dictionary.[60] This intercultural work, however, does not appear to have made much of an impression on Hojeda, whose response to the growing hysteria about Jews and other heretics, real or imagined, was to reaffirm the founding myths of Christian Spain while writing against Judaism. His effusive description of Christian sacrifice in *La Christiada* can be partly explained by the context of the suppression of crypto-Judaism in Lima. Nonetheless, it makes his silence about Amerindian suffering stand out even more.

---

59. Felipe Guamán Poma de Ayala, *Nueva corónica y buen gobierno*. 2:738.

60. Some of the members of the Academia Antártica were Spaniards and others were *criollos*, but they all had a humanist training, and there seems little doubt that they identified culturally with Spain, a fact that helps to explain their apparent ability to dissociate from some of the abuses of the Indians taking place throughout the region. See Trinidad Barrera, introduction to *Primera parte del Parnaso Antártico de Obras Amatorias*, 25. On the Quechua grammar of Domingo de Santo Tomás, see Rolena Adorno, *Guaman Poma: Writing and Resistance in Colonial Peru*, 23.

5

Gendering the Imperial Monarchy
Lope de Vega's *Jerusalem conquered*

Lope de Vega's "tragic epopee" (*epopeya trágica*), *Jerusalem conquered* (1609), is an epic that inserts an imaginary Spanish military presence into the coalition of European forces that waged the Third Crusade to liberate the Holy Land from Muslim occupation in 1189. Lope's poem is, thus, a pro-Castilian revision of Tasso's *Gerusalemme Liberata* (*Jerusalem delivered*), and indeed, of history itself. This is a text that tramples the Aristotelian precepts prevalent at the time of its composition to an extent that appears to have made even the poet, himself, uneasy. Arthur Terry writes that Lope de Vega appeals to Aristotle's distinction between poetry and truth "to justify his own departures from 'truth'; in Lope, however, it serves only to reveal his failure to reflect seriously on the epic theory with which he attempts to impress his readers." Felisa Guillén, in contrast, analyzes the poem's prologue to the count of Saldaña, claiming that its contents are an important indicator of Lope's attempt to grapple with literary theory and establish the theoretical framework for the poem. She concludes by describing—accurately, it would seem—the poet's awkward predicament when she writes, "In this second part of the prologue to his *Jerusalem*, Lope has withdrawn from his positions, little by little and through multiple subterfuges, to the point where he finally concedes that the only historically true thing in his poem is the role of protagonist that he assigns to Richard [of England]."[1] Nonetheless, there is a long critical tradition of negative judgments against *Jerusalem conquered:* that it is uneven; that it is impossible to determine the beginning, middle, and end of the poem; that it suffers from "undigested *culteranismo*"; that it lacks a solitary hero; and that the only thing about the poem that can provoke wonder (*maravilla*) is the ridiculousness of its plot.[2] In this case, however, the poet's attitude toward

---

1. Arthur Terry, *Seventeenth-Century Spanish Poetry: The Power of Artifice*, 194; Felisa Guillén, "Épica, historia y providencialismo en la España del siglo 17: El caso de la *Jerusalén Conquistada*," 51.

2. The most valuable summary of the epic's critical tradition appears in volume 3 of the edition of Joaquín de Entrambasaguas. Guillén similarly reviews some of the most

literary precepts is perhaps not as consequential as that Lopean act of imaginative voluntarism by which he incorporated Spain into the Crusade. In this chapter I will argue that this fanciful feat of national inscription into Crusade history is a means to an end, a deployment of the pen against the past in the name of the future. For once the poet had put Spain into the Third Crusade, he could insert the Crusade into his heroic vision of Spanish history: it was the perfect tautology designed to give Spain the national literary epic that Lope de Vega claimed she lacked, and whether or not factual history substantiated the plot was evidently a matter of secondary importance to the poet.

What *Jerusalem conquered* offers is a rhetorical construct that corresponds to that epic vision. It is a text that demarginalizes the case of Spain by centering Alphonse VIII of Castile, placing him in the thick of the campaign against Saladin alongside Richard of England, called "Lion-heart," and Philippe-Auguste of France. The poet makes his intention to ransom Spain's glory from oblivion explicit: the Spanish heroes, submerged in silence by Tasso, will write their own history, "so that the truth will remain distinct" (para que quede la verdad distinta).[3] The spirit behind the fashioning of the Spanish heroic self here is, therefore, both corrective and ethnocentric: the Spanish monarchy is in the Lopean *epos* an equal partner in a European (Christian) alliance arrayed against an Islamic "other."

By linking this imagined illustrious past to the Habsburg dynasty through prophecy, among other means, Lope de Vega figures forth an arrangement of Spanish imperial monarchy in the early seventeenth century, one that is inherently gendered, as these pages aim to demonstrate. Chapter 3 has shown the degree to which feminism and poststructuralist theories have the power to coax from Golden Age texts meanings hidden from more traditional approaches. We have also seen that Golden Age foundational myths, such as the ones that underlie many epic poems of the period, set in place a suggestive correlation between the female body, viewed as one site of coercion against alterity, and the body politic. This chapter will pursue the same line of thought, to explore the ways in which female "otherness" is routinely neutralized in order to enhance a Castilian heroic identity that is, in the final analysis, male.

---

important criticisms that Pedro de Torres Rámila and Juan Pablo Mártir Rizo leveled at *Jerusalem conqered* as early as 1617. See "Épica, historia y providencialismo," 83–85.

3. All quotations of *Jerusalem conquered* are taken from the critical edition of Joaquín de Entrambasaguas, and hereafter appear in the text by book, octave, and where pertinent, lines, in this case, 17.25.4. Entrambasaguas numbers the lines, but not the stanzas. I have made my own numbering of the stanzas, excluding from my count a sonnet that summarizes the plot, which appears above the text proper at the beginning of each book.

Prophetic Power and the Structuring of Political Identity

As noted other places in this book, prophecy is a convention of epic poetry that serves as a vehicle for aggrandizement of group and state identity. It was crucial to Diego de Hojeda's writing of ecclesiastic and universal history, and it plays a primary role in Lope de Vega's reworking of history from the perspective of literary self-fashioning. Guillén also understands this, though she frames her discussion in the somewhat inelastic terms of Fichter's model of "dynastic epic."[4] By dint of recurrent invocations to superhuman powers, epic texts depend to an important extent on the device of foretelling the future to create the illusion that they are inspired or sacral. Moreover, by invoking the myth of a just and bounteous society that coincides with the plenitude of imperial rule, prophetic revelations and dreams generally point beyond the plot line of the epic to some golden age that lends transcendental meaning to the main narrative. This device is in evidence in the epic of antiquity (Aeneas's prophetic dream on the shore of the Tiber in book 8 of the *Aeneid*, for example), and in virtually all epic of the Renaissance. Because these prophecies are ideological representations of an ideal order, they must be viewed as essentially political.

By including a brief disquisition on the subject of prophecy in *Jerusalem conquered*, Lope shows more than a passing interest in its importance for epic. However, one may have cause to wonder what it means that this explanation of two kinds of prophecy is uttered by a satanic figure:

> If, of the two kinds of prophecy,
> it is the one used to threaten Niniveh,
> and the blessed king, whereby his days increased,
> since in the end he achieved pardon through penitence:
> so let Jerusalem cry like Ezekiel,
> let her go out to the town square like Niniveh,
> her head covered in ashes,
> and God will return her to greatness.

> But if the prophecy is perforce
> of predestination, what can man attempt,
> what does he wish, what can he try with weapons?
> For it will be so, though the earth be astonished.

> (Si dos maneras hay de Profecías,
> La una con que a Nínive amenaza,
> Y al santo Rey, pues aumentó sus días,
> Que al fin por penitencia el perdón traza:
> Llore Jerusalén como Ezequías,

---

4. See "Épica, historia y providencialismo," 166–70.

> Y salga como Nínive a la plaza,
> Cubierta de ceniza la cabeza,
> Y volverála Dios a su grandeza.
>
> Mas si su Profecía es por ventura
> De predestinación, [¿]lqué intenta el hombre,
> Qué quiere con las armas qué procura
> Pues ha de ser, aunque la tierra asombre?)
>   (18.84–85)

Clad as "Discord" (*Discordia*), the Devil appears to Richard to convince him that he must return home immediately because Philip of France, his erstwhile comrade-in-arms, has invaded England. To assuage Richard's guilt over abandoning the Crusade, Discord leads him to accept historical inevitability, as revealed in prophecy. Discord claims that there is, on the one hand, "the prophecy of threat" (*profecía de amenaza*), the desired end of which is to effect repentance. The example cited is Nineveh, a city spared destruction by heeding the prophecy of Jonah. "Prophecy of predestination" (*profecía de predestinación*), on the other hand, reveals the ordering of unavoidable future events. Thus Discord can argue that only "when God wishes it, God absolute" (Cuando lo quiera Dios, Dios absoluto, 18.88.2) will Jerusalem be freed from the "African yoke" (*yugo de África*), with or without Richard's help. Accepting this well-reasoned logic, Richard departs, and the coalition, always fraught with internal tension, dissolves. There is sufficient truth in Discord's argument to persuade Richard, but not enough to caution him of the negative consequences of his actions (the violent storm that will overtake his fleet, and his subsequent imprisonment by the duke of Austria). Guillén, who takes the position that free will, not predestination, informs an "epic subplot" of *Jerusalem conquered*, argues that Discord's comments cannot be taken at face value because the speaker is untrustworthy.[5] The problem is that prophecy can only be refuted or proven by hindsight. Indeed, there seems to be as much predestination as warning in Discord's words to Richard. But whichever kind of prophecy Lope de Vega intended this to be, his highlighting of the passage suggests how conscious the poet was of the literary and propagandistic usefulness of prophecy in establishing the political program of the epic.

The three most important prophecies in *Jerusalem conquered* are ones of predestination, which does not mean they are devoid of exemplarity, a quality Guillén associates with some of the episodes that constitute what she calls the "tragic subplot" of the epic. In the first prophecy, a captive Spanish pilgrim to the Holy Land encapsulates for Saladin the history of

5. Ibid., 143.

the Castilian kingdom, predicting a Christian victory over "the Turk," a designation Lope uses very loosely in a way that exemplifies the homogenization of the "other" that occurs in Orientalist texts, a phenomenon also witnessed in Rufo's *La Austriada*.[6] Lope, who probably has the more recent Ottoman Turks in mind, retrojects this generalized ethnic identity back onto Saladin, who—for chronological reasons—would have to have been a Seljuk. Saladin, however, was not a Turk, but a Kurd, and he belonged to one of the Atabeg dynasties that followed the disintegration of the Seljuk empire. Although adequate to his poetic purposes, Lope's generic *turco* is inadequate, as are all stark ethnic or religious categories, to the task of discussing the mixed multicultural populations of Saladin's region.

It is perhaps appropriate that the prophetic voice here should belong to the ex-centric figure of the pilgrim. The prophecy fashions an image of the origins of Castilian monarchy that begins ingloriously with the story of Roderick, the last Visigoth king. Drawing on sources like Alphonse X's *Crónica general* (*General chronicle*), the chronicle of Johannes Nauclerus (1516), and Miguel de Luna's *Verdadera historia del rey don Rodrigo* (*True history of the king don Roderick*, 1592 and 1600), Lope de Vega details Roderick's misguided breaking of the locks on the Tower of Hercules, his discovery within the tower of a canvas that predicts the imminent occupation of Spain by Moors, and his cupidity, which provoked a woman's desire for revenge and led to the Arab invasion (A.D. 711). Israel Burshatin writes of the version of this story contained in the *Crónica sarracina* (*Saracen chronicle*), "In contrast to the continuities of epic, fissures and disruptions prevail in a world on the brink of disaster . . . In place of Cidian mastery over word and sword, stands King Roderick's intemperance."[7] In the same spirit, the pilgrim's tale in *Jerusalem conquered* exposes an "un-epic moment" or a vulnerable point in the royal line, a line broken when Roderick had his way with Don Julian's daughter, Florinda, also known as La Cava.

In the pilgrim's version of the story, ironically, the problem is not that Roderick has forced himself on the woman against her will, but that Florinda has grown resentful because his enthusiasm for her has waned:

> Deadly displeasure went with Roderick,
> and with Florinda remained vengeance,
> which suggested to her the must unjust act
> our memory can recall of any woman;

6. Guillén, "Épica, historia y providencialismo," 163. On the homogenization of the "other" in Orientalist texts, see Edward W. Said, *Orientalism*, 101–2, 239–40.

7. Israel Burshatin, "The Moor in the Text: Metaphor, Emblem, and Silence," in *"Race," Writing, and Difference*, ed. Henry Louis Gates, Jr., 123.

it is said that not seeing the king's pleasure,
but rather such a change after so much love
was the cause, for the woman who has been enjoyed
feels more hated than forced.

(Fue con Rodrigo este mortal disgusto,
Y quedó con Florinda la venganza,
Que le propuso el hecho más injusto
Que de muger nuestra memoria alcanza;
Dícese que no ver en el Rey gusto,
Sino de tanto amor tanta mudanza
Fue la ocasión, que la muger gozada
Más siente aborrecida que forzada.)
(6.43)

Here, as Virués does in *El Monserrate*, Lope de Vega erases the rape by making the pilgrim hold the scorned woman responsible for the Arab invasion and the end of the Visigoth line. According to this account, the beautiful woman constitutes a dangerous fault line running beneath the Castilian monarchy. This representation of La Cava as the cause of disruption and the object of wrath is particularly important for Lope's structuring of the epic, since it thematically connects the beginning of the poem and its end.

In his oral history of the kingdom, the pilgrim does not shy away from acknowledging the consolidation of Muslim power in Iberia. He describes how the impact of the Moorish attack stripped Roderick of the signs of his office, just as the winds of approaching winter tear the leaves from a tree:

Thus Roderick on the last
miserable day of this unhappy war
lay on the ground, where the majesty
had already fallen from his shoulders:
there lay the torn royal purple
stained in blood, stained in sweat,
there the green laurel, and the scepter of gold:
his body was the tree; the Moor, the wind.

(Así Rodrigo el miserable día
Último de esta guerra desdichada
Quedó en el campo, donde ya tenía
La majestad del hombro derribada:
Allí la rota púrpura yacía
Teñida en sangre, y en sudor bañada,
Allí el verde laurel, y el cetro de oro,
Siendo el árbol su cuerpo, el viento el Moro.)
(6.63)

The tree simile, which recurs in the prophetic discourses of the poem, must be read as a symbol of the Castilian throne, a genealogy or "family tree" of royalty. Lope thereby seems to suggest that though the reign of a given monarch is inconsequential or even unhappy, what counts is the rootedness and continued expansion of the organism to bring forth future kings that restore integrity to the state. In a similar vein, the pilgrim claims that Ferdinand I inherited the throne of Castile, "propagating the trunk of Pelayo" (el tronco de Pelayo propagando, 6.81.4), and that Alphonse VIII can count both Pelayo and Ruy Díaz de Bivar (el Cid) among his predecessors. This prophecy thus connects the Castilian hero of *Jerusalem conquered* to the Visigoth kings and to the leaders of the *Reconquista*, a domestic crusade already being waged on Iberian soil. The pilgrim's vision ends with the prediction of Saladin's defeat, based on the success of the Reconquest to date:

> Spanish shores have contained the men,
> and contain them today, from one sea to the other,
> who, at the expense of their blood, in total war
> took back everything from Oviedo to Seville:
> if gallant Alphonse of Castile comes
> to conquer this holy ground,
> when you put your Moons up against his Suns,
> he will show you who the Spanish are.

> (Los hombres que ha tenido, y que hoy encierra
> Del uno al otro mar la Hispana orilla,
> A costa de su sangre, a pura guerra
> Ganaron desde Oviedo hasta Sevilla:
> Si a conquistar esta sagrada tierra
> Gallardo viene Alfonso de Castilla,
> Quando pongas tus Lunas a sus Soles,
> El te dirá quien son los Españoles.)
> (6.89)

Hearing Alphonse extolled for his role in freeing Spain from Moorish domination, Saladin is infuriated and orders that nine captive Spanish knights do hand-to-hand combat with Saracen peers. The Christians prevail, whereupon the Muslim onlookers slaughter the nine Spaniards. In this act, the author uses stereotypical images of the Moor, present in Spanish writing since the Middle Ages, according to which they are either vilified as barbarians, dogs, and traitors, or idealized to mirror the virtues of Christian knighthood.[8] Both tendencies are evident in Lope de Vega's epic where, for the sake of military parity and decorum, Saladin and his high-ranking troops are generally portrayed in a favorable light. For example, Lope creates a catalogue of the flower of Spanish chivalry (12.87–97) made up of knights from

8. Ibid., 117.

prominent aristocratic families throughout the peninsula who make themselves subjects, which is to say they voluntarily assume a "subjected state" when they place themselves in the service of Alphonse of Castile.[9] This is followed by a parallel review of the best Islamic warriors (13.1–10). Likewise, Saladin proves his chivalry by liberating two captured Spanish Crusaders, but only because he is discriminating enough to prefer Spaniards over other Christians, as the text makes explicit. Speaking to Alphonse, the newly freed Garcipacheco can then say of the Ayubbite sultan:

> "The world has not seen, Lord," he says,
> a man as brave as this Persian.
> Speaking in peace, he is a second Numa,
> and in war, he comes before Trajan:
> I noted his ingenuity, his solemn conduct,
> his ability to dissemble, his heroic hand,
> and if he loses Asia, it will not be
> because he is not a strong and prudent captain.
>
> He can endure affront, even when he knows
> that punishment is in his hand and his strength,
> he puts his strong heart under lock and key,
> yet shows love and deference to the enemy;
> his mien is unassuming, his soul staid, he is
> rough with his son, elusive with his best friend;
> if he loses Jerusalem's fortress,
> a secret deity and force constrain him.
>
> (No ha tenido, señor le dice, el mundo
> Un hombre del valor deste Persiano,
> Es hablando en la paz Numa segundo,
> Y en la guerra, primero que Trajano:
> Noté su ingenio, y proceder profundo,
> Su disimulación, su heroica mano,
> Y si éste pierde el Asia, no es defecto
> De no ser Capitán fuerte, y discreto.
>
> Sabe sufrir la injuria, cuando sabe
> Que está en su mano, y fuerzas el castigo,
> Su fuerte corazón cierra con llave,
> Y muestra amor, y estima al enemigo:
> Humilde tiene el rostro, el alma grave,
> Áspero al hijo, incierto al más amigo,
> Si de Jerusalén pierde la fuerza
> Deidad secreta le constriñe, y fuerza.)
> (15.163–64)

9. For the difficulties inherent in assuming the "subject's" compliance with a given subject-position, see Paul Smith, preface to *Discerning the Subject*, xxxi.

Valor, gravity, restraint, respect for the enemy, humility, a healthy detachment from his subjects: these are all characteristics that generally correspond to the representation of Alphonse and Richard in *Jerusalem conquered*. Saladin Ayubi's portrait, juxtaposed to that of the European kings, reinforces the ideological underpinnings of what is essentially the same sympathetic representation already claimed for the Christian monarchs.

But the occasional positive representation of the "other" cannot be separated from issues of positionality in the speech act. When he tells Saladin the story of Roderick in tragic terms, the pilgrim's subject-position is unmistakably Eurocentric. One cannot fail to see the irony in his sorrowfully relating to a Muslim leader something that the latter could only perceive as the triumph of his coreligionists in taking the better part of Iberia. Moreover, Saladin would already have known of Islamic presence and culture inside the peninsula: the Arabs had invaded Spain more than four hundred years earlier. Said points out that one of the deep ideological fissures in texts like Lope's is the basic assumption that the Oriental cannot tell his own story and therefore needs a European to tell it for him. Accustomed as students of the Golden Age are to discourse that laments the "fall" of Christian Spain, they may read the pilgrim's account of Moorish occupation almost without realizing that he is Orientalizing the Orient (in the terms of Said) for an interlocutor, Saladin, whose real position is not acknowledged, since he has no voice of his own.[10]

The other two prophecies of "predestination" in *Jerusalem conquered* are not as elaborate as what we have just seen. Nonetheless, they are indispensable in textually constructing a subjective Castilian ethnos or group identity. Both prophecies continue to elaborate the two connected motifs: expansion of the Spanish crown and the *Reconquista*. The first takes place in Sicily, where the Christian forces put to port on their way to the Holy Land. There, beneath a cliff beaten by the waves, the Christian kings come upon the dwelling of the prophetic abbot Joachim of Fiore, an historical figure. Guillén argues that due to the broad acceptance of the abbot's interpretation of history and "its influence in attributing a messianic destiny to the Spanish monarchy, it is not strange that the Joachimite prophetic program should shape the ideological substratum upon which *Jerusalem conquered* is constructed, just as it had that of the *Dragontea*."[11] Lope refers to Joachim's powers in the following terms:

> There lived the holy Joachim the monk,
> endowed with a prophetic spirit,
> he who wrote on tablets of marble

10. Said, *Orientalism*, 20, 67.
11. Guillén, "Épica, historia y providencialismo," 117.

things future, which now we see as past.

> (Aquel santo Joaquín monje vivía
> De espíritu profético dotado,
> El que en losas de mármol escribía
> Lo futuro, que hoy vemos ya pasado.)
> (7.47.1–4)

The similarities between the monk's vatic powers and the pilgrim's unworldly voice are readily apparent. Joachim issues a warning to the kings: their military victory is assured as long as they can keep the peace between them. The monk then turns to the real object of his prophecy: the future of Alphonse's line. Just as in the speech of Discord, elements of "warning" blend together with others of "predestination" in this prophecy, which makes the prophecies of *Jerusalem conquered* somewhat more complicated than Guillén claims.[12] The more important issue, perhaps, is whether or not Lope's poetic practice squares with his theoretical statements about prophecy, stated directly or through his characters. It would appear that they do not always do so, making it somewhat difficult to evaluate the ideological currents in his work, which are not fixed, but somewhat fluid. In the present vision, Alphonse learns that the thrones of Spain and England will be intertwined through his marriage to Eleanor (Leonor), whom Lope erroneously identifies as the daughter of Richard the "Lionheart,"[13] and that their offspring will produce illustrious kings. Notice the reappearance in Joachim's speech of the tree symbol:

> The branches of its generous trunk
> will continue to propagate this line,
> until they are transferred and grafted
> onto Austria, and honored by her heroic name.

> (Iránse en esta línea propagando
> Las ramas de su tronco generoso,
> Hasta que insertas queden trasladadas
> En Austria, y de su nombre heroico honradas.)
> (7.54.5–8)

The Spain of the Hapsburgs is evoked in allusions to the virtue and might of Charles V, and to the American discoveries that barely made the world large enough to accommodate Philip II, "that so great a Sun should not fit in such a small sphere" (porque no cupiera / tan grande Sol en tan pequeña Esfera, 7.57.7–8). This is Lope de Vega's allusion to Philip II's

---

12. Ibid., 138.
13. The woman Alphonse VIII married in 1170 was Eleanor, daughter of Henry II of England.

182 Myth and Identity in the Epic of Imperial Spain

motto after Spain's annexation of Portugal, *Non sufficit orbis* (the world is not enough), a phrase intended to express Philip's achievements in augmenting the realms of his father, whose *Plus ultra* ("Onwards and upwards") was now deemed insufficient to the expanse of the empire. Lope then evokes the militant orthodoxy of Philip III, "bolt of lightning to the vile heretic, knife to the Moor" (Rayo al Hereje vil, cuchillo al Moro, 7.58.7). Through Alphonse, the poet links the mythical past of Pelayo and el Cid to the Habsburg king whose favor he so obviously curries in the seventeenth century, as evidenced by the fact that he dedicated *Jerusalem conquered* to Philip III.[14]

> You shall be, Alphonse, your ancestors'
> glory; to your future heirs you shall be
> a Sun whose transparent rays
> imitate divine resplendence.
>
> (Serás Alfonso de tus ascendientes,
> Gloria, y de tus futuros sucesores
> Un Sol de cuyos rayos transparentes
> Imiten los divinos resplandores.)
> (7.67.1–4)

Thus, this prophecy places Alphonse VIII at the center of Spanish history by showing, though somewhat erroneously from a historical standpoint, that he redeems Spain from Muslim bondage.

The third prophecy merely completes the previous one. In a battle won by the Christian forces, the Egyptian soothsayer Mafadal falls prisoner to Alphonse. Mafadal had earlier sent a boat loaded with poisonous snakes to try to keep the Christian forces from coming ashore off Jerusalem. The serpent-laden boat leaves little doubt that Lope de Vega associates Eastern peoples—Muslims, in particular—with ferocious and venomous animals, the same ones used to symbolize the deadly "other" in virtually all the Golden Age epics. Of this we have seen abundant examples in *El Monserrate* and in *La Christiada*. When asked to reveal the future of the Catholic kingdoms, Mafadal shows Alphonse VIII a mirror that reflects "the living portraits of the successive kings of Spain." In this mirror, Alphonse sees the faces of his grandson Ferdinand, liberator of Seville, and his great-grandson, Alphonse X, "the Wise," maker of just laws. The suc-

---

14. For Habsburg cultural renderings of the imperial theme, see Geoffrey Parker, *The Grand Strategy of Philip II*, 3–5. See also Elizabeth R. Wright's examination of Lope's attempts to manipulate the patronage system in the unstable political atmosphere at Philip III's court, "The Poet as Pilgrim: Lope de Vega and the Court of Philip III, 1598–1609," 268. Wright interprets the Crusades in *Jerusalem conquered* as an allegory for "battles within the royal palace."

cessors to the Spanish throne appear one after the other, but only that of the Catholic Kings seems to merit Lope's special attention:

> That Ferdinand the Fifth, who divided
> Moorish and Hebrew blood from that of nobles,
> which it so infests and spoils,
> takes command of the open field,
> combed hair bathing his face
> in light; his divine Hypsicratea[15]
> with her ancient headdress looking like
> the golden age, which returned in them both.

> (Aquel Fernando Quinto, que de España
> La sangre dividió Mora, y Hebrea
> De la noble, que tanto infesta y daña,
> El campo descubierto señorea:
> El peinado cabello el rostro baña
> De luz, y su divina Ipsicratea
> Con las tocas antiguas parecía
> El siglo de oro, que en los dos volvía.)
> (13.157)

It might seem puzzling that Lope simultaneously lavishes praise on the ecumenical Alphonse X, also known as the "King of Three Religions," and on Ferdinand V, architect of the expulsion of the Jews and later of the Moriscos from Spain. But one must remember that Lope composed his text in the years immediately preceding the first major Morisco expulsion (1609), with which its publication coincided. In this prophecy, *Jerusalem conquered* shows explicit acceptance of the Spanish crown's policies directed at achieving religious and ethnic purity, political policies that were as homogenizing as Lope's own literary representations of the "infidel," and certainly more devastating in real, human terms. After the laudatory words for Spain's champions of "cleanliness of blood" (*limpieza de sangre*), the Habsburg kings pass by in quick review. When the mirror darkens, Alphonse asks to be shown the face of his betrothed. The prophecy ends with a glimpse of Eleanor doing needlework in a London castle, cloistered in a woman's space—a reminder, perhaps, that the Western self has a domestic female "other" that cannot be eliminated, so it must be disempowered. The place of women in Golden Age epics is located either away

---

15. Hypsicratea, wife of Mithridates and queen of Pontus, is remembered for dressing like a man and enduring great hardship to accompany her husband to war. Her story appears in Boccaccio's *Concerning Famous Women*, chapter 76. Lope de Vega probably had access to the Spanish translation published by Pablo Hurus (Zaragoza, 1494).

from home and at risk, or encloistered, yet still somehow in jeopardy. Partial exceptions are some of Ercilla's Araucanian women, especially Fresia, and Lope's own character, Ismenia. What seems clear, in any event, is that the epic narrative of imperial monarchy is always gendered, though in ways that are not entirely predictable.

The position of Alphonse in this case appears analogous to that of Saladin in the pilgrim's prophecy but, in fact, it is not. By asking for information about the enemy, Saladin prompted the pilgrim to recount the historical narrative of a powerful Castilian elite. In contrast, Alphonse VIII, a European king, has traveled to the Middle East not only to make war, but also to have the future of his own line revealed to him by a Moorish magician. Lope couches this unorthodox foretelling of the future in careful terms by establishing pagan ownership of the mirror and by creating a somewhat sinister character in Mafadal. But what primarily sets this prophecy apart from the pilgrim's vision is that Alphonse is not shown a set of completed facts about which he might have an alternative interpretation and evaluation, but rather the glorious tomorrow of his own dynasty. Significantly, he shows no curiosity about the East, its people or culture, only a desire to conquer them. The adequate sign for this in the text is the mirror itself, which can do nothing more than passively reflect the face of the person standing in front of it. It is congruous with the "mysterious" powers the West has always imputed to Orientals that Alphonse would ask a Moor for answers about the future of his Christian state. But it is also poignantly ironic that the Moorish voice in Spain is being officially silenced even as Lope prepares to publish his poem.[16]

The purpose of all three prophecies is to establish an important link between the plot of the poem (Middle Eastern conquest), and the specific case of the Spanish struggle against Islam (the *Reconquista*), which serves as a backdrop to the Crusade for Jerusalem. That connection forged, Lope's text must be read as a testament to the global significance of the war against Muslim power. In addition, the prophecies serve the function of binding together the destinies of England and Spain. It is well known that Philip III pulled back from the full-scale military aggression against the Protestant North that had characterized his father's reign, only to redouble his efforts against Islam at home and abroad. The new political situation led him to nurture his dynastic connections with the royal houses of Europe. The necessity of an enduring peace with England is a notion that underlies the whole text of Lope de Vega. The

16. See Burshatin, "The Moor in the Text," 132.

Peace of London was signed on August 27, 1604, when Lope's *Jerusalem conquered* was nearly finished.[17] This helps to make it more understandable that he would privilege the position of an English king in his poem.

Just as Lope de Vega inserted Spain into the Third Crusade, in a bold poetic move that textualized a European will-to-power against a fascinating but terrible "other" perceived as militarily equal but ethnically inferior, he managed, through the prophecies of *Jerusalem conquered,* to inscribe Alphonse VIII of Castile into a central position within Spanish monarchic history. This is a history he narrates as a fragile construct, due to the monarchs' vulnerability to women. In this text, prophecy connects national history, a history Goethe and Schiller called the "absolute past," with the action of the epic and with the future of the Spanish state, a state that sees itself solidly within the European camp, especially now that extreme measures have been taken to render Spanish society ethnically homogeneous. Prophecy, however, has also served to uncover a fault line in the foundations of the imperial monarchy. This fault line has a name: La Cava. The pilgrim's tale has given us the first demonizing representation of woman in the epic. In contrast to *El Monserrate,* however, which poetically grounded the foundation of the Virgin's shrine at Montserrat in the victimization of a single, nameless woman, *Jerusalem conquered* contains several important female characters and at least suggests a comparatively broad spectrum of representational possibilities for women. The case of Ismenia shows the extent to which this is true.

The Destiny of Ismenia

Jerusalem conquered, like many other Golden Age epics, constructs a Spanish sense of self in the process of, and at the expense of, suppressing or absorbing difference, both ethnic and sexual. The character of Ismenia, princess of Limassol (Limisol) and Limenia, who fights side by side with the Christian soldiers to retake Jerusalem, offers a particularly complex illustration of this way of writing Spanish heroic identity.

It is reading about female heroic figures that drives Ismenia to study martial arts: her models are Penthesilea, a legendary Amazon of post-Homeric lineage, Camilla, leader of the Volscians, and Semiramis, widow of Ninus and legendary queen of Assyria, who subjugated numerous Asian territories and built the city of Babylon. Lope de Vega, who explicitly compares his character to Hippolyta, queen of the Amazons, also calls her

---

17. See Antonio Ubieto, et al., *Introducción a la Historia de España,* 365. Wright places the celebration of the signing of the treaty with England in 1605. See her "Poet as Pilgrim," 271.

"princess of Limisol," thereby invoking the name of a land in the *Orlando Furioso*, one where the women go off into battle and the men stay at home spinning (canto 19). These elements combine to establish a first textual link between Ismenia and the mythical woman who wages war separate from men, the Amazonian figure who represents a real threat to the established social order.[18] However, the toponymic echo from the *Furioso* must be considered in the larger context of Ismenia's Cypriot origins, since she is a native of the island that is dedicated to Venus. The destiny of Lope's heroine, thus, is marked equally by the goddess of love and by Mars, god of war.

Indeed, it is this apparent conflict that motivates the character of Ismenia. When she meets Alphonse VIII of Castile, the princess of Limenia falls in love with him and decides to join the Crusade dressed as a man so that she may remain close to him. In this sense, the Amazonian subtextuality is displaced and remains partially unfulfilled. Instead, the character seems to branch off in the direction of the "manly woman" (*mujer varonil*) that abounds in the Golden Age *comedia*, and in the literature of the period, generally: a woman who dresses like a man for a particular motive (such as pilgrimage or vengeance) but recovers her original gender role by the end of the work.[19] However, the female character in *Jerusalem conquered* also breaks the mold of the typical *mujer varonil*. When, in a declaration of love, Ismenia decides to reveal her identity to the Castilian king, he rejects her in the name of his engagement to Eleanor. Unbeknownst to Ismenia, Garcerán Manrique, the Spanish hero, has overheard her disclosure. His initial reaction of relief suggests his hope that, now that her secret is out, he will no longer have to contend on the battlefield with a very competitive rival. In possession of this information, then, Garcerán Manrique falls in love with Ismenia, despite her obstinate love for the king of Castile. It is perhaps revealing that Lope puts Ismenia in a position of vulnerability before allowing her to return Garcerán's affections. Pursued by ten enemy soldiers, the woman warrior falls to the ground half dead (17.172). Garcerán Manrique carries her to safety, and she has a kind of epiphany that it is God's will that she return his love ("Que ya conozco que lo quiere el cielo," 18.45.8). Immediately, the Spaniard and the Cypriot make wedding plans.

It is, above all, Ismenia's transvestism that allows the princess to enter unnoticed a world of men. When she dresses in men's clothing, Ismenia passes herself off for her brother, Dinodoro, usurping his identity along with his arms. This is an important detail because at the end of the text, when Ismenia no longer needs the disguise, Dinodoro appears to retrieve

---

18. See William Blake Tyrrell, *Amazons: A Study in Athenian Mythmaking*, 88–112.

19. On the figure of the *mujer varonil*, see especially Melveena McKendrick, *Woman and Society in the Spanish Drama of the Golden Age*.

his "weapons, and the decorum of the Kings of Cyprus" (las armas, y el decoro / De los Reyes de Chipre, 18.107.2–3). Nevertheless, during her cross-dressing period, Ismenia takes control of the signs of the masculine gender code, displaying them with such excellence that the other soldiers are taken in, believing her to be a prince and brave comrade-in-arms. The difference between her sex and her gender, which is made manifest partly in her behavior, is resolved in favor of the latter: Ismenia masters the masculine code, "covers" herself with male "otherness," and reconstructs her gender. But as Dianne Dugaw argues, "Gender coding is not just about difference. It is about dominance." The woman who passes for a man encodes herself "in the language of gender *deceptively*," continues Dugaw, so that she becomes "ungrammatical, subversive, a lying sign." One effect of her farce is to show how arbitrary all gender identity is, since it is a social construction. In other words, as Judith Butler has cogently argued, gender is above all performative.[20] Accordingly, in the same way that Ismenia dresses like a man, she also "un-dresses" when she chooses to, easily recovering her previous gender code. The voluntary revelation of her secret enhances the character's subjectivity and her agency. Only when she wants, and to whom she wants, does she reveal her sex.

But, as noted above, there is an uninvited witness to this "dis-covery": Garcerán Manrique. His interference in the scene constitutes a violation of Ismenia's will as a subject, as her subsequent rejection of him makes clear. Manrique's resolution is firm, however. Under the pretext of recovering some feathers, which she had pulled from his helmet during his escape on the night of her conversation with Alphonse, Manrique approaches Ismenia. The motives of love and war become interwoven from the moment that the Spaniard insults her, and Ismenia, to defend herself, proposes that they disarm to engage in bodily combat, "the body naked of betrayal and steel" (desnudo el cuerpo de traición y acero, 13.53.8). Stripped of weapons as well as clothing (*vestidos*), Ismenia throws herself into the fight, which Lope represents in boldly erotic terms.[21]

---

20. Dianne Dugaw, *Warrior Women and Popular Balladry, 1650–1850*, 165; on the nonexistence of fixed gender identities, see Judith Butler, *Gender Trouble: Feminism and the Subversion of Identity*, chapter 1. Marjorie Garber studies cross-dressing in the military during the modern period and calls attention to the special appeal of dressing in uniform. See her *Vested Interests: Cross-Dressing and Cultural Anxiety*, 54–59.

21. This type of amorous struggle has an interesting precedent in medieval literature, where the *serranas* of Juan Ruiz's *Libro de buen amor* viewed combat as an appropriate prelude to the sexual act. See Estelle Irizarry, "Echoes of the Amazon Myth in Medieval Spanish Literature," in *Women in Hispanic Literature: Icons and Fallen Idols*, ed. Beth Miller, 61.

The two now embrace, now release one another,
now position themselves better, now plan a new ruse,
they grab arms first, then shoulders,
then finally they cling to whole bodies:
take care, famed Ismenia, not to be burned
by the concealed flames that embrace you;
careful, don't let Deianira put on you,
new Alcides, the shirt of Nessus.[22]

Watch out, for Garcerán is a Lernaean hydra,
who breathes fire from his wounded chest,
for as he wants to declare his love,
it comes out broken up in timid sighs:
Garcerán fights with little strength
to make the tight embrace last longer,
he plans new tricks with his feet,
holding fast, like the vine to the elm.

(Ya se abrazan los dos, ya se desasen,
Ya se ponen mejor, ya otro ardid trazan,
Ya los brazos, y ya los hombros asen,
Ya finalmente el cuerpo todo enlazan:
Guarda famosa Ismenia no te abrasen
Las encubiertas llamas que te abrazan,
Que no te ponga nuevo Alcides, mira,
La camisa de Neso Deyanira.

Guarda que es Garcerán sierpe Lernea,
Que fuego espira del herido pecho,
Porque como decir su amor desea,
Sale en suspiros tímidos deshecho:
Con pocas fuerzas Garcerán pelea,
Para que dure aquel abrazo estrecho,
Por que si con los pies ardides traza
Es que como la vid al olmo enlaza.)
(13.57–58)

Ismenia's removal of armor and clothing is tantamount to her "taking off" a previously assumed gender. This situation indicates a joining of contraries: love/war, Venus/Mars, woman/man. In these circumstances, it seems slightly ironic that Alphonse should come upon the fighting couple and protest that Manrique is too far from the scene of battle: "Are you so far from the assault, and naked?" (Tan lejos del asalto

---

22. Fearing the loss of Hercules's love, Deianira sends him a tunic soaked in the poisonous blood of Nessus. When Hercules puts on the tunic, he is poisoned and dies. See Ovid, *Metamorphoses* 9.138 ff.

estas desnudo?, 13.89.4). For the moment, the adoring Garcerán is not interested in any combat but this one.

To be able to remain in the Holy Land, Ismenia must do more than dress like a man. She must perform well in combat, since her skills as a soldier are an important part of that typically masculine behavior that she must exhibit so as to not be discovered. It is important to appreciate the extent to which Ismenia is efficient and convincing as long as she dresses and does battle like a man. From the moment of her arrival in the Holy Land, her commanders send her on dangerous missions (9.103–4). Farther ahead, and immediately after discoursing on her amorous predicament, she struggles valiantly against seven men, until Garcerán Manrique comes to her aid (10.138). When a dispute arises over who deserves the sword of the fallen Christian hero Juan de Aguilar, Ismenia demonstrates her valor by fighting with exceptional ferociousness to raise the banner of the cross in the highest battlements of Ptolemais, a city controlled by the enemy (11.40–43).

Ismenia's soldierly perfection is not unproblematic, however, in the context of her love. She imagines that Alphonse will not be able to love the same person he has seen in battle:

> How can he love me, he who today watched me
> drive the Turkish troops from a wall,
> stained in blood, I who resist their furor
> with rough, hard, manly furor:
> if, instead of silk and gold, I wear steel,
> and attempt to show such ferociousness,
> even if I call myself by my own name,
> Alphonse will not love a woman who is so much a man.

> (Cómo me ha de querer, quien hoy me ha visto
> Teñida en sangre despejar un muro
> De Turca gente, y que el furor resisto
> Con varonil furor áspero y duro:
> Si en vez de seda, y oro, acero visto,
> Y tal ferocidad mostrar procuro,
> Aunque diga que soy mi propio nombre,
> Alfonso no querrá mujer tan hombre.)
> (11.61).

The female character is torn; in order to maintain the gender illusion she has created, she must try to achieve fame, just as a man would do. She believes, however, that her very prowess in battle makes her undesirable in the eyes of a man like Alphonse:

> I myself am my own impossibility,

for the more I desire fame and renown,
the more do I endorse the belief that I am a man.

(Yo misma soy el imposible mio,
que cuanto más procuro fama y nombre,
más firmo la opinión de que soy hombre.)
(11.56.6–8)

Thus, Ismenia sums up and simultaneously subverts the heroic code according to which a man fights to win fame, all the while expecting the reward of love (woman) as compensation for his efforts. Where the epic ideal itself is concerned, the effect of introducing a woman into the masculine world of warfare is, at the very least, parodic. Dugaw suggests that one effect of the woman warrior character in analogous texts is that her presence inverts the European heroic model: "Relying on this gendered ideal, the Female Warrior motif by its reversing of roles simultaneously exposes the seams (so to speak) of the ideal. Moreover, this heroic reversal actually in some sense collapses the opposition between male Glory and female Love, for the heroine plays out both ideals herself."[23]

Ismenia's cross-dressing constitutes something more than a clever ruse on the part of a woman who wants to be close to her beloved. This representation of the transvestite woman, like all cases of literary transvestism, shows signs or possibilities of homosexuality and especially of androgyny. It seems as if Lope de Vega had given free rein to his poetic imagination in the scenes in which Ismenia must fulfill her role as a man in the company of a woman who is in love with her/him, the beautiful slave Melidora. This episode has more or less serious ramifications that indirectly touch on the sexuality of other characters, especially that of Garcerán Manrique. Ismenia captures Melidora, a woman from Macedonia carried into captivity by the Saracen Branzardo. Melidora, always dressed in woman's clothing, is nonetheless described according to the terms of *varonil* women: "A man in bravery, a woman in stubborn determination" (Hombre en valor, muger en la porfía, 12.120.8). Ismenia convinces her to surrender, and from the moment that Melidora lays eyes on her, the slave falls hopelessly in love.

Thus speaking Ismenia, she lifted the visor
of her helmet, and uncovered her face;
no imperial eagle could resist so great a sun,
which causes the heavenly one to halt:
as soon as she was seen by Melidora,
though from a distance, she stares at the light,

23. Dugaw, *Warrior Women*, 191.

> the sun is not the less beautiful because it is distant,
> if its reflections burn on a pyramid.
>
> (Esto diciendo Ismenia, alzó la vista
> De la celada, y descubrió la cara,
> Que no hay ave Imperial que se resista
> A tanto sol, que el de los cielos para:
> Luego que fue de Melidora vista,
> Aunque de lejos en la luz repara,
> Que el sol no es menos bello por más lejos,
> Si en pirámide abrasan sus reflejos.)
> (12.125)

Perhaps because Ismenia identifies with her emotional vulnerability, the woman warrior takes pity on Melidora and decides to have the slave taken to her own tent, publicly insinuating that she wants to enjoy her sexually. Garcerán Manrique, who is in love with Ismenia, engages in conjectures about the true sexual identity of the two women with his confidant, Osorio. In a situation where the sexual codes begin to blur, he thinks Melidora might even turn out to be a man who has gotten inside Ismenia's tent with the intention of raping her. Although Manrique reiterates that he has overheard Ismenia's revelations about her own sexual identity and her love of Alphonse, his friend advises him to trust his eyes instead of his ears, because:

> "it is impossible that Ismenia's exploits,"
> Osorio responds, "could be executed
> by the arm of a woman . . ."
>
> (Las hazañas de Ismenia no es possible
> [Osorio le replica] que ser puedan
> de brazo de muger . . .)
> (12.137.1–3)

Under false pretense, the two men enter Ismenia's tent for confirmation of Melidora's sex. When Ismenia arrives, Manrique pretends to be a servant so that he can stay to serve dinner. What he sees makes him every bit as jealous as if Melidora were a man:

> Ismenia is equally gallant without her armor;
> Melidora sighs as she looks at her,
> Garcerán sighs, and she, forgetting herself,
> is amazed by his masculine presence:
> in the end she is loved as a man and as a woman,
> she loves as a woman, she stares like a man,
> to achieve the effect of covering over her name

and her womanly identity with manly actions.

> (Gallarda queda Ismenia desarmada,
> Melidora mirándola suspira,
> Suspira Garcerán, y ella olvidada
> De su presencia varonil se admira:
> En fin por hombre, y por muger amada
> Ama como muger, como hombre mira,
> A efeto de poder cubrir el nombre,
> Y el ser mujer con las acciones de hombre.)
> (12.144)

When the dinner is concluded, Manrique leaves hurriedly, but he remains just outside the tent, peering in. He is a knight turned voyeur.

Jealousy is not the only problem that affects Garcerán Manrique, for his own sexuality is in the balance during these scenes in which the representation of Ismenia approaches hermaphroditism. These are moments of generalized sexual confusion and, in Manrique's case, of absolute consternation, for what his eyes see is at odds with what his ears have heard. In his bewilderment, he even starts to believe that he is in love with another man: "In such confusion, he arrives at a state in which he believes that he loves one whom he believes to be a man" (Y en tanta confusión a estado viene, / Que piensa que ama a quien por hombre tiene, 12.149.7–8). Ismenia, meanwhile, solves her most immediate problem by encouraging Melidora to entertain hopes of marriage after converting to Christianity. In this way, the Ismenia character facilitates a linkage of the themes of religion and sexual identity in Lope de Vega's crusading epic. In the end, though, Melidora disappears from view and is not mentioned again.

In the broader context of inflexible gender construction that informs *Jerusalem conquered*, the Melidora episode stands out as an important site of fluid sexual (not just gender) identity. When Ismenia enters the tent with the beautiful slave woman and removes her armor, she sees and feels like a woman, but she is seen both as a man and as a woman. When Lope de Vega blends into this deliberate sexual ambiguity the dismay of Garcerán Manrique (who was privy to Ismenia's secret), *Jerusalem conquered* becomes downright carnivalesque. The system of gender codes that had appeared relatively stable until Ismenia went to war is now decentered, upset. War, of course, is about destabilizing all sorts of codes, so it could be that what happens here is emblematic of a more inclusive chaos. Nonetheless, while the rest of the work constructs gender according to the more or less rigid needs of primary epic (in other words, of epic before Ariosto), here sex is seen to be fluid enough to create a deeply ambiguous effect.

This is not so far-fetched if we consider that in the Renaissance, medicine itself remained fairly confused about sexual identity. Thomas Laqueur has shown that Renaissance doctors believed that there was one sex shared by men and women, so that, in contrast to twentieth-century views on this subject, sex was thought to be more fluid, gender less so.[24] The contemporary state of medical knowledge may help to account for the abundance of cross-dressing episodes in the *comedia* and for the androgyny that can be found in the pastoral novel. It also may suggest that such scenes were, in the Golden Age, something more than evidence of a literary convention. One thinks, for example, of the cross-dressed shepherdess of Montemayor's *La Diana*, whose name is also Ismenia, pursued by another shepherdess whom Ismenia rejects, pretending instead to be her cousin, Alanio.[25] Judging by all the sexual confusion that Montemayor's shepherdess generates in the other characters, it is not unthinkable that she was the model for the Ismenia of the *Jerusalem conquered*. The most likely model for Lope's Ismenia character, however, comes from a twelfth-century Byzantine novel by Eustathius Macrembolites titled *De Ismeniae et Ismenes amoribus libellus* (*The book of the loves of Ismenia and Ismene*), in which cross-dressing plays an important role.[26]

The anticipated marriage of the Lopean Ismenia and Garcerán Manrique is, among other things, a way of striving for textual closure, though this type of dénouement would seem to correspond better to the world of the *comedia* (where Lope knew almost intuitively how to end a play). In *Jerusalem conquered*, on the other hand, the poet has attempted to construct a quasi-historical universe and, in the princess of Limassol, a figure who is not comic, but heroic. Matrimonial bliss may seem an inappropriate manner of closure for the epic, yet there are precedents for the themes of marriage and return to domesticity even since the beginning of the genre. Marriage plays an important role in the *Odyssey*, and the *Orlando Furioso* also includes an important dynastic marriage. Thus Ismenia's destiny does not necessarily diminish the stature of her character, which brings great dignity to Lope de Vega's poem. At the end of the text, the coalition of Christian forces is seriously fragmented, and the European monarchs abandon the Crusade in less than perfect circumstances, yet Ismenia's conduct remains chivalrous from beginning to end.

It is true that Ismenia's marriage to Garcerán Manrique suggests that the heroine ultimately accepts the position of dependency that the "natur-

24. See Thomas Laqueur, *Making Sex: Body and Gender from the Greeks to Freud*, chapter 4. I owe this reference to my colleague Rebecca Haidt.

25. See John T. Cull, "Androgyny in the Spanish Pastoral Novels," 329.

26. *De Ismeniae et Ismenes amoribus libellus* appears in a modern collection titled *Il Romanzo bizantino del 12 secolo*, ed. Fabrizio Conca. There is also an Ismenia in a pastoral play by Lope de Vega titled *Los Amores de Albanio e Ismenia*. The date of composition of the play is uncertain. I am indebted to Antonio Carreño for the latter reference.

al order" would seem to have designated for her and for uppity women like her. In contrast to what happens to the male soldiers, Ismenia is vanquished not on the battlefield, but rather in the battle of love: the woman warrior finally surrenders and assumes the role of the Spanish hero's wife. Consequently, Ismenia not only takes on a paradigmatic feminine role, but her national difference is suppressed in the process of enhancing the Castilian ethnos that assimilates her. Lope de Vega's text thus reaffirms and promotes the patriarchal and early nationalist values prevalent in Golden Age epic, generally, while at the same time placing marriage for love on a modern plane that fits well with incipient bourgeois ideology, a view that would have been unacceptable to Tasso.[27] Nonetheless, what stands out about the Ismenia figure is not her belated "rehabilitation," nor her restoration to femininity—a move that is thoroughly canonical in the texts of this period—but rather the heroine's efforts to insert herself into the action of epic (the patriarchal code-text par excellence), and the vicissitudes that mark her trajectory as a woman warrior. For Ismenia occasionally corrupts the ideological base of Lope de Vega's text: the heroine, in her ability to negotiate both gender codes perfectly, proves that neither is superior to the other, and that the idea of supremacy itself is a rationalization of power fabricated a posteriori. As noted in chapter 3, there would be no need to constantly reaffirm and promote the values of patriarchy and state if they were predestined and stable. The subversion and upheaval that Ismenia's presence provokes in the *Jerusalem conquered* seem to indicate that, on some level, the poet himself knew intuitively that those values, the very ones that inform his text, were vulnerable. This could well be the greatest irony in the poem Lope de Vega wanted to be Spain's national epic.

The "Beautiful Jewess" in Jerusalem conquered

The last section of this chapter will continue to develop the argument that *Jerusalem conquered*, no less than the other epics of imperial Spain analyzed in this book, attempts to establish a dominant identity for the Spanish imperial monarchy in ways that consistently involve suppressing difference. Mieke Bal writes that such textual dominance is, "although present and in many ways obnoxious, not unproblematically established," a situation that makes possible a certain amount of deviance.[28] Lope's first version of the "Jewess of Toledo" legend manifests both of these tendencies: a scripting of "otherness" that relates to Christian male interest, and a small measure of deviance.

27. See Lillian S. Robinson, *Monstrous Regiment: The Lady Knight in Sixteenth-Century Epic*, 220.
28. Mieke Bal, *Lethal Love: Feminist Literary Readings of Biblical Love Stories*, 3.

As the previous chapters suggest, alterity in Golden Age epic is almost always racialized and frequently gendered. In this legend that Lope de Vega embeds into book 19 of the *Jerusalem conquered*, the "other" is both: Raquel, "the Jewess of Toledo." We have already seen how the European leaders return to their respective kingdoms when the Christian forces are torn apart by discord. Having left the Turks far behind, Alphonse VIII of Castile now takes measures to shore up his victories in the *Reconquista* by marrying Eleanor. But there is another "other" nearby whom Lope considers a threat to more than just the king's marriage. She is Raquel, "The Jewess of such great beauty that she achieved fame in all lands circled by the Sun" (La hermosura mayor en una Hebrea / Que tuvo fama en cuanto el Sol rodea, 19.112.7–8). For her, the monarch forsakes both wife and kingly duty. Finally, his grandees put Raquel to death, ending a public love affair that supposedly lasted some seven years.

The earliest written account of the Castilian king's love for a Jewish woman called Fermosa ("Beautiful") appears to be the *General chronicle* of "Alphonse the Wise," but the literary reincarnations of the woman extend at least into the eighteenth century and well beyond the borders of Spain. Lope de Vega recycles the figure of the "beautiful Jewess" twice: once in *Jerusalem conquered*, and again in a play titled *Las paces de los Reyes y Judía de Toledo* (*The reconciliation of the kings and Jewess of Toledo*, 1617). The seventeenth century offers several other versions of the legend, such as Mira de Amescua's *La desgraciada Raquel* (*The unfortunate Raquel*, 1635). The best known of all the Spanish works that recount this tale of adulterous love and death is García de la Huerta's play, *Raquel* (1778). The details of these versions vary slightly. One important variant is the length of the liaison, reduced from seven years to seven months by the time the *Tercera crónica general* (*Third general chronicle*) was composed (1344). Another is the circumstances of Raquel's execution and the monarch's reaction to it. The *General chronicle* says that "counts, rich men and gentlemen" (condes y ricos hombres y caballeros) distracted the king by engaging him in conversation while others went to the Jewish woman's room. "Others went to the Jewess, and as they found her on a noble dais, they slit her throat and those of all who accompanied her, then they left. And when the king found out about this, he was so distraught that he knew not what to do, for he loved her so much that he was willing to go to ruin for her (fueron otros a do estaba la judía: y como la hallasen en muy nobles estrados: degolláronla y a cuantos con ella estaban: y fuéronse luego. Y como el rey supo este [sic] fue muy cuitado que no sabía qué hacer: que tanto la amaba que se quería por ella perder).[29] In Lope's *Jerusalem conquered*, the monarch is

29. Quoted in G. Cirot, "Alphonse le Noble et la Juive de Tolède," 290.

away hunting when the grandees break into Raquel's quarters and pierce her breast with their swords. As mentioned in chapter 1, seventeenth-century Spanish theater bears an explicit interdiction against drawing one's sword in the king's presence. Since Lope de Vega was so accustomed to the conventions of the theater, it is reasonable that the playwright's work would differ from the *General chronicle* on this point. On learning of the murder, Lope's Alphonse is inclined at first to seek vengeance, but "honor," the awareness that the men have acted in his true interest, makes him desist. In J. B. Diamante's *La judía de Toledo* (*The Jewess of Toledo*, 1667), in contrast, the monarch exits the stage to punish the assassins, while García de la Huerta makes him pardon them.

The critical history of the "Jewess of Toledo" legend has had a historicist bent. Menéndez y Pelayo upholds the verisimilitude of the tale, which came under attack in the late seventeenth century and throughout the eighteenth.[30] Cirot attempts to separate legend from history, concluding that the liaison is believable since Alphonse VIII and Eleanor would have married quite young and waited to have children until after the extramarital affair had ended. René Andioc is more interested in the ideological ramifications of mobilizing the legend within a particular historical context. His study of García de la Huerta's *Raquel* emphasizes the significance of the story during Charles III's reign. Andioc argues that Raquel represents a nonaristocratic social group that has illegally captured state power. For the French scholar of eighteenth-century literature, the drama itself is an embodiment of the playwright's own aristocratic and antiabsolutist beliefs.[31] E. Lambert's comparative study links the Spanish versions of *La judía de Toledo* to later literary works that treat the theme elsewhere. Arguing that the love of Alphonse and Raquel is a variant of the biblical Esther story, Lambert lays out the connection between García de la Huerta's play and the French novel of Jacques Cazotte, *Rachel ou la Belle Juive* (*Rachel or the beautiful Jewess*, 1788), a German play, Brandes's *Rahel oder die schöne Jüdin* (*Rachel or the beautiful Jewess*, 1789), and an Austrian play Lambert found superior to everything else in the tradition, Grillparzer's *Jüdin von Toledo* (*Jewess of Toledo*).

Only Edna Aizenberg acknowledges a link between ethnicity and gender in the character of Raquel, at the same time registering the complaint that previous scholarship on the Jewish minority in medieval Spain had not made significant space for Jewish women. "The female of the faith,"

---

30. Ibid., 294.

31. René Andioc interprets Raquel's murder to be García de la Huerta's allusion to the aristocratic uprising against the King's Minister Squillace (Esquilache). See his introduction to *Raquel*, by García de la Huerta, 19–30.

writes Aizenberg, "has generally been left out of the picture, often mentioned only in passing, or has been the object of very narrowly focused attention, not the kind of attention that would allow a generalized picture of the Jewess to emerge." Drawing on feminist theory and ethnic studies scholarship that details an enduring representation of the Jewess as "fictional sex symbol" in works written by men, Aizenberg's article concludes that though both Judaism and Christianity frowned on inter-ethnic sexual relations in Spain's Middle Ages, the Christian-authored "sexualized Jewess tales" manipulated this disapproval to underplay "the negative power of the Christians while thrusting the Jews into the role of the stiff-necked folk who contravene and object."[32]

Although Lope de Vega's *Jerusalem conquered* is the first literary rendition of the legend, none of these studies analyzes Lope's treatment of the Raquel figure here or in his later play. Lambert even goes so far as to assert that the Lopean version of the love affair merits no comment because it did not influence the later "Jewess of Toledo" texts. In the same vein, Andioc finds that the influence of Ulloa de Pereyra and Diamante on García de la Huerta was far greater than that of Lope de Vega.[33] Since the particulars of the plot in the eighteenth-century play fundamentally coincide with those of the Raquel story in *Jerusalem conquered*, it is strange that Andioc should take this position. García de la Huerta even takes character names (Garcerán Manrique, for example) from Lope de Vega's epic. In fact, all the most significant elements in the later versions of the Raquel story are already present in *Jerusalem conquered*. Lope's account may actually show more traces than do the later versions of misogynist ideology and of that same anti-Semitic discourse documented in the epic of Diego de Hojeda (see chapter 4). Nevertheless, by reading Lope de Vega's text against the grain, so to speak, it is also possible to appreciate the delicate subjectivity that the poet gives to the character of the beautiful Jewess, a subjectivity that manages to partially disrupt the otherwise sexist and anti-Semitic representation of the woman as object of desire and of ethnic fury.

The "Jewess of Toledo" episode in *Jerusalem conquered* opens with an account of the king's love for Raquel. The narrator justifies Alphonse VIII's

---

32. Edna Aizenberg, "Una Judía Muy Fermosa: The Jewess as Sex Object in Medieval Spanish Literature and Lore," 187; and 190. Sexualized Jewess stories of this type are still marketable in Spain and other places. Two examples are these historical novels available in bookstores in Madrid during the 1990s: the fourteenth edition of the translation of Lion Feuchtwanger's *La Judía de Toledo* and Yael Guiladi's *Orovida: Una mujer judía en la España del siglo 15.*

33. E. Lambert, "Alphonse de Castille et la Juive de Tolède," 374; Andioc, introduction, 18.

straying from his marriage with the statement that love must be unattainable: "For if love is not Tantalus, I do not believe that desire has living strength" (Que en no siendo amor Tántalo, no creo / Que tenga vivas fuerzas el deseo, 19.111.7–8). Since Eleanor is safe at home, and his desire for her has waned (inevitably, according to the narrator), the monarch looks elsewhere for love or pleasure and thus he comes upon Raquel, here likened explicitly to Bathsheba, Dalilah and Io, while Lope's Alphonse is called a restless Jacob (19.113–14). According to the words of the text, Raquel's power over the king is greater than the influence of the stars: she has taken over his intellectual faculties, paralyzing him as a remora halts a vessel:

> It is astonishing to see a woman paralyze
> the elevated thought of a king so wise,
> as a small remora stops the ship
> which presses its weight against the sea's shoulder.

> (Admira ver que el alto entendimiento
> De un Rey tan Sabio una mujer detiene,
> Como pequeña rémora la nave
> Que oprime el hombro al mar con peso grave.)
> (19.115.5–8)

In Spanish literature of the time, the reference to the two biblical beauties constitutes a commonplace code used both to praise women's beauty and to demonize women in a specifically sexual way. Inasmuch as the allusion is to Jewish women, it also encodes anti-Semitism when used in this manner. The references to the remora and to Io, on the other hand, constitute classical allusions to adulterous desire and female jealousy that, mobilized in this context, have clear sexist markings. More importantly, Lope's choice of metaphor for the Jewish woman, a remora on the ship of state, a parasite living off the monarchy and hindering its progress, identifies the deepest fear that seventeenth-century Spaniards held about the "New Christian" or *converso* element amongst them: that invisibly, imperceptibly, this domesticated "other" could still pollute the body politic from within. We have already seen evidence of this anxiety in Rufo's *La Austriada*. Thus, the real danger is that Raquel will displace the Christian monarch. This fear is realized when the text makes the woman intervene in state policy. Although her own words later contradict the negative motivation imputed to her here, we read that "The laws issued from Raquel's own hand" (Raquel daba las leyes de su mano, 19.122.1). The narrator says that Castile's king has metamorphosed into a lion running away from fire or an elephant frightened by a "vile animal" (19.116.1–2), a man who no longer attends to the governance of his kingdom and subjects. As if he were nostalgically gazing back on the epic battles of the first eighteen books of *Jerusalem conquered*, the narrator

affirms that the Castilian monarch's taste for war has given way to a prefer-
ence for the softer battle of love, insinuating that the king, through loving a
Semitic woman, has grown effeminate. Contact with a decadent Eastern
"other" encodes the same risk of feminization we have noticed in *La
Araucana* and *La Christiada*. Alphonse's problem is that he is no longer him-
self. In loving the Hebrew woman, the Castilian sovereign has put aside his
Western maleness and "gone Oriental." The narrator says he has "forgotten"
himself and his reason:

> There is nothing that reason can now discern,
> his senses are suspended, his soul bathed
> in sweet oblivion, also his faculties; he is
> incapable of distinguishing between them to use them.

> (No hay cosa ya que la razón discierna
> Suspensos los sentidos, y bañados
> De dulce olvido el alma, y sus potencias,
> Sin conocer, ni usar sus diferencias.)
> (19.117.5–8)

So Lope's Alphonse, who supposedly starts to take on the beautiful
Raquel's Semitic "otherness," grows irrational and undiscerning. As the
head is the center of the body, so the monarch is always the locus of sover-
eignty. But as Michel Foucault points out, it is necessary to understand not
just how monarchic power constitutes itself as absolute and sufficient, but
how it is applied at the extremities of sovereignty, through an apparatus
that subjects, excludes, and disciplines in its name.[34] The grandees consti-
tute a social group that lies close to the head and center of the social body
and they are an important part of such an apparatus. They perceive Raquel
as an encroaching threat of contamination that they must exterminate. The
irony in this case is that they must contravene the monarch's will to do so.

Taking advantage of Alphonse's absence from the city, the gentlemen
and nobles conspire to murder the Jewish woman. They unite under the
leadership of Illán Pérez de Córdoba, described as a "prudent elder" (pru-
dente viejo). Pérez de Córdoba's speech develops a parallel between
Raquel's people and other racial groups to whom Castile bears an adver-
sarial relationship. In reminding his coconspirators that many of them
would risk life and limb to rescue their king from Moors and Turks, the
wise old man links the *Reconquista* to the Crusades. As we shall see in a
moment, he also claims that Alphonse's dalliance with Raquel keeps him
from fighting against the Moors, thereby intermixing Jews and Muslims to

34. Michel Foucault, *Power/Knowledge: Selected Interviews and Other Writings
1972–1977*, 97.

activate the whole discursive formation of anti-Semitism as he connects Jewish history to the king's perilous position at the side of Raquel. A key expression of this discourse is an allusion to the destruction of Jerusalem:

> "The destruction which endures and lives until today
> could be seen on the tragic walls
> of the Hebrew people, ever infamous and hard-hearted;
> even the wall was softer and easier to punish."
>
> ("Allí la destruición que hoy vive y dura
> En sus trágicos muros contemplastes
> Del pueblo Hebreo, siempre infame y duro,
> Que aun fue más blando a su castigo el muro.")
> (19.126.5–8)

These four lines invoke one of the most hackneyed utterances of anti-Jewish ideology: that the Jews are a hard and obstinate people who saw the Messiah but reviled him and instigated his death. This belief surfaces throughout Diego de Hojeda's *La Christiada*, as we have seen. By likening the walls of Toledo to those of Jerusalem, Pérez de Córdoba emphasizes that the Castilian city, successfully recaptured from the Moors, is now vulnerable to Jewish attack through the person of Raquel:

> Alphonse lies sleeping in shameful lethargy,
> in the arms of a beautiful Jewess,
> having so completely forgotten that he is king
> that the Moorish enemy criticizes his baseness:
> for seven years you have permitted him to love
> the beautiful Raquel, so that he is
> the slave of this people—he who ought to be
> the Titus Caesar of their blood one day.
>
> (Yace dormido en un letargo infame,
> Alfonso en brazos de una hermosa Hebrea,
> Tan fuera de pensar que Rey se llame
> Que el Moro opuesto su bajeza afea:
> Siete años ha que permitís que ame
> A la bella Raquel, para que sea
> Esclavo desta gente, el que devía
> Ser Tito César de su sangre un día.)
> (19.128)

By telling the grandees that it is they who have allowed the liaison to continue, while simultaneously conjuring the image of Titus, the conspiratorial elder induces them to do what he implies the monarch should, but cannot, do: get rid of the Jewess.

Lope contextualizes the figure of Raquel in a formulaic anti-Semitism that serves to deeply racialize his representation of the female "other." Then, through the words of the conspiracy's leader, he likens the Jewish woman to Calypso and Circe, the same spellbinding females of Homeric provenance that played an important role in the demonization of woman in *El Monserrate*. Pérez de Córdoba also compares Raquel to Helen of Troy and to La Cava.

> What Calypso, what Circe, what betrayals
> have deceived our Ulysses in this fashion?
> just look how he honors his Castles and Lions,
> English roses and French lilies:
> will we, along with other nations, have to battle
> with another captain, grandson of Anchises,
> over this new Helen, or will the mountain
> reduce Spain through another Cava?

> (¿Qué Calipso, qué Circe, qué traiciones
> Tienen así nuestro engañado Ulises?
> Bien honra sus Castillos y Leones,
> Inglesas rosas, y Francesas lises:
> Habemos de tratar varias naciones
> Con otro Capitán nieto de Anquises,
> Por esta nueva Elena, o la montaña
> Ha de cifrar, por otra Cava a España?)
> (19.129)

In this way, the poet connects the Alphonsine love affair to the pilgrim's story of Roderick, the last Visigoth king (book 6). Guillén has also noticed that *Jerusalem conquered* establishes a parallel between the Jewess and La Cava that suggests the love affair's tragic outcome. Citing the dialogue between the Castilian nobles and the Jewess, she writes:

> The interlocutors allude to the parallel between the Jewess and La Cava, either to ratify it or to give the lie to it, suggesting another correspondence, by extension, between the punishment which looms over King Alphonse and the misfortune suffered by Don Roderick because of his illicit conduct . . . According to this parallel formation, Alphonse VIII's love for the Jewess is foreshadowed by Don Roderick's passion for La Cava, and therein lies the fatalism which encircles it.[35]

Lope de Vega makes the analogue between La Cava's story and that of the Jewess Raquel textually explicit. The two narratives join to form a thematic nucleus that contains very dissimilar elements: in La Cava's story, lust,

---

35. Guillén, "Épica, historia y providencialismo," 159–60.

sexual violence, revenge, and loss of kingdom; in Lope's version of the *judía de Toledo* legend, obsessive love, neglect of kingly duty, and finally, assassination of the woman. The common elements seem to be the sway of female charms over monarchs, and the threat they supposedly represent to good governance. Raquel, however, has two problems that La Cava does not have. She is Jewish, and she is in an adulterous relationship with a Christian man, either by choice or because she is in love (a circumstance that may remove choice). The state may actually be threatened in both stories, but there is no cabinet conspiracy to get rid of La Cava. Alphonse VIII is just as guilty of adultery as is Raquel, but he does not have to pay for his sin directly, only indirectly, when his son is killed by a falling roof tile, leaving Alphonse without an heir. Raquel alone pays such a direct price. Perhaps by taking a closer look at Lope's representation of the beautiful Jewess, as it takes shape in the verbal pattern of the Castilian nobles' conspiracy to take her life, it will be possible to deduce that religion or ethnicity accounts for the sharp difference in the treatment of the two women, La Cava and Raquel.

The passage, partially cited above, reassembles the themes of treachery, contentiousness, and deceitfulness long used to stereotype and denigrate both women and Jews. Lope summons what are, by the seventeenth century, clichéd expressions to determine a specific kind of female and ethnic "otherness" for the Raquel character, even before she enters the text. The intertextualities that the poet marshals deliberately seek out fatal identifications between women, Jews and Moors. As Harriet Goldberg points out, in medieval Spain the belief that the Jews had collaborated in the Moorish invasion was common; indeed, it was often thought that Count Don Julian himself was a Jew, an idea that Lope does not adduce, but that creates even greater affinity between La Cava and Raquel. The speech of Illán Pérez de Córdoba is a kind of compendium of seventeenth-century anti-Semitic thought, not substantively different from the discursive formation present in *La Christiada*. It reminds us of how prevalent racializing language of this type was in early modern Spain. If, indeed, Spanish society in the twelfth century was characterized by a certain tolerant coexistence of the three faiths, this cannot be inferred from Lope de Vega's later poetic recreation of that century. Instead, there is in *Jerusalem conquered* an unmistakable hatred of the Semitic "other" that is made explicit toward the end of Illán Pérez de Córdoba's speech, when he refers to the Jews as a "lowly, abhorred nation" (baja nación aborrecida, 19.132.6). Could it be that Lope mobilizes the image of the Jews as a despised people so that Raquel's murder will feel more like an inevitability than an instance of violence against women that has both the structure and the degrading force of a gang rape?[36]

36. Harriet Goldberg, "Two Parallel Medieval Commonplaces: Antifeminism and Antisemitism in the Hispanic Literary Tradition," 97–98, in *Aspects of Jewish Culture*

The grandees enter Raquel's room while the king is away. Alphonse's absence constitutes a particular vulnerability that is textually reiterated by the image of the open, unguarded door. Encountering no resistance, the men penetrate the woman's quarters with swords drawn. The psychosexual implications of Lope's organization of the scene seem unavoidable. Under these dire circumstances, the textual emphasis on the woman's beauty is discordant, to say the least, but it reaffirms the irresistible power Lope de Vega and other Christian writers attributed to the Jewish female as object of sexual desire. The observation that the sight of Raquel's face momentarily checks the assassins' fury means that they are as vulnerable as the monarch to her physical charms. However, instead of resulting in increased sympathy for the woman's plight, this renewed appreciation of Raquel's physical appeal has the effect of displacing the ultimate responsibility for her destiny onto her body, which is always the site for racialized and gendered expression.

Speaking for the group, Illán Pérez repeats the charge that Raquel is "La Cava reborn." The leader then bemoans the loss of the monarch's reason, too long subject to the Jewish woman's power, "held fast by the bonds of your pleasure" (de los lazos de tu gusto asida, 19.137.3). Lope thus frames the necessity for Raquel's death in terms of the hierarchical opposition reason/pleasure (*razón/gusto*), but the unreasonable behavior of the grandees instantly undercuts the force of the binary opposition. The woman responds to their accusations with cogent arguments that further annul the simple opposition between reason and pleasure that the Castilian nobles have invoked as a pretext for killing her. Raquel answers that she is no Cava, since the king never forced her. She goes on to say that had she been raped, she has no father who would bring Moors to Spain. She wonders what harm she can bring to Castile if she neither complains nor seeks vengeance. Finally, the Jewish woman proposes a less bloody but equally effective solution to the problem the grandees face. She asks them to banish her.

> Take me from here to where I will not
> be seen by the king, send me to a foreign land,
> do not pierce my breast, hideous deed,
> which will make you detestable in Spain:
> for you know that when Alphonse sees
> that my blood bathes his royal bed,

---

in the Middle Ages, ed. Paul E. Szarmach. On the association between "normal" sex, force, and rape, see Andrea Dworkin, *Pornography: Men Possessing Women*, 164–65.

he will die of anguish, and thus,
whoever brings death to the king is a traitor.

(Llevadme desde aquí donde no sea
Vista del Rey, pasadme a tierra extraña,
No me paséis el pecho, hazaña fea,
Que os ha de hacer infames en España:
Que bien sabéis que cuando Alfonso vea,
Que su cama Real mi sangre baña,
Morirá de dolor, y desta suerte
Será traidor quien diere al Rey la muerte.)
(19.140)

Raquel's voice twists the commonplace assumption that Jews are traitorous by adducing the grandees' own treachery. She is the epitome of rationality. In fact, her speech constitutes a counterdiscourse: it is the flip side of a much older misogynous discourse that deemed women and women's language unreasonable, passionate, animalistic, in contrast to the supposedly self-evident reasonableness of men's language. Her words deconstruct the opposition inherent in Illán Pérez de Córdoba's argument. The "prudent elder" refuses her terms precisely because, as he puts it, the king is so accustomed to enjoying her pleasure/taste (*gusto*) that he will search her out, even if she is exiled. In the words of Pérez de Córdoba, the king must suffer a great sorrow (*disgusto*); his addiction to this *gusto* must be broken.

In the end, the Jewish woman's arguments cannot sway the grandees. Despite their protestations about reason, they have always known they have the power to look for a solution to a problem of state not in the abstract, but in the body of the woman and the Jew. It is the body that, according to David Theo Goldberg, "materially grounds racialized expression, investing racist expression with its power of discrimination between and over the excluded and included, naturalizing and normalizing the violence of dismissal, dispersal, indeed, all too often, disappearance."[37] Raquel, whose "otherness" Lope objectified, gendered, and racialized from the beginning by naming her "beautiful Jewess" (*hermosa hebrea*), displays a fine-tuned reason that falls on the deaf ears of those Castilian nobles for whom the Semitic woman signifies imminent danger of contagion, partly because they, like the king, are presumably susceptible to her enchantments. *Jerusalem conquered* constructs the Raquel figure as what Stephen Greenblatt has called "the other of the other," that is, a strange people living inside Christendom and threatening it with disease. Since, as witnessed in the var-

37. David Theo Goldberg, *Racist Culture: Philosophy and the Politics of Meaning,* 53–54.

ious chapters of this book, anti-Semitism may actually have served as the *Urtext* for the writing of alterity in Golden Age epic, generally, what happens to the Jews in these poems can just as easily happen to the Araucanian Indians or to the Moriscos. Greenblatt's claim, therefore, that the Jews were the single "other" that was distinctively "unredeemable" because it could not be "included in the larger sphere of metaphoric understanding" that applies to other groups perceived as strange or different is ultimately not true.[38] In fact, it may be very significant that of all the characters who perish in Lope de Vega's vast epic, this one vulnerable Jewish female is the only one to articulate her defense in words against a band of armed men acting in the name of their Christian sovereign. To a point, Raquel's small voice destabilizes these men and their reasons. Lope de Vega seems, as if in spite of himself, to be captivated by this voice and its power. The poet's sympathy for his own doomed character, evident in the reasonable words he gives her, suggests the small measure of deviance that the dominant writing of otherness can occasionally allow. To disembody those words and restore an order they want very much to believe is natural and fated, the Castilian grandees contrive to murder the beautiful Jewess of Toledo.

Raquel's end, though violent and tragic in ways that are probably closely related to her religious and ethnic identity, fits into a pattern of neutralization that affects all the female characters in *Jerusalem conquered*. The monarchy itself seems to be "built" on a fault line associated with a misogynous construct of femininity, beginning with the exemplary tale of Roderick and La Cava. Ismenia achieves marvelous deeds in the fight for Jerusalem, but Lope finally marries her off to Garcerán Manrique. She returns her sword to her brother and presumably moves to Spain. Further demonstration of Lope de Vega's writing of "otherness" efficiently absorbed can be found in the case of Sibyla, queen of Jerusalem and wife of Guido, who commits suicide when her children die of starvation during the siege of the city (book 4), and in the commodified status of Isabela, the sister who survives Sibyla and is passed from husband to husband because she alone offers access to the throne of Jerusalem. Alphonse VIII's own wife, Eleanor, though never in any physical danger, is subjected to neglect and betrayal, which she suffers in silence, primarily because the poet gives her no voice and no space in the epic. The poet, in conclusion, offers his readers a fascinating, sometimes magnificent, ensemble of female characters. He then takes them back, one by one, leaving only Christian men in the king's army and in all positions of state power and authority. *Jerusalem conquered* is doubtless a much more elaborate, complex

---

38. Stephen Greenblatt, *Marvelous Possessions: The Wonder of the New World*, 50–51.

text than *El Monserrate*. Here however, as in the text of Virués, the construct of imperial monarchy that emerges is already fully gendered. And here, as in *El Monserrate*, the spaces left for women are private, not public, and very restricted: the husband's house or a convent. What is different is that Lope de Vega dazzles his readers with several truly remarkable women before he "writes them out" of his text and out of the public sphere that corresponds to the epic genre.

Conclusion
The Cultural Role of Epic Then and Now

When the five epics studied in this book came on the Spanish literary scene, they were already in competition with a variety of literary discourses. Petrarchist lyric, which had enjoyed a position of considerable strength at the court of Charles V, flourished during the late sixteenth and early seventeenth centuries. The romances of chivalry, enormously popular in the first half of the sixteenth century, shared in the aristocratic ethos of the epics, at least on a fictional level, while in the second half of the century, it was the pastoral novel that enchanted and entertained large numbers of Spanish readers. Between these two literary modes, the year 1554 brought a book that would, together with *La Celestina* (already a Golden Age "best-seller") mark the beginnings of an early Spanish realism: *La Vida de Lazarillo de Tormes* (*Lazarillo de Tormes's life*). With its moralizing and its intense focus on the baser aspects of social life, the picaresque novel promoted a disturbingly pessimistic view of the earthly advancement to which marginalized and disenfranchised groups could aspire. The Spanish national theater flourished at this time, and the first years of the seventeenth century saw the arrival of Cervantes's *Don Quijote de la Mancha*, the first modern novel. During this whole period there was also an abundance of religious and devotional works of many kinds. All these discursive types coexisted in the Spain that witnessed the flowering of the learned epic. To be deliberately reductive, their primary themes were love in its many forms, death, honor, and, in the picaresque, abjection.

In this cultural context, the specific role of epic was to project an idealized image of the social group to which its writers belonged, a high-ranking group that understood its interests to be compatible with those of the monarchy and with the imperial project. It is in this sense that the epics of the imperial age lay claim to the events that they themselves depict as triumphal. Although they do not extol empire in so many words, they always align themselves with imperial power, even when they seem to eschew atrocities occurring within the context of conquest. To some extent, Alonso de Ercilla (a king's man), Cristóbal de Virués and Juan Rufo Gutiérrez (both soldiers at Lepanto), Diego de Hojeda (a missionary to Peru), and Lope de Vega (who dedicated his poem to Philip III) all placed their pens in the service of Habsburg monarchy and the defense of the faith, which were, for them, synonymous.

The epic is perhaps the purest Renaissance discourse, in the sense in which Walter Cohen uses this term, to refer to a classicizing discourse of empire that was hegemonic.[1] Delving deep into an ancient past in order to compete with it and to bask in the glow of its prestige, Spanish-language imperial epic shies not from associating political power and religion. On the contrary, the political program of epic is constituted only when these elements are purposefully joined to form a construct that clearly foreshadows the writing of the nation-state in the nineteenth century. The link between church and state is taken for granted in all the epics, even when religion is not the focal point nor the teaching of the faith a main objective.

Preferring to paint a rosy picture of the character and enterprise of the Spaniards, the epics show no tolerance for representation of the abject, unless it be in association with the condition of the enemy, as proof of his/her need for redemption—a classic justification for colonialism.[2] In this sense, the epic "other" almost always appears degraded and, consequently, ripe for conquest. The Spanish male heroic imaginary is thereby represented as glorious but also, by degrees, honorable, compassionate, and chivalrous. The character of the poet gives assistance to several Amerindian widows in *La Araucana,* for example, which serves to enhance his own figure by establishing his identity as a life-restoring liberator, full of moral vision and magnanimity.

Love may enter the epics, but only in a subplot or as a secondary theme, and hardly ever on the part of the Spaniards, who presumably are concerned with more important matters. It is assumed that they will find the reward of love waiting for them once they have proved themselves in battle. Furthermore, there is no domesticity here—only its remnants, visible in the widowed women of Arauco who honor their fallen husbands. Ercilla permits the Araucanian characters to love and to marry, but his own character can only project his desire for conjugal love into the future by means of prophecy. Similarly, Virués creates the character of Lijerea, a Moorish woman who puts on armor to rescue her husband who has been captured by the Christians. When the husband sees her blood-stained clothes, he realizes she has been killed in battle and dies of anguish (canto 11). None of the Spanish men, however, shows a lasting bond with a woman during the action of the epic. On the Christian side, only Lope's Ismenia seems inclined

---

1. Walter Cohen, "The Discourse of Empire in the Renaissance," in *Cultural Authority in Golden Age Spain,* ed. Marina S. Brownlee and Hans Ulrich Gumbrecht, 265–66.
2. See David Spurr, *The Rhetoric of Empire: Colonial Discourse in Journalism, Travel Writing, and Imperial Administration,* 77–80.

to go to war to be near the man she loves. As we have seen, she disguises her motive as well as her sex under a man's armor, but in the end she renounces the soldier's life to marry a Spanish caballero.

So, with the possible exception of Lope's Garcerán Manrique and Ismenia, the Spanish heroes do not love happily. How could they, when the texts routinely represent woman as pernicious, an ever-present threat? When sexual intimacy with women does occur on the Spanish side, it takes the form of lust that quickly brings about the hero's downfall. Virués's *El Monserrate* is all about the hero's attempt to save himself after having given in to this passion, the same one that led to disaster for Roderick the Visigoth. Lope's Alphonse VIII is devoted to Raquel, the "Jewess of Toledo," but this illicit love is intended to demonstrate the Castilian monarch's lassitude and weakness at the end of the poem. The epics exalt the reputations of legendary women like Dido (*La Araucana*) and Hypsicratea (*Jerusalem conquered*), but the female characters who inhabit their pages do not, as a rule, fare any better than the enemy "other." In the case of the "beautiful Jewess," who is *both*, the love affair results in the woman's assassination. Other female characters belonging to the enemy camp simply disappear without authorial comment. We are never told what happens to Melidora (the slave enamored of Ismenia), to Haxa (the Moorish slave in *La Austriada*), or to Ercilla's Guacolda (wife of Lautaro, presumably killed at Mataquito). The poets forget about these characters, or they do not deem it important to recount their end. Either way, such gaps form a disturbing pattern that probably relates to the writers' decision, conscious or not, to use exclusionary structures of representation.[3] All in all, the poetic universe of epic is too fraught with imminent danger for fulfilling romantic relationships to develop, at least among Christian knights bent on victory.

The Golden Age epic, therefore, was not particularly well equipped to address two of the important themes that other literary discourses of the time treated extremely well. The only way it could do so was to construe them antithetically, as a moral warning of dangers to be avoided (lust rather than love), or as a way of debasing the enemy and morally justifying his defeat (abjection). The other two great Golden Age themes, honor and death, were thoroughly compatible with the ethos of epic. The Spanish poems regularly articulated these themes and combined them in the notion of honorable death, which in the epic was not a high-sounding metaphor but a real possibility that surrounded the characters and could touch their lives at any moment.

One thing that distinguished epic from the other literary discourses of

3. Ibid., 93.

the age was its ability to create a genealogy that exalted and legitimized the political status quo. Genealogies, as we have seen throughout this book, are crucial to all epic, partly for their ability to show a venerable origin, and partly as a show of deference to the foundational texts of the genre. Through allusion, as David Wyatt remarks, epics "uncoil a time-line within themselves; they station themselves within the historical line of earlier epics."[4] In a manner analogous to Virgil's use of the prophetic dream in the *Aeneid*, the poems studied in this book all invoke the past to shift the magnificence of the body politic in their own time to the foreground. Even when they narrate recent history or a biblical story, the epics reach deep into the national past to ratify imperial monarchy of the sixteenth and seventeenth centuries. Ercilla pretends to anticipate the defeat of the Ottoman Turks at Lepanto and to survey Spanish discoveries by misreporting his writing time. Rufo traces the origins of John of Austria to endow his hero with a Christian sense of mission and a redemptive role. Virués reaches into the legends of medieval Catalonia, only to bring the Catholic Kings to the sanctuary on Montserrat and to view, from a distance, Philip II's palace at El Escorial. Diego de Hojeda fills his epic on the passion of Christ with prophetic vistas whose purpose is to construct a heroic Catholic identity that is explicitly linked to Spanish nation. Lope de Vega, meanwhile, turns to Roderick the Visigoth to ground a future vision of pan-Iberian monarchy presided over by Philip III. This strategy validates a present that is depicted, according to the imperial myths that anchor these epics, as complete, peaceful, harmonious, and just—except, of course, for the occasional excesses of conquest that "tarnish" Spanish victories, to use Ercilla's words.

More than any other Golden Age discourse, the epic figures forth a world that appears uncomplicatedly torn by forces of good and evil. This is accomplished in part by voyages of war and conquest, historical and metaphorical, that consistently pit the heroes of the poems against an enemy who serves to reinforce a strong sense of Spanish heroic identity created partly by means of the genealogies alluded to above. Each epic, in its way, tells the story of going to war against an enemy "other" depicted as worthy of defeat by means of a range of representational strategies that the epics recycle and transfer from one target group to another. The opponent can be located as far away as Chile or as close as the hero's inner demons, but the epics always depict him or her according to a pattern of representation that ultimately connects the enemy to a comprehensive symbolization of evil with deep religious connotations. By inference, the

4. David Wyatt, "Star Wars and the Productions of Time," 602.

Spanish heroes are associated with good, even when their conduct does not live up to the code of Christian chivalry that is an organizing principle in these poems. The world of epic may contain colorful characters and episodes, as Homer taught us well. But finally it is a black-and-white world that does not use gray shadings to advantage.

Four hundred years after the Spanish epics were written, in a medium that the Golden Age bards could never have imagined, film writer/director George Lucas divided his fictional world in a remarkably similar way. The first installment of the *Star Wars* trilogy (1977) is the product of belief systems dominant in the U.S. during the latter part of the twentieth century; at the same time, it stubbornly adheres to ancient ways of structuring its fictional universe. Here, as in the epics of the Golden Age, good and evil forces pull the characters first this way, then that. Now, as then, hegemonic culture, which never refers to itself as "imperial," triumphs in the end.

In the *Star Wars* trilogy, Hollywood has given us a narrative that assumes the conquest of space by humans, and for better or worse, it has given us an epic for our time. Although Lucas may not have been consciously aware of all that was involved in writing great epic, he has invited us to consider the trilogy in the context of heroic narrative by recalling the epic as the source of his inspiration. Lucas has said that he wrote *Star Wars* out of nostalgia for the *Odyssey* and stories like it, yet, except for an occasional mention of the movies' "epic myth," only Wyatt has taken Lucas's statement seriously enough to examine his films as epic. Other critics simply treat them as updated space opera, or as a mélange of ingredients taken from pulp magazines such as *Flash Gordon*, 1950s science fiction films like *Forbidden Planet*, classics such as *The Wizard of Oz*, and Westerns such as John Ford's *The Searchers*.[5] Even Wyatt does not attempt to link the trilogy and the political environment in which it was written. If recent work on epic has taught us anything, however, it is that the connection between epic and empire is strong and unavoidable, even in cases where the writer strives to execute an "alternative" epic that critiques the genre from within.[6] Hip critics like John Rieder boldly affirm that "in the name of nostalgia for an active, self-confident America the film treats us to a veritable celebration of violent racism, imperialism, and male chauvinism." Rieder, however, does not develop this line of thought in a substantive analysis of the ideological foundations of *Star Wars*, except to notice

5. See Andrew Gordon, "Star Wars: A Myth for Our Time," 74–78. Wyatt's study is the aforementioned "Productions of Time."

6. See David Quint, *Epic and Empire: Politics and Generic Form From Vergil to Milton*, 368. Quint makes this point not in reference to Renaissance epic, but to Sergei Eisenstein's 1938 "film epic," *Alexander Nevsky*.

that the "rebels are clean, white Americans who befriend life-like machines," while the Empire's "vaguely Prussian militarists are machine-like men" and "the odd extraterrestrial stands in for ethnic variation in traditional American style." The most daring criticisms of *Star Wars* take its "imperialist" slant for granted, yet they avoid the topic of empire, focusing instead on the trilogy's extension of Orientalism into deep space (admittedly, a colonialist representational strategy).[7] Of what does the "imperialist" bent of *Star Wars* consist, and to what extent are Lucas's films epic? Let us take a closer look.

It is perhaps ironic that an especially Aristotelian stroke of genius leads Lucas to open his story in medias res with episode 4, *A New Hope*. The temporal parameters of the trilogy are identical to those of classical and Renaissance epic, but with a twist, so to speak. The first words to flash across the screen, "A long time ago in a galaxy far, far away," show that Lucas pretends to recount a very old story. From the technology in evidence in the films, however, and from the fact that intergalactic travel is a routine occurrence, we must deduce that this is the future of our own time. *Star Wars* takes for granted the conquest of space, the "final frontier," retrojecting it onto a mythical remote past and establishing the presence of earthlings in other galaxies. This move inverts the usual procedure in the epic poems examined in this book, which invoked the past to create a pedigree and a sense of identity for the present, then triumphantly projected these onto the future.

At the same time, however, Lucas remains very interested in genealogy, which he uses in the way that Juan Rufo, for example, employed it to show the lineage of his hero. Accordingly, at the end of the trilogy's second installment, *The Empire Strikes Back*, the wicked figure of Darth Vader, symbolically robed in black, identifies himself as the biological father of Luke Skywalker, Lucas's hero. This inauspicious origin is, however, partly deceptive, because the very thing that made Vader vulnerable to attack by the forces of evil, known in the trilogy as the "dark side," was his extraordinary sensitivity to the positive side of the same energy field, known as the "Force." Deep down, therefore, Darth Vader is just a hero who took a wrong turn. He lingered among the enemy and assimilated his ways, but he is still eminently salvageable. The hermit Juan Garín (*El Monserrate*) articulates this message, but Homer and Virgil had already demonstrated that the epic hero's dangerous negotiation with the powers of an evil "other" could be overcome. Odysseus stayed with Circe for a whole year, and Aeneas dallied

7. John Rieder, "Embracing the Alien: Science Fiction in Mass Culture," 33–34. See also Jeffrey A. Weinstock's "Freaks in Space: 'Extraterrestrialism' and 'Deep-Space' Multiculturalism."

with Dido of Carthage, but both men left these apparently menacing women behind in the end, having recovered their sense of mission and a desire to return to domesticity. So the young Skywalker does not have to feel ashamed of his origins. On the contrary, the "Force" remains strong in his family, as we learn in the trilogy's third installment, *Return of the Jedi*, when Luke discovers that he has a twin sister, the princess Leia Organa. (This is one of several romance elements that enter into Lucas's epic world.)

In contrast to the conventions of Golden Age epic, *Star Wars* does not use genealogy to legitimize a political situation already in existence, at least not directly. Within the boundaries of its fiction, the hero opposes the status quo. Luke Skywalker and his band of "Alliance" rebels, whom the three films refer to as "freedom fighters," struggle against the evil Galactic Empire and its political program, known as the "New Order" (a term coined either by George Lucas or George Bush). Their objective is to recover a form of government already lost when the trilogy opens: that of the Old Republic, which had been gradually perverted by corruption and overbureaucratization, then taken over by the Empire. *Star Wars*, then, fits neatly into David Quint's ambiguous category of "epic of the losers," though in this case the "losers" triumph in the end. It is no accident that the three main characters of the trilogy, Luke Skywalker, Princess Leia, and Han Solo (who joined the Alliance almost by accident and is repeatedly criticized for caring too much about money), look and sound utterly North American. In this, Rieder is quite right. The utter Americanness of the heroes suggests that Lucas, through his characters' struggle and the myths of republicanism that inspire it, has executed a monumental feat of displacement in order to legitimize an extratextual political status quo that is, roughly speaking, that of the last decades of the Cold War, in which the United States was said to be one of two geopolitical superpowers. George Lucas, after all, was born in 1944 and grew up during the 1950s, a period in U.S. cultural history so stultifying that only bold avant-garde writers could begin to articulate a devastating critique of it in 1956, when Allen Ginsberg's "Howl" was published. Lucas's displacement is to project empire into space and onto a fictional enemy, while refraining from even an indirect critique of U.S. imperialism.

Evidence for this idea lies in the strategies used to represent the Galactic Empire, the multilayered but always malevolent "other" everywhere in evidence in the *Star Wars* trilogy. Any viewer schooled in World War II films, fictional or documentary, makes an automatic association, one that is probably conscious, between the emperor's subordinates and those of Hitler. The uniforms worn by the officer class who supervises the Empire's attack on various rebel bases are eerily similar to those worn by officers of the Third Reich. The emperor's foremost infantrymen are the vinyl-clad "Imperial Stormtroopers," whose faces are completely covered, rendering them the more inhuman. Mixed in with these Nazi-like elements are others that recall, in a stereotypical way, the military police uniform (the greatcoat and fur hat, or *ushanka*) of the former Soviet Union. In the same vein, the emperor's "Royal Guard" dresses in red from head to toe. Subtly reproducing on the big screen a political discourse about "Soviet Imperialism" that was very strong in the United States during the 1970s and 1980s, Lucas effortlessly collapses his image of purported Nazis into another of Red Army wannabes. The result is an apparently seamless representation of the Galactic Emperor as a "generic dictator" who exists outside of real history, yet who stirs well-known connotations of Nazism and the "red menace" that resonated in U.S. culture during the period in which these films were produced. The trilogy effectively expounds the message (one that still has much currency in U.S. culture) that there is no substantive difference between fascism and socialism, and that both are equally evil. Herein lies at least part of the trilogy's "ideological limitations," to which Rieder only alludes in passing. Herein, too, lies a significant part of its relationship to U.S. imperialism, which exists in *history*, rather than just in a story.

The connection between the Galactic Empire and the extraterrestrial "others" so abundant in the trilogy seems tenuous at first. However, since the Empire has banned nonhuman life forms from the Imperial City, there is a strong bias in favor of humans, which in these films, as Jeffrey A. Weinstock and others assert, almost always means white American males. The nonhuman life-forms can be friendly or hostile, but they all occupy a subaltern position from the perspective of both Empire and Alliance. The best study of "Extraterrestrialism" in *Star Wars* is that of Weinstock, who argues that the "aliens" of the trilogy are really a holdover from the American freak show, which had become extinct in the 1940s largely because it could not compete with science fiction films. "The freak show," writes Weinstock, "the exhibition of difference for amusement, the apex of terrestrial 'political incorrectness,' is alive and well in space." Weinstock shows that the "freaks" of *Star Wars* carry Orientalist codes to other galaxies, where they are used to depict truly horrifying characters such as Jabba the Hutt as a decadent and degenerate sultan. To the extent that Orientalism is bound up with an ascendant West whose codes for scripting identity and difference are inherently racist, the ideas embodied in these creatures are thoroughly consistent with an ideology of empire that vibrates all through the *Star Wars* trilogy. According to this logic, Weinstock finds that Chewbacca the Wookie, sidekick of lead character Han Solo (played by Harrison Ford), is an updated version of the "missing link," or hirsute man, while the adorable Ewoks of Endor "play on an equally stereotypical construction of the 'primitive' African pygmy tribe living in the jungle, astounded by the white man's technological 'magic' and too simple to be devious."[8] These examples suffice to suggest that even the "acceptable" nonhumans are racialized in ways consistent with a colonialist system of representation. Needless to say, all of this is hauntingly reminiscent of the codes of Renaissance epic.

It is in its disengagement from history that *Star Wars* falls apart as epic. On the level of metaphor, as mentioned above, there is a quasi-historical connection between the trilogy's enemy powers and the world in which we live, but genuine epic would not dissemble that connection or try to pass it off as fiction. Indeed, what gives such amazing force to the *Iliad*, the *Aeneid*, and the *Araucana* is precisely this bold advertisement of the link between the text and political power in the real world. The dehistoricization of empire in *Star Wars* creates some artistic problems for Lucas because it results in war that seems poorly justified and in flat characters.

The epics of imperial Spain, as we know, established a tight link between religion and the state, one that they manipulated to justify war and conquest. *Star Wars* does not display an analogous connection; in fact, there is no faith with a large following in evidence in the trilogy. There is, of course, the "Force" and those who believe in it, the Jedi Knights, who are said to be defenders of the Old Republic and the guardians of justice and peace. However, the important subtext for the Jedi Knights is not epic, but the novels of chivalry, whose action was also apparently detached from history. The Jedi code can be favorably compared with an unwritten chivalric code for the knights of the romances of chivalry, many of the tenets of which appear, recontextualized, in Golden Age epic. Luke Skywalker must learn self-restraint to become a Jedi, and he must walk a spiritual path of sorts. But since the *Star Wars* Jedi live in a secular world where spiritual motivations are almost completely lacking, other characters (Han Solo and Jabba the Hutt, for example, both of whom Lucas connects to the vice of greed) laugh at them for believing in "old ways." Because the Old Republic exists outside history and even outside the temporal limits of the trilogy, it is hard to muster enthusiasm about its defense, so that phrases like "freedom fighters" turn out to be nothing but fluff. As Wyatt points out, the trilogy suffers from an "aneaesthesia of the heart" that rubs off on the spectator, who can watch the destruction of an entire world (Alderaan) without feeling a thing.[9] In the end, the only motivation the trilogy adduces for the fight against the Empire is a family one: Luke's father was a Jedi, and he wants to claim his legacy. Family

---

8. Weinstock, "Freaks in Space," 328–33.
9. Wyatt, "Productions of Time," 609.

can constitute an important motivating force in epic (Aeneas carries his aged father, Anchises, out of the ruins of Troy), but by itself it is insufficient.

The lack of a historical context also has a direct impact on our ability to gauge the exemplarity of the characters. Let us consider the case of the *Star Wars* women, for example. Princess Leia is a leading character in the trilogy, but she is, in Andrew Gordon's words, a "confusing figure" because she serves too many functions in the narrative. "As composite woman," writes Gordon, "Leia is Goddess, Whore, Lover, Mother, Sister, and Castrating Bitch all at once: tempting but taboo." On the surface, her status appears somewhat improved from that of the women in classical and Renaissance epic, but since she lives outside history, we cannot know how emancipated she really is. The only female character to whom we can compare her is Mon Mothma, organizer of the Alliance to Restore the Republic. Mon Mothma, however, only appears for one brief moment at the end of *Return of the Jedi* to announce the plans for the Battle of Endor, which brings an end to the Empire.[10] The idea behind her character is extremely important, but since Lucas makes her practically invisible, the viewer never develops any feelings about her one way or the other. The women of this postmodern epic do not have to dress as men to succeed, it is true, but they are also free of inner conflict and historical specificity, which makes for extremely weak character development. The doubts and hesitations of Lope de Vega's Ismenia, for example, draw us closer to her than we ever get to Leia Organa.

So, while the organization of time and great themes of epic past (honor, death, the promise of love, even the critique of greed) live on in the *Star Wars* trilogy, Lucas's decision to separate his films from all but a metaphoric remnant of our own time ultimately renders them somewhat flat and empty. As Renaissance epic did, he tries to use a "good war story" to temporarily anchor his viewers in an idealized fictive sense of who they are. In contrast to the epics of imperial Spain, however, the heroes and villains of the *Star Wars* trilogy exist outside the processes of history. There is, thus, no sense of the nation's evolution that is so crucial to epic. What we are left with is a momentarily enticing story. Perhaps it is no accident that one of the most poignant moments in the whole *Star Wars* trilogy is the scene in *Return of the Jedi* where the protocol droid C-3PO relates the story of the Galactic Civil War for the assembled Ewoks in a language only they can understand. With Luke Skywalker, Leia Organa, and Han Solo, we look on as the droid punctuates his war narrative with thundering sound effects

10. Andrew Gordon, "The Power of the Force: Sex in the Star Wars trilogy," 196. For the details of Mon Mothma's character, see Bill Slavicsek, *A Guide to the "Star Wars" Universe*, 308-9.

and occasionally recognizable names. Is this George Lucas, writer of post-modern epic, winking back at Homer? If we could understand the words, and if the outcome were crucial to our real history, perhaps the droid's story would have all the necessary power to return us to the origins of the genre. As it is, our view of C-3PO's war story must be filtered through pre-vious experience with historical genres such as epics. Such genres spring from deeply rooted cultural myths and are shaped by writers into power-ful ideological dramas in which the stakes are always high and the state always enduring.

Bibliography

Adorno, Rolena. *Guaman Poma: Writing and Resistance in Colonial Peru.* Austin: University of Texas Press, 1986.

Aguirre Beltrán, Gonzalo. *La población negra de México: Estudio etnohistórico.* 1946. Reprint. Mexico: Fondo de Cultura Económica, 1972.

Aizenberg, Edna. "Una Judía Muy Fermosa: The Jewess as Sex Object in Medieval Spanish Literature and Lore." *La Corónica* 12 (1984): 187–94.

Albarracín Sarmiento, Carlos. "El poeta y su Rey en *La Araucana.*" *Filología* 21 (1986): 99–116.

Alegría, Fernando. *La poesía chilena: Orígenes y desarrollo del siglo 16 al 19.* Berkeley: University of California Press; Mexico: Fondo de Cultura Económica, 1954.

Alfonso el Sabio. *Primera crónica general de España que mandó componer Alfonso el Sabio y se continuaba bajo Sancho 4 en 1289.* Edited by Ramón Menéndez Pidal. 2 vols. Madrid: Bailly-Bailliere, 1906.

Alter, Robert, and Frank Kermode, eds. *The Literary Guide to the Bible.* Cambridge: Harvard University Press, 1987.

Anderson, Benedict. *Imagined Communities. Reflections on the Origins and Spread of Nationalism.* 1983. Rev. ed. London: Verso, 1991.

Andioc, René. Introduction to *Raquel,* by García de la Huerta. Madrid: Castalia, 1970.

Anzaldúa, Gloria. *Borderlands/La Frontera: The New Mestiza.* San Francisco: Aunt Lute Books, 1987.

Ariosto, Ludovico. *Orlando Furioso.* Translated by Sir John Harington. Edited by Rudolf Gottfried. 1963. Reprint. Bloomington: Indiana University Press, 1975.

Aristotle. *Poetics.* Translated by Richard Janko. Indianapolis: Hackett, 1987.

Armstrong, John Alexander. *Nations before Nationalism.* Chapel Hill: University of North Carolina Press, 1982.

Aubrun, Charles V. "Poesía épica y novela: El episodio de Glaura en *La Araucana* de Ercilla." *Revista Iberoamericana* 21 (1956): 261–73.

Avalle-Arce, Juan Bautista. "El poeta en su poema (El caso Ercilla)." *Revista de Occidente* 32 (1971): 152–70.

Bakhtin, Mikhail M. *The Dialogic Imagination.* Edited by Michael Holquist. Translated by Caryl Emerson and Michael Holquist. Austin: University of Texas Press, 1981.

Bal, Mieke. *Lethal Love: Feminist Literary Readings of Biblical Love Stories.* Bloomington: Indiana University Press, 1987.

Balbuena, Bernardo de. *El Bernardo, o victoria de Roncesvalles.* Edited by Cayetano Rosell. Bibilioteca de Autores Españoles 17, 139–399. Madrid: Rivadeneyra, 1851.

Bartra, Roger. *Wild Men in the Looking Glass: The Mythic Origins of European Otherness.* Translated by Carl T. Berrisford. Ann Arbor: University of Michigan Press, 1994.

Bataillon, Marcel. "The Idea of the Discovery of America among the Spaniards of the Sixteenth Century." In *Spain in the Fifteenth Century, 1369–1516,* edited by Roger Highfield, translated by Frances M. López-Morillas, 426–64. New York: Harper and Row, 1972.

Berger, Philippe. *Libro y lectura en la Valencia del Renacimiento.* Valencia: Alfons el Magnanim, Institució Valenciana d'Estudis i Investigació, 1987.

Bergmann, Emilie. *Art Inscribed: Essays on Ekphrasis in Spanish Golden Age Poetry.* Cambridge: Harvard University Press, 1979.

Bernheimer, Richard. *Wild Men in the Middle Ages: A Study in Art, Sentiment, and Demonology.* Cambridge: Harvard University Press, 1982.

Beverley, John R. "Gracián and the Baroque Overvaluation of Literature." Paper presented at MLA, Washington, D.C., December 1989.

Bhabha, Homi K., ed. *Nation and Narration.* London: Routledge, 1990.

Bitton, Livia E. "The Jewess as a Fictional Sex Symbol." *Bucknell Review* 21 (1973): 63–86.

Bloom, Harold. *The Anxiety of Influence: A Theory of Poetry.* New York: Oxford University Press, 1973.

———. *A Map of Misreading.* Oxford: Oxford University Press, 1975.

Boccaccio, Giovanni. *Concerning Famous Women.* Translated by Guido A. Guarino. New Brunswick, N.J.: Rutgers University Press, 1963.

———. *De las ilustres mujeres.* Madrid: Real Academia Española, 1951. (Facsimile edition of 1494, Paulo Hurus, Zaragoza.)

Böhm, Günter. *Nuevos antecedentes para una historia de los judíos en Chile colonial.* Santiago: Editorial Universitaria, 1963.

Bouterwek, Frederick. *History of Spanish and Portuguese Literature.* Translated by Thomasina Ross. 2 vols. London: Boosey and Sons, 1823.

Braudel, Fernand. *The Mediterranean and the Mediterranean World in the Age of Philip II.* Translated by Siân Reynolds. 2 vols. New York: Harper and Row, 1966.

Brooke, Christoper. *The Monastic World, 1000–1300: The Rise and Development of the Monastic Tradition.* London: Paul Elek, 1974.

Brown, Michael, ed. *Approaches to Antisemitism: Context and Curriculum.* New York and Jerusalem: American Jewish Committee and International Center for University Teaching of Jewish Civilization, 1994.

Burns, Norman T., and Christopher J. Reagan, eds. *Concepts of the Hero in the Middle Ages and the Renaissance.* Albany: State University of New York Press, 1975.

Butler, Judith. *Gender Trouble: Feminism and the Subversion of Identity.* New York: Routledge, 1990.

Camões, Luiz de. *The Lusiads.* Translated and edited by Leonard Bacon. New York: Hispanic Society of America, 1950.

Campbell, Lily B. "The Christian Muse." *Huntington Library Bulletin* 8 (1935): 29–70.

Cardaillac, Louis. *Moriscos y cristianos: Un enfrentamiento polémico (1492–1640).* Preface by Fernand Braudel. Translated by Mercedes García Arenal. Madrid: Fondo de Cultura Económica, 1979.

Caro Baroja, Julio. *Los moriscos del Reino de Granada: Ensayo de historia social.* Madrid: Instituto de Estudios Políticos, 1957.

Castillo, Ana. *Massacre of the Dreamers: Essays on Xicanisma.* New York: Plume, 1995.

Cavafy, Constantine. *The Complete Poems.* Translated by Rae Dalven. New York: Harcourt, 1948.

Cerdan, Francis, ed. *Hommage à Robert Jammes.* (Anejos de *Criticón,* 2 vols.). Toulouse: Presses Universitaires du Mirail, 1994.

Cervantes Saavedra, Miguel de. *Don Quijote de La Mancha.* Edited by Martín de Riquer. Barcelona: Juventud, 1966.

Cevallos, Francisco Javier. "Don Alonso de Ercilla and the American Indian: History and Myth." *Revista de Estudios Hispánicos* 23 (1989): 87–97.

Chadwick, Henry. *The Early Church.* Vol. 1 of *The Pelican History of the Church.* Reprint. New York: Penguin Books, 1982.

Chenu, M.-D. *Nature, Man, and Society in the Twelfth Century: Essays on New Theological Perspectives in the Latin West.* Translated by Jerome Taylor and Lester K. Little. Chicago: University of Chicago Press, 1968.

Chevalier, Maxime. *L'Arioste en Espagne, 1530–1650: Recherches sur l'influence du "Roland furieux."* Bordeaux: Institut d'Études Ibériques et Ibéro-Américaines de l'Université de Bordeaux, 1966.

———. *Lectura y lectores en la España del Siglo 16 y 17.* Madrid: Ediciones Turner, 1976.

Chorpenning, Joseph F. "The Monastery, Paradise, and the Castle: Literary Images and Spiritual Development in St. Teresa of Avila." *Bulletin of Hispanic Studies* 62 (1985): 245–57.

Cirot, G. "Alphonse le Noble et la Juive de Tolède." *Bulletin Hispanique* 24 (1922): 289–306.

Cohen, Walter. "The Discourse of Empire in the Renaissance." In *Cultural Authority in Golden Age Spain,* edited by Marina S. Brownlee and Hans Ulrich Gumbrecht, 260–83. Baltimore: Johns Hopkins University Press, 1995.

Colombí-Monguió, Alicia de. *Petrarquismo peruano: Diego Dávalos y Figueroa y la poesía de la Miscelánea Austral.* London: Tamesis, 1985.

———. "Teoría y práctica de la poética renacentista: de Fray Luis a Lope de Vega." In *Actas del 8 Congreso de la Asociación Internacional de Hispanistas,* 323–31. Madrid: Istmo, 1986.

Conca, Fabrizio, editor. *Il Romanzo Bizantino del 12 Secolo.* Classici Greci. Torino: Unione Tipografico-Editrice Torinese, 1994.

Corcoran, Sister Mary Helen Patricia. Introduction to *La Christiada,* by Diego de Hojeda. Edited by Mary Helen Corcoran. Washington, D.C.: Catholic University Press, 1935.

Covarrubias, Sebastián de. *Tesoro de la Lengua Castellana o Española.* Edited by Martín de Riquer. Barcelona: Alta Fulla, 1987.

Cruz, Anne J. *Imitación y transformación: el petrarquismo en la poesía de Boscán y Garcilaso de la Vega.* Purdue University Monographs in Romance Languages. Amsterdam: John Benjamins, 1988.

Cull, John T. "Androgyny in the Spanish Pastoral Novels." *Hispanic Review* 57 (1989): 317–34.

Culler, Jonathan. *The Pursuit of Signs: Semiotics, Literature, Deconstruction.* Ithaca, N.Y.: Cornell University Press, 1981.

Curtius, Ernst Robert. *European Literature and the Latin Middle Ages.* Translated by Willard R. Trask. Bollingen Series 36. New York: Pantheon Books, 1953.

Davis, Elizabeth B. "Hagiographic Jest in Quevedo: Tradition and Departure." *Modern Language Notes* 104 (1989): 315–29.

———. "La Nueva España y la ideología imperial: la épica del siglo 17." In vol. 2 of *Historia de la literatura mexicana,* edited by Raquel Chang-Rodríguez. Mexico: Siglo 21, in press.

———. "The Politics of Effacement: Diego de Hojeda's Humble Poetics." *Bulletin of Hispanic Studies* 71 (1994): 339–57.

———. "Rape and Repentance: Virués' *El Monserrate* and Reading Golden Age Foundational Myths." *Calíope* 2 (1996): 32–53.

———. "'Woman, Why Weepest Thou?': Re-visioning the Golden Age Magdalen." *Hispania* 76 (1993): 38–48.

Delaney, John J., and James Edward Tobin. *Dictionary of Catholic Biography.* Garden City, N.Y.: Doubleday, 1961.

Deleuze, Gilles, and Felix Guattari. *Kafka: Toward a Minor Literature.* Translated by Dana Polan. Minneapolis: University of Minnesota Press, 1986.

Deyermond, Alan. "El hombre salvaje en la novela sentimental." In *Actas del II Congreso Internacional de Hispanistas,* edited by Jaime Sánchez Romeralo and Norbert Roulssen, 265–72. Nijwegen: Asociación Internacional de Hispanistas, 1967.

Di Cesare, Mario A. *Vida's "Christiad" and Vergilian Epic.* New York: Columbia University Press, 1964.

Domínguez Ortiz, Antonio. *Instituciones y sociedad en la España de los Austrias.* Barcelona: Ariel, 1985.

———. *La Sociedad Española en el Siglo 17.* 2 vols. Granada: Universidad de Granada, 1992.

Donno, Elizabeth Story, ed. *Elizabethan Minor Epics.* London: Routledge and Kegan Paul, 1963.

Dudley, Edward, and Novak, Maximillian E., eds. *The Wild Man Within: An Image in Western Thought from the Renaissance to Romanticism.* Pittsburgh: University of Pittsburgh Press, 1972.

Dugaw, Dianne. *Warrior Women and Popular Balladry, 1650–1850.* Cambridge: Cambridge University Press, 1989.

Dupláa, Cristina, and Gwendolyn Barnes, eds. *Las nacionalidades del Estado español: Una problemática cultura.* Minneapolis: University of Minnesota Press, 1986.

Durand, José. "Caupolicán. Clave historial y épica de La Araucana." *Revue de Littérature Comparée* 52 (1978): 367–89.

———. "El chapetón Ercilla y la honra araucana." *Filología* 10 (1964), 113–34.

Durling, Robert M. *The Figure of the Poet in Renaissance Epic.* Cambridge: Harvard University Press, 1965.

Dworkin, Andrea. *Pornography: Men Possessing Women.* New York: Plume, 1989.

Eagleton, Terry. *Against the Grain: Essays 1975–1985.* London: Verso, 1986.

Elkin, Judith L. "Imagining Idolatry: Missionaries, Indians, and Jews." In *Religion and Authority of the Past,* edited by Tobin Siebers. Ann Arbor: University of Michigan Press, 1993.

Elliott, Alison Goddard. *Roads to Paradise: Reading the Lives of the Early Saints.* Hanover, N.H.: University Press of New England, 1987.

Elliott, John H. *Imperial Spain, 1469–1716.* New York: St. Martin's Press, 1963.

———. *Spain and Its World, 1500–1700: Selected Essays.* New Haven: Yale University Press, 1989.

Ercilla y Çúñiga, Alonso de. *La Araucana.* Madrid: Pierres Cossin, 1569.

Ercilla, Alonso de. *La Araucana*. Edited by Isaías Lerner. Madrid: Cátedra, 1993.

———. *La Araucana*. Edited by Marcos A. Morínigo and Isaías Lerner. 2 vols. Madrid: Castalia, 1987.

———. *La Araucana*. Edited by Antonio de Sancha. Madrid: Antonio de Sancha, 1776.

Escalante, Bernardino de. *Discursos de Bernardino de Escalante al Rey y sus Ministros, 1585–1605*. Edited by José Luis Casado Soto. Servicio de Publicaciones, Universidad de Cantabria. Salamanca: Europa Artes Gráficas, 1995.

Estudios dedicados a Menéndez Pidal. Madrid: Consejo Superior de Investigaciones Científicas, 1953.

Fetterley, Judith. *The Resisting Reader: A Feminist Approach to American Fiction*. Bloomington: Indiana University Press, 1978.

Feuchtwanger, Lion. *La judía de Toledo*. Translated by Ana Tortajada. 1954. Reprint. Madrid: Edaf, 1992.

Fichter, Andrew. *Poets Historical: Dynastic Epic in the Renaissance*. New Haven: Yale University Press, 1982.

Flavius, Josephus. *The Jewish War*. Translated by William Whiston. Israel: Steimatzky, 1980.

Florit, Eugenio. "Los momentos líricos de *La Araucana*." *Revista Iberoamericana* 33 (1967): 45–54.

Foucault, Michel. *Power/Knowledge: Selected Interviews and Other Writings, 1972–1977*. Translated by Colin Gordon, Leo Marshall, John Mepham, and Kate Soper. Edited by Colin Gordon. New York: Pantheon Books, 1972.

Fox, Dian. *Kings in Calderón: A Study in Characterization and Political Theory*. London: Tamesis, 1986.

Garber, Marjorie. *Vested Interests: Cross-Dressing and Cultural Anxiety*. New York: Routledge, 1992.

García de la Huerta, Vicente. *Raquel*. Edited by René Andioc. Madrid: Castalia 1970.

Gates, Henry Louis, Jr., ed. *"Race," Writing, and Difference*. Chicago: University of Chicago Press, 1986.

Gaylord [Randal], Mary. *The Historical Prose of Fernando de Herrera*. London: Tamesis, 1971.

Gilman, Sander L., and Steven T. Katz. eds. *Anti-Semitism in Times of Crisis*. New York: New York University Press, 1991.

Goic, Cedomil. "Poética del exordio en *La Araucana*." *Revista Chilena de Literatura* 1 (1970): 5–22.

Goldberg, David Theo. *Racist Culture: Philosophy and the Politics of Meaning*. Oxford: Blackwell, 1993.

González Echevarría, Roberto, and Enrique Pupo-Walker, eds. *Cambridge History of Latin American Literature.* 3 vols. Cambridge: Cambridge University Press, 1996.

Gordon, Andrew. "The Power of the Force: Sex in the *Star Wars* Trilogy. In *Eros in the Mind's Eye: Sexuality and the Fantastic in Art and Film,* edited by Donald Palumbo, 193–207. New York: Greenwood Press, 1986.

———. *"Star Wars:* A Myth for Our Time." In *Screening the Sacred: Religion, Myth, and Ideology in Popular American Film,* edited by Joel W. Martin and Conrad E. Ostwalt, Jr., 73–82. Boulder: Westview Press, 1995.

Greenblatt, Stephen. *Marvelous Possessions: The Wonder of the New World.* Chicago: University of Chicago Press, 1991.

———. *Shakespearean Negotiations: The Circulation of Social Energy in Renaissance England.* Berkeley: University of California Press, 1988.

Greene, Roland. "'This Phrasis is Continuous': Love and Empire in 1590," *Journal of Hispanic Philology* 16 (1992): 237–52.

Greene, Thomas M. *The Descent from Heaven: A Study in Epic Continuity.* 1963. Reprint. New Haven: Yale University Press, 1970.

———. *The Light in Troy: Imitation and Discovery in Renaissance Poetry.* New Haven: Yale University Press, 1982.

Guamán Poma de Ayala, Felipe. *Nueva crónica y buen gobierno.* Edited by John J. Murra, Rolena Adorno, and Jorge L. Urioste. Madrid: Siglo 21, 1987.

Guiladi, Yael. *Orovida: Una mujer judía en la España del siglo 15.* Translated by Manuel Pereira. Barcelona: Edhasa, 1996.

Guillén, Felisa. "Ekphrasis e imitación en la Jerusalén conquistada." *Hispania* 78 (1995): 231–39.

———. "Épica, historia y providencialismo en la España del siglo 17: El caso de la *Jerusalén Conquistada."* Ann Arbor: University Microfilms International, 1989.

Hale, David George. *The Body Politic: A Political Metaphor in Renaissance Literature.* The Hague: Mouton, 1971.

Hall, Stuart, and Paul du Gay, eds. *Questions of Cultural Identity.* London: Sage, 1996.

Hart, Thomas. "The Author's Voice in *The Lusiads." Hispanic Review* 44 (1976): 45–55.

———. "The Idea of History in Camões's *Lusiads." Occidente* 36 (1972): 83–97.

———. *"The Lusiads* and the Modern Reader." *Emory University Quarterly* 19 (1963): 1–7.

Herrera, Fernando de. *Relación de la guerra de Chipre y suceso de la batalla naval de Lepanto.* Sevilla: Alonso Picardo, 1572. Reprint. Vol. 21 of

Colección de Documentos Inéditos para la Historia de España. Edited by Miguel Salvá and Pedro Sainz de Baranda. Madrid: Viuda de Calero, 1852.

Highet, Gilbert. "Classical Echoes in *La Araucana.*" *Modern Language Notes* 62 (1947): 329–31.

Higgins, Lynn A., and Brenda R. Silver, eds. *Rape and Representation.* New York: Columbia University Press, 1991.

Hojeda, Diego de. *La Christiada.* Edited by Sister Mary Helen Patricia Corcoran. Washington, D.C.: Catholic University Press, 1935.

———. *La Cristiada.* Edited by Frank Pierce. Salamanca: Anaya, 1971.

Homer. *The Iliad.* Translated by Richmond Lattimore. Chicago: University of Chicago Press, 1951.

———. *The Odyssey.* Translated by Robert Fitzgerald. New York: Anchor Books, 1963.

———. *The Odyssey of Homer.* Translated by Richmond Lattimore. 1965. Reprint. New York: Harper and Row, 1967.

Horace. *Odes and Epodes.* Translated by C. E. Bennett. Loeb Classical Library. Cambridge: Harvard University Press, 1988.

Hurtado de Mendoza, Diego. *Guerra de Granada hecha por el rey D. Felipe II contra los Moriscos de aquel reino, sus rebeldes.* Servicio de Publicaciones, Universidad de Cádiz. Chiclana: Lipper, 1990. (Facsimile edition of Barcelona, 1842.)

Isaac, Jules. *Genèse de l'antisémitisme.* Paris: Calman-Levy, 1956.

Jakobson, Roman. *Selected Writings.* Edited by Stephen Rudy. 6 vols. Netherlands: Mouton, 1981.

Johnson, Barbara. *A World of Difference.* Baltimore: John Hopkins University Press, 1987.

Kaminsky, Amy K. *Reading the Body Politic: Feminist Criticism and Latin American Women Writers.* Minneapolis: University of Minnesota Press, 1993.

Kossoff, David, and José Amor y Vázquez, eds. *Homenaje a William L. Fichter.* Madrid: Castalia, 1971.

Krieger, Murray. *Ekphrasis: The Illusion of the Natural Sign.* Baltimore: Johns Hopkins University Press, 1992.

Kurth, Burton O. *Milton and Christian Heroism: Biblical Epic Themes and Forms in Seventeenth-Century England.* Berkeley: University of California Press, 1959.

Lagos, Ramona. "El incumplimiento de la programación épica en *La Araucana.*" *Cuadernos Americanos* 238 (1981): 157–91.

Lambert, E. "Alphonse de Castille et la Juive de Tolède." *Bulletin Hispanique* 25 (1923): 371–94.

Lapesa, Rafael. "*La Jerusalén* de Tasso y la de Lope." In *De la Edad Media a nuestros días*, 264–85. Madrid: Gredos, 1967.

Laqueur, Thomas. *Making Sex: Body and Gender from the Greeks to Freud.* Cambridge: Harvard University Press, 1990.

Leal, Luis. "*La Araucana* y el problema de la literatura nacional." *Vórtice* 1 (1974): 68–73.

Lerner, Isaías. "Ercilla y Lucano." In *Hommage à Robert Jammes* (Anejos de *Criticón*, 1), 683–91. Toulouse: Presses Universitaires du Mirail, 1994.

———. "Garcilaso en Ercilla." *Lexis, Revista de Lingüística y Literatura* 2 (1978): 201–21.

———. Introduction to *La Araucana*, by Alonso de Ercilla. Madrid: Cátedra, 1993.

———. "Para los contextos ideológicos de *La Araucana*: Erasmo." In *Homenaje a Ana María Barrenechea*, edited by Lía Schwartz Lerner and Isaías Lerner, 261–70. Madrid: Castalia, 1984.

Lewalski, Barbara Kiefer. *"Paradise Lost" and the Rhetoric of Literary Forms.* Princeton, N.J.: Princeton University Press, 1985.

Lewis, Bernard. *Cultures in Conflict: Christians, Muslims, and Jews in the Age of Discovery.* New York: Oxford University Press, 1995.

Lida de Malkiel, María Rosa. *Juan de Mena: poeta del prerrenacimiento español.* Publicaciones de la Nueva Revista de filología hispánica. Mexico: Colegio de México, Fondo de Cultura Económica, 1950.

Lockhart, James. *Spanish Peru, 1532–1560. A Social History.* 2nd ed. Madison: University of Wisconsin Press, 1994.

Lockhart, James, and Otte, Enrique, eds. *Letters and People of the Spanish Indies: Sixteenth Century.* Cambridge: Cambridge University Press, 1976.

Lucan. *The Civil War.* Translated by J. D. Duff. Loeb Classical Library. Cambridge: Harvard University Press, 1988.

Lucas, George. *Star Wars: The Empire Strikes Back.* Directed by George Lucas. Produced by Gary Kurtz. 128 min. CBSFox/Lucasfilm, 1980. Special edition, 1997. Videocassette.

———. *Star Wars: A New Hope.* Directed by George Lucas. Produced by Gary Kurtz. 124 min. Twentieth Century Fox/Lucasfilm, 1977. Special edition. 1995. Videocassette.

———. *Star Wars: Return of the Jedi.* Directed by Richard Marquand. Produced by Howard Kazanjian. 134 min. CBSFox/Lucasfilm, 1983. Special edition, 1997. Videocassette.

Lukács, Georg. *The Theory of the Novel.* Translated by Anna Bostock. Cambridge: Massachusetts Institute of Technology Press, 1971.

Madrigal, Luis Iñigo. *Historia de la literatura hispanoamericana*. 2 vols. Madrid: Cátedra, 1982.

Malvern, Marjorie M. *Venus in Sackcloth: The Magdalen's Origins and Metamorphoses*. Carbondale: Southern Illinois University Press, 1975.

Mariscal, George. *Contradictory Subjects: Quevedo, Cervantes, and Seventeenth-Century Spanish Culture*. Ithaca, N.Y.: Cornell University Press, 1991.

Martínez Millán, José, et al. *La corte de Felipe II*. Madrid: Alianza, 1994.

Martz, Louis L. *The Poetry of Meditation: A Study in English Religious Literature of the Seventeenth Century*. Rev. ed. New Haven: Yale University Press, 1962.

Mas, Albert. *Les Turcs dans la Littérature Espagnole du Siècle d'Or: (Recherches sur l'évolution d'un thème littéraire.)*. 2 vols. Theses, Memoires and Studies. Paris: Centre de Recherches Hispaniques, Institut d'Études Hispaniques, 1967.

Mazur, Oleh. "The Wild Man in the Spanish Renaissance and the Golden Age: A Comparative Study." Ann Arbor: University Microfilms International, 1982. (Facsimile of 1966 dissertation).

McKendrick, Melveena. *Woman and Society in the Spanish Drama of the Golden Age*. Cambridge: Cambridge University Press, 1974.

Medina, José Toribio. *Historia del Tribunal del Santo Oficio de la Inquisición de Lima*. 2 vols. Santiago: Fondo Histórico y Bibliográfico J. T. Medina, 1956.

———. "Las mujeres de *La Araucana* de Ercilla." *Hispania* 11 (1928): 1–12.

———. *Vida de Ercilla*. México: Fondo de Cultura Económica, 1948.

Menéndez y Pelayo, Marcelino. *Historia de las ideas estéticas en España*. 3rd ed. 2 vols. Madrid: Consejo Superior de Investigaciones Científicas, 1962.

Meo Zilio, Giovanni. *Estudio sobre Hernando Domínguez Camargo y su "San Ignacio de Loyola, Poema Heroico."* Florence: Casa Editrice G. d'Anna. Universitá degli Studii di Facultá di Magistero, Istituto Ispanico, 1967.

Mexía, Diego. *Primera Parte del Parnaso Antártico de obras amatorias*. Edited by Trinidad Barrera. Rome: Bulzoni, 1990.

Meyer, Sister Mary Edgar. *The Sources of Hojeda's "La Christiada."* Ann Arbor: University of Michigan Press, 1953.

Miller, Beth, ed. *Women in Hispanic Literature: Icons and Fallen Idols*. Berkeley: University of California Press, 1983.

Morley, S. Griswold, and Richard W. Tyler. "Los nombres de personajes en las comedias de Lope de Vega." *University of California Publications in Modern Philology* 55 (1961): 1–294.

Münzer, Hieronymus. *Itinerarium Hispanicum Hieronymi Monetarii.* Edited by Ludwig Pfandl. *Revue Hispanique* 48 (1920): 1–178.

Murrin, Michael. *History and Warfare in Renaissance Epic.* Chicago: University of Chicago Press, 1994.

Navarrete, Ignacio. *Orphans of Petrarch: Poetry and Theory in the Spanish Renaissance.* Berkeley: University of California Press, 1994.

———. "Renaissance Nationalisms: Introduction." *Comparative and General Literature* 39 (1990–91): 23–24.

Nicolopulos, James R. "Pedro de Oña and Bernardo de Balbuena Read Ercilla's Fitón." *Latin American Literary Review* 26 (1998): 100–19.

———. "Prophecy, empire and imitation in the *Araucana* in the light of the *Lusíadas.*" Ann Arbor: University Microfilms International, 1992.

———. "Reading and Responding to the Amorous Episodes of the *Araucana* in Colonial Peru." *Calíope* 4 (1998): 227–47.

Ovid. *Metamorphoses.* Translated by Frank Justus Miller. Revised by G. P. Goold. Loeb Classical Library. Cambridge: Harvard University Press, 1984.

Pagden, Anthony. *The Fall of Natural Man: The American Indian and the Origins of Comparative Ethnology.* Cambridge: Cambridge University Press, 1982.

———. *Spanish Imperialism and the Political Imagination: Studies in European and Spanish-American Social and Political Theory, 1513–1830.* New Haven: Yale University Press, 1990.

Parker, Geoffrey. *Philip II.* 3rd ed. Chicago: Open Court, 1995.

———. *The Grand Strategy of Philip II.* New Haven: Yale University Press, 1998.

Parkes, James. *The Conflict of the Church and the Synagogue: A Study in the Origins of Antisemitism.* 1934. Reprint. New York: Atheneum, 1969.

Pastor, Beatriz. *Discursos narrativos de la Conquista: Mitificación y emergencia.* Rev. ed. Hanover, N.H.: Ediciones del Norte, 1988.

Peña, Margarita. "La poesía épica colonial: La épica sagrada." *Plural (segunda época)* 20–22:240 (1991): 108–13.

———. "La poesía épica en la Nueva España (Siglo 16)." In Vol. 1 of *Historia de la literatura mexicana,* edited by Beatriz Garza Cuarón and Georges Baudot, 450–60. Mexico: Siglo 21, 1996.

Pérez de Villagrá, Gaspar. *Historia de la Nueva México, 1610.* Edited by Alfred Rodríguez and Joseph P. Sánchez. Albuquerque: University of New Mexico Press, 1992.

Pérez-Torres, Rafael. *Movements in Chicano Poetry: Against Myths, Against Margins.* Cambridge: Cambridge University Press, 1995.

Peristiany, J. G., and Julian Pitt-Rivers, eds. *Honor and Grace in Anthropology.* Cambridge: Cambridge University Press, 1992.

Perry, Mary Elizabeth. *Gender and Disorder in Early Modern Seville.* Princeton, N.J.: Princeton University Press, 1990.

Pierce, Frank. *Alonso de Ercilla y Zúñiga.* Amsterdam: Rodopi, 1984.

———. "The *canto épico* of the Seventeenth and Eighteenth Centuries." *Hispanic Review* 15 (1947): 1–48.

———. "*La creación del mundo* and the Spanish 'Religious Epic' of the Golden Age." *Bulletin of Hispanic Studies* 17 (1940): 23–32.

———. "History and Poetry in the Heroic Poem of the Golden Age." *Hispanic Review* 20 (1952): 302–12.

———. "Hojeda's *La Christiada.* A Poem of the Literary Baroque." *Bulletin of Spanish Studies* 17 (1940): 203–18.

———. "*La Jerusalén conquistada* of Lope de Vega: A Reappraisal." *Bulletin of Spanish Studies* 20 (1943): 11–35.

———. Introduction to *La Cristiada,* by Diego de Hojeda. Edited by Frank Pierce. Salamanca: Anaya, 1971.

———. "The Literary Epic and Lope's *Jerusalén conquistada.*" *Bulletin of Hispanic Studies* 33 (1956): 93–98.

———. "The Place of Mythology in *The Lusiads.*" *Comparative Literature* 6 (1954): 97–122.

———. *La poesía épica del Siglo de Oro.* Translated by J. C. Cayol de Bethencourt. 2nd ed. Madrid: Gredos, 1968.

———. "The Poetic Hell in Hojeda's *La Christiada:* Imitation and Originality." In Vol. 4 of *Estudios dedicados a Menéndez Pidal,* 469–508.

———. "Some Aspects of the Spanish 'Religious Epic' of the Golden Age." *Hispanic Review* 12 (1944): 1–10.

———. "Some Themes and their Sources in the Heroic Poem of the Golden Age." *Hispanic Review* 14 (1946): 95–103.

———. "The Spanish 'Religious Epic' of the Counter-Reformation: A Survey." *Bulletin of Spanish Studies* 18 (1941): 174–82.

Pigman, G. W. III. "Versions of Imitation in the Renaissance." *Renaissance Quarterly* 33 (1980): 1–32.

Putnam, Michael C. J. *The Poetry of the "Aeneid."* 1965. Reprint. Ithaca, N.Y.: Cornell University Press, 1988.

Quevedo, Francisco de. *Obra poética.* Edited by José Manuel Blecua. 4 vols. Madrid: Castalia, 1969.

Quint, David. *Epic and Empire: Politics and Generic Form from Virgil to Milton.* Princeton, N.J.: Princeton University Press, 1993.

———. "Epic and Empire." *Comparative Literature* 41 (1989): 1–32.

———. "Voices of Resistance: The Epic Curse and Camões's Adamastor." In *New World Encounters,* edited by Stephen Greenblatt, 241–71. Berkeley: University of California Press, 1993.

Rabasa, José. "Aesthetics of Colonial Violence: The Massacre of Ácoma in Gaspar de Villagrá's *Historia de la Nueva México*." *College Literature* 20 (1993): 96–114.

———. *Inventing America: Spanish Historiography and the Formation of Eurocentrism*. Norman: University of Oklahoma Press, 1993.

Resnick, Seymour. "The Jew as Portrayed in Early Spanish Literature." *Hispania* 34 (1951): 54–58.

Rhodes, Elizabeth. "Spain's Misfired Canon: The Case of Luis de Granada's *Libro de la oración y meditación*." *Journal of Hispanic Philology* 15 (1990): 43–66.

Rieder, John. "Embracing the Alien: Science Fiction in Mass Culture." *Science-Fiction Studies* 9 (1982): 26–37.

Robinson, Lillian S. *Monstrous Regiment: The Lady Knight in Sixteenth-Century Epic*. New York: Garland, 1985.

Romero, Hector. "*La Araucana* a través de los antologistas." In *The Two Hisperias: Literary Studies in Honor of Joseph G. Fucilla on the Occasion of his 80th Birthday*, edited by Américo Bugliani, 367–89. Madrid: Porrúa, 1977.

Ruether, Rosemary R. *Faith and Fratricide*. New York: Seabury Press, 1974.

Rufo, Juan. *La Austriada*. Edited by Cayetano Rosell. Bibilioteca de Autores Españoles 29. Madrid: Rivadeneyra, 1854.

Said, Edward W. *Orientalism*. New York: Vintage, 1979.

Sancha, Antonio de. Introduction to *La Araucana*, by Alonso de Ercilla. Madrid: Antonio de Sancha, 1776.

Santa Teresa de Jesús. *Libro de la Vida*. Edited by Otger Steggink. Madrid: Castalia, 1986.

———. *Obras completas de Santa Teresa*. Edited by Efrén de la Madre de Dios and Otger Steggink. Madrid: Biblioteca de Autores Cristianos, 1967.

Sayce, R. A. *The French Biblical Epic in the Seventeenth Century*. Oxford: Clarendon Press, 1955.

Scaliger, Julius Caesar. *Select Translations from Scaliger's Poetics*. Translated by Frederick Morgan Padelford. Yale Studies in English 26. New York: Henry Holt, 1905.

Schwartz Lerner, Lía. "Tradición literaria y heroínas indias en *La Araucana*," *Revista Iberoamericana* 38 (1972): 615–25.

Simon, Marcel. *Verus Israël: Étude sur les relations entre Chrétiens et Juifs dan l'empire romain*. 1948. Reprint. Paris: E. de Boccard, 1964.

Sismondi, J. C. L. Simonde de. *Historical View of the Literature of the South of Europe*. 2 vols. 2nd ed. London: H. G. Bohn, 1846.

Slavicsek, Bill. *A Guide to the Star Wars Universe*. 2nd, rev. ed. New York: Ballantine Books, 1994.

Smith, Paul. "Preface." *Discerning the Subject.* Minneapolis: University of Minnesota Press, 1988.

Smith, Paul Julian. *Representing the Other: "Race," Text and Gender in Spanish and Spanish American Narrative.* Oxford: Clarendon Press, 1992.

Spingarn, Joel Elias. *A History of Literary Criticism in the Renaissance.* New York: Macmillan, 1899.

Spurr, David. *The Rhetoric of Empire: Colonial Discourse in Journalism, Travel Writing and Imperial Administration.* Durham, N.C.: Duke University Press, 1993.

Stage International de Tours 1966. *Théorie et Pratique Politiques à la Renaissance.* Paris: J. Vrin, 1977.

Stone, Oliver. *Wall Street.* CBS/Fox, 1987. Videocassette.

Suárez de Figueroa, Cristóbal. *Hechos de D. García Hurtado de Mendoza, quarto Marqués de Cañete,* 103–4, *apud* Antonio de Sancha, Introduction to *La Araucana,* by Alonso de Ercilla, xx–xxi. Madrid: Antonio de Sancha, 1776.

Szarmach, Paul E., ed. *Aspects of Jewish Culture in the Middle Ages.* Albany: State University of New York Press, 1979.

Tanner, Marie. *The Last Descendant of Aeneas: The Habsburgs and the Mythic Image of the Emperor.* New Haven: Yale University Press, 1993.

Tasso, Torquato. *Discourses on the Heroic Poem.* Translated by Mariella Cavalchini and Irene Samuel. Oxford: Clarendon Press, 1973.

Terry, Arthur. *Seventeenth-Century Spanish Poetry: The Power of Artifice.* Cambridge: Cambridge University Press, 1993.

Ticknor, George. *History of Spanish Literature.* 3 vols. New York: Harper and Brothers, 1849.

Triviños, Gilberto. "Bernardo del Carpio desencantado por Bernardo de Balbuena." *Revista Chilena de Literatura* 16 (1980): 315–38.

———. "Nacionalismo y desengaño en *El Bernardo* de Balbuena." *Acta literaria* 6 (1981): 93–117.

Tyrrell, William Blake. *Amazons: A Study in Athenian Mythmaking.* Baltimore: Johns Hopkins University Press, 1984.

Ubieto, Antonio, et al. *Introducción a la historia de España.* Barcelona: Teide, 1963.

Van Horne, John. "The Attitude toward the Enemy in Sixteenth Century Spanish Narrative Poetry." *Romanic Review* 16 (1925): 341–61.

———. *"El Bernardo" of Bernardo de Balbuena.* Urbana: University of Illinois Press, 1927.

Vega Carpio, Lope Félix de. *Jerusalén Conquistada.* 3 vols. Edited and annotated by Joaquín de Entrambasaguas. Madrid: Consejo Superior de Investigaciones Científicas, 1951.

———. *Las paces de los reyes y judía de Toledo.* Edited by James A. Castañeda. Salamanca: Anaya, 1971.

Vida, Marco Girolamo. *The De Arte Poetica of Marco Girolamo Vida, 1517.* Translated and edited by Ralph G. Williams. New York: Columbia University Press, 1976.

———. *The Christiad.* Edited and translated by Gertrude C. Drake and Clarence A. Forbes. Carbondale: Southern Illinois University Press, 1978.

Virués, Cristóbal de. *Historia del Monserrate.* Edited by Cayetano Rosell. Biblioteca de Autores Españoles 17. Madrid: Rivadeneyra, 1851.

———. *El Monserrate Segundo.* Edited by Mary Fitts Finch. Valencia–Chapel Hill: Albatros, 1984.

Virgil. *Eclogues, Georgics, Aeneid.* Translated by H. R. Fairclough. 2 vols. Loeb Classical Library. Cambridge: Harvard University Press, 1986.

Von Dem Bussche, Gastón, ed. *Homenaje a Ercilla.* Concepción: Instituto Central de Lenguas, Universidad de Concepción, 1969.

Von Hallberg, Robert, ed. *Canons.* Chicago: University of Chicago Press, 1984.

Voragine, Jacobus de. *The Golden Legend.* Translated by Granger Ryan and Helmut Ripperger. 1941. Reprint. New York: Longmans, 1948.

Warnke, Frank J. *Versions of Baroque.* New Haven: Yale University Press, 1972.

Weinberg, Bernard. *A History of Literary Criticism in the Italian Renaissance.* 2 vols. Chicago: University of Chicago Press, 1961.

Weinstock, Jeffrey A. "Freaks in Space: 'Extraterrestrialism' and Deep-Space Multiculturalism." In *Freakery: Cultural Spectacles of the Extraordinary,* edited by Rosemarie Garland Thomson, 327–37. New York: New York University Press, 1996.

Whinnom, Keith. "The Problem of the Best-seller in Spanish Golden-Age Literature." *Bulletin of Hispanic Studies* 57 (1980): 189–98.

White, Florence Donnell. *Voltaire's Essay on Epic Poetry: A Study and an Edition.* New York: Phaeton Press, 1970.

Williams, A. Lukyn. *Adversus Judaeos: A Bird's-Eye View of Christian 'Apologiae' Until the Renaissance.* London: Cambridge University Press, 1935.

Williams, Charles Allyn. "Oriental Affinities of the Legend of the Hairy Anchorite." *University of Illinois Studies in Language and Literature* 10 (1925): 9–56; 11 (1926): 57–139.

———. "The German Legends of the Hairy Anchorite." *University of Illinois Studies in Language and Literature* 18 (1935): 1–48.

Williams, James G., ed. *The Girard Reader.* New York: Crossroad, 1996.

Williams, John D. "The Savage in Sixteenth-Century Spanish Prose Fiction." *Kentucky Foreign Language Quarterly* 3 (1956): 4–46.

Wilson, Diana de Armas. "'Vuela por alta mar, isleño esquife': Antonio de Viana's *Conquista de Tenerife* (1604)." *Calíope* 3 (1997): 24–36.

Wittreich, Joseph Anthony, Jr. *Visionary Poetics: Milton's Tradition and his Legacy.* San Marino, Calif.: Henry E. Huntington Library, 1979.

Woodward, Kenneth L. *Making Saints: How the Catholic Church Determines Who Becomes a Saint, Who Doesn't, and Why.* 1990. Reprint. New York: Simon and Schuster, 1996.

Wright, Elizabeth. "Epic and Archive: Lope de Vega, Francis Drake and the Council of Indies." *Calíope* 3 (1997): 37–56.

———. "The Poet as Pilgrim: Lope de Vega and the Court of Philip III, 1598–1609." Ph.D. diss. Ann Arbor: University Microfilms International, 1998.

Wyatt, David. "*Star Wars* and the Productions of Time." *Virginia Quarterly Review* 58 (1982): 600–15.

Yates, Frances A. Astraea: *The Imperial Theme in the Sixteenth Century.* London: Routledge and Kegan Paul, 1975.

Zeitlin, Froma I. "Playing the Other: Theater, Theatricality, and the Feminine in Greek Drama." In *Nothing to Do with Dionysos?: Athenian Drama in Its Social Context,* edited by John J. Winkler and Froma I. Zeitlin, 63–96. Princeton, N.J.: Princeton University Press, 1990.

Index

Abjection: as justification for colonialism, 208
Academia Antártica, 171
Academic boundaries, 18
Adorno, Rolena: on "world-upside-down," 72n17
Aemulatio, 63; in *La Austriada*, 84
Aeneas's shield, 77, 79
Aeneid (Virgil), 79, 81
Affected modesty, 1, 55
Aizenberg, Edna: on sexualized Jewess tales, 197
Albaicín. *See La Austriada*
Albarracín Sarmiento, Carlos: on Ercilla and Philip II, 27, 31; on denunciation of Spanish greed, 96
Alegría, Fernando: on Ercilla's allegiance to Philip II, 30; on Araucanian dissension, 41
Alonso de Armería, Fray, 156, 158
Alphonse VIII (of Castile). *See Jerusalem conquered*
Alphonse X (of Castile), 182
Alpujarra: rebellion in, 61
Alterity. *See* Otherness
Amazons, 185–86
American Indian, 39
Anderson, Benedict: on print-languages, 14, 103
Andioc, René: on García de la Huerta's *Raquel*, 196; on Lope de Vega's lack of influence on García de la Huerta, 197
Anti-Semitism: as ultimate European discourse of otherness, 159, 205; vs. "Jew-hatred," 159–60; in the Gospels, 160–61; influence on Hojeda of patristic, 163–67; discursive formation of, 200
"Anxiety of influence," 62–63
Arab invasion of Spain, 177, 180
La Araucana: nationalist readings of, 20; absence of Spanish hero in, 21; contradictions in, 20; testimonial perspective of, 24; recent historical events in, 24; *verismo* of, 25; apostrophes to

Philip II in, 31–37; memory in, 33, 36; betrayal in, 44, 47, 48, 50; battle of Mataquito in, 44, 49; execution of Caupolicán in, 34–35; expedition to the south in, 36; as source for Rufo's battle of Lepanto, 77–78
—characters: Fresia, 26; Caupolicán, 26, 34, 41, 48; Galbarino, 35, 48, 66; Lautaro, 36, 48; Peteguelén, 41; Marcos Véaz, 36, 48; Rengo, 43–44, 84; Andrea the Genoese, 22; Tucapel, 42–44; Colocolo, 42, 66; Ercilla, 25; Philip II, 38; Araucanian widows, 208
—themes: nobility as service, 21–39; critique of greed, 66–68; promotion of imperial program and discoveries, 23
Ariosto, Ludovico: *Orlando Furioso*, 4; imitation of, 5; his influence on Spanish epic, 12; his Limassol as place of gender role reversal, 186
Armstrong, John A.: on emergence of national subjectivity, 13
La Austriada: taking of Morisco prisoners in, 70–71; sack of Válor in, 71; similes in, 82–83; evacuation of Albaicín in, 90–93; repression of deportation narrative in, 93; textual disruption in, 96
—characters: Zaide and Haxa, 68; marquis of Mondéjar, 69; Abenhumeya, *rey chico*, 69; Luis Fajardo, marquis of Los Vélez, 72; Alí-Bajá, 79; Luchalí (Ochalí), 79
—themes: false honor, 72; pillage and military indiscipline, 75; greed and death, 73–74; apparent riches vs. honor, 75; appetite vs. discipline and reason, 75
Auto de fe of Lima (1639), 170
Avalle-Arce, Juan Bautista, 25n10

Bakhtin, Mikhail: "Epic and Novel," 6n11; privileges the modern, 15
Bal, Mieke: on textual dominance and deviance, 194